BEHIND THE PLAYDOUGH CURTAIN

A Year in My Life as a Preschool Teacher

PATTI GREENBERG WOLLMAN

Charles Scribner's Sons
New York London Toronto Sydney Tokyo Singapore

CHARLES SCRIBNER'S SONS
Rockefeller Center
1230 Avenue of the Americas
New York, NY 10020

Manufactured in the United States of America

10   9   8   7   6   5   4   3   2   1

Library of Congress Cataloging-in-Publication Data
Wollman, Patti Greenberg.
    Behind the playdough curtain: a year in my life as a preschool
teacher/Patti Greenberg Wollman.
        p.   cm.
    1. Wollman, Patti Greenberg.   2. Preschool teachers—United
States—Biography.   I. Title.
LA2317.W65A3   1994
372.21—dc20   94–8583   CIP

ISBN 0-684-19665-4

NOTE TO THE READER

This is a true and faithful rendering of the events in one year of my life as a preschool teacher. The names and physical descriptions of the people involved have been changed, as have the names of the school and the synagogue.

CONTENTS

To Bernice Kaufman
a director of rare insight and compassion;
a woman of wit, grace and courage,
this book is affectionately dedicated.

BEHIND THE PLAYDOUGH CURTAIN

. . .

ACKNOWLEDGMENTS

There are many people I would like to thank for helping me with the birth of this book. My agent, Nancy Trichter, offered to represent me when I had written only twelve pages. Her belief in my ability sustained me through the difficult period of composition. Her talent in her profession is exceeded only by her ability to be a friend. I am equally grateful to my editor, Edward Chase, for his enthusiasm, his kindness and his gentle help in guiding this first-time author through the mystifying wilderness of publishing. His suggestions were invaluable and his patience unbounded. With his strong intelligence and his endearing sense of humor, he is truly one of a dying breed: an author's editor.

I am indebted to my publisher, Barbara Grossman, for her support and her many helpful editing suggestions. She has my respect along with my appreciation. Thanks also to Mark LaFlaur for his work on my book and his friendly conversation. I always felt better after talking to him.

My friends and family were a wonderful resource during the writing of my journal as well as its transformation into a book. They stuck by me when I was always tired from teaching all day and writing all night. They listened to my agonies over the turn of a phrase with minimal complaint. They encouraged me to believe I had talent as well as stamina. My thanks to Janet for her important suggestions and her contribution of the book's title. Thanks to Kimba for her unerring moral acuity which helped me see what I could and could not write. A thank-you is insufficient for the help I received from Alexandra, my friend and colleague. I couldn't have done it then and I couldn't do it now without her friendship, her intelligence and her ability to understand just about everything.

To Cathy, Josh, Marianne and Phyllis (in alphabetical order), I offer my sincere thanks and overwhelming gratitude. In an increasingly hostile world, where I stand without the comfort of my sibling, it is good to know that familial love can be generated without the existence of blood ties. You are, and you always will be, my brother and my sisters.

Finally more love and gratitude goes to my family than I could ever express. To my children Ben and Laura: your pride in my writing was an unquenchable aid to me. I could see through your eyes that I was becoming the role model I wanted to be. Thank you both for understanding when I was preoccupied or when dinner wasn't on the table. (And thanks to the guys at Samba's Deli for providing it so often with their ever-ready smiles!)

Thanks to my parents, who have believed in me as long as I can remember. They struggled through the hard times with undiminished love and pride. I hope they enjoy the good times to the hilt: they deserve it.

From my parents, I learned about the beauty and sanctity of a happy marriage. I was lucky enough to find that joy myself, albeit in middle age. To my dear husband Warren, much love and many kisses. You were the first one to tell me that I had to write these stories down. What would I have done without your 5 A.M. coffees and your constant concern? I am a lucky woman and I know it.

One of the most important things I have learned is that writing a book is in a very real sense a team effort. I'm the one who spent those predawn hours at the computer, but it never would have happened without the people who believed in me. My love and thanks to you all.

PREFACE

Jamie P., at three years and two months of age, was the oldest child in my class. He was also the only child not toilet trained. With a large, sweet face atop a small, broad body, Jamie was oddly built. Wearing Pampers made the awkward job of walking even more difficult: he looked like a rectangle with legs.

Jamie's parents were concerned. Their son seemed to have the pieces in place. He urinated in a toilet with no problem. He knew when he had to make a bowel movement. We knew, too: in school, he would crawl off to our house area, lie in the doll bed and sing. (When Jamie stopped singing, we had a job to do!) Why wouldn't he take that final step toward independence?

I didn't know the answer, but I had an idea. Maybe Jamie needed to watch another child in our class use the toilet—to see that it was easy to do. I invited him along one day when I was taking Emily to the bathroom. To my surprise, he came willingly.

Emily had just turned three, and was even smaller than Jamie. But she was fully trained: she hopped right onto the seat. Jamie watched her intently. After a minute, he turned to me and said with great thoughtfulness:

"She's not falling in."

"No," I replied. "And neither will you."

Two days later, Jamie was out of Pampers completely. He hadn't been able to tell us the problem, but he responded beautifully when we solved it.

• • •

Preschool teachers do a lot more than play games and bandage scraped knees. But this seems to be a well-kept secret. I've been a teacher for nearly twenty years, and the question I'm most frequently asked by the parents of my students is still "What do you do with them all day?"

I understand why parents ask: it's because they cannot tell, even by observing, what the answer is. It's like looking into a funhouse mirror; everything they see is distorted. A parent's presence changes the delicate balance between teachers and students. All the good stuff happens when no one else is in the room.

Three- and four-year-olds can learn a great deal during the course of a school year. They can identify letters and shapes, and begin to understand the most basic concepts of numbers. They are exposed to the scientific principle of forming a hypothesis and testing it. (What do you think will happen to the snow in this bowl if I put the bowl on top of the radiator?) They learn respect for other living things by taking care of classroom pets and by planting seeds and helping them grow. They prepare for reading and writing by working with toys that improve their small motor and hand-eye coordination. They experiment with proportion and balance as they build with blocks.

But the most important things that preschool children learn in their first year are not academic. They are: 1) how to get along with people who aren't their relatives and 2) the simple idea that acquiring knowledge is an enjoyable activity. This is, in fact, the civilizing year for children.

In order to communicate these two concepts, a teacher must be an actor, singer, orator and clown. Can you tell a story that has children listening in complete silence and awe? Can you read a book while holding it up so the pictures are always visible? Can you make children laugh just by asking a question? Can you teach children to mime a song after they've sung it? Can you put on a tape and get children to dance with you?

On a more important level, can you praise with enthusiasm? Can you remember that every successful step a child takes is a small miracle? Can you act excited when a child accomplishes something that you always knew he or she was capable of? Can you run this show when you're sick or angry or just plain tired of it all? It's a tall order, requiring both talent and application.

Now, a teacher can be Mary Martin, Meryl Streep and Charlie Chaplin all rolled into one, but no child will learn in a threatening or hostile atmosphere. Children must feel safe in a classroom. So, while using his or her acting skills, a teacher must also engage in policework. Teachers discipline, negotiate, restrain, get tough with, ease up on and generally provide their own thin blue line between civilization and chaos.

When disciplining children, my version of jail is "time out." A child sits on a chair and may not get up until I say so. Naturally, I sit next to the child for a time and discuss the offense. But I put the chair right near the action. While we are talking, the perpetrator can see all the fun he or she is missing. Some kids do heavy "seat time" in the beginning of school. Some of them cry. None of them like it at first. But they quickly learn that the rules protect everyone, as long as those rules are consistently applied.

If the classroom is in working order, with the children playing happily and safely, then the teachers can begin to see what the *issues* are. In educational parlance, an issue is an ongoing difficulty. If Johnny skins his knee, it's an event. If Johnny isn't interested in doing any artwork, it's a problem. If Johnny is always tired and cranky because his parents don't have a consistent bedtime for him—that's an *issue*.

A three- or four-year-old won't plop down in my lap and recite his or her life history. A teacher is like a detective, gleaning clues from the behavior and language of the child, and from conversations with the parents. Like a detective, I may ask direct questions and receive evasive answers. My best tools are observation, logical thinking, intuition and luck.

Suppose that three-and-a-half-year-old Sally bites her class-mate Jimmy. Perhaps she's angry and momentarily forgets to use her words. This is more common to a two-and-a-half-year-old, who may not know many words to express anger. But it can still happen a year later.

Suppose that Sally bites Jimmy again, and even again. (It's often the same victim—someone the biter either loves or hates.) Now we have an issue. What's going on in Sally's head? Is she actually angry at the victim, who may be bothering her inside or outside the classroom? Is she angry about something else that is going on at home? Does she, for example, have a younger sibling who bites? Has her mother recently gone back to work? Is her father away a lot? Or, more seriously, is Sally witness to a lot of fighting between grown-ups? Biting can express anxiety as well as anger. In this case, we need to find out what is happening at home.

In order to help the child, the teacher must work with the parents: there can be no real change in a child's life without their understanding and cooperation. When talking to parents, I frequently feel like uttering Sergeant Friday's "Just the facts, ma'am." But parents don't always *know* the facts—that is, they don't always know which facts will help. So a teacher must *listen* and *sift*. I use all my experience and skill—and a large dollop of luck—to figure out the correct problem and a workable solution to it.

Unlike a detective, who has on his side the coercion of the law, a teacher cannot force parents to accept the truth about their child. Often, the skills of a diplomat are necessary to convince parents without hurting their feelings. Sometimes it's a fairly easy task: "Your child needs to spend more time alone with you." Sometimes it's a hard one: "I'm pretty sure your baby-sitter is hitting your child. You're probably going to have to fire her."

It doesn't matter how famous, ambitious or successful you are in the real world. Your child is your vulnerable spot—the soft underbelly of every parent. Telling parents the truth is often the toughest work in town.

• • •

Preschool teaching is most difficult, however, because it is a twenty-four-hour-a-day job. We can't leave our troubles at the office: they come home with us, invading our conversation and our dreams. Our students are in our hearts every moment from September to June. With this in mind, I decided to keep a journal for a year to illustrate the glories and difficulties of teaching in a preschool classroom. It seemed like such a simple idea. Each night, I'd write down what had occurred that day and how my assistant Cathy and I had handled any problems.

I taught at the Congregation Beth-El Nursery School, in New York City. As in all the best schools in the progressive tradition, our underlying philosophy was that children learn by doing—by handling objects while counting them, for example, or by making books to help them learn to read. This year, however, despite my enlightened intentions, I was in for the struggle of a lifetime.

Cathy and I had the Class from Hell, aptly named by a colleague who had dared to spend an hour in our room. Nearly all the kids had *issues*. Some came in lugging their private burdens; some had traumas thrust upon them during the year. But at one time or another, their emotional lives rattled like the chains of Jacob Marley's ghost.

How was I to handle the crises and tragedies that cropped up in our room all year long? I couldn't acquire an instant Ph.D. in Psychology, or a specialty in running trauma workshops. All I had were the tools of my trade. I used my detective skills to find out what was the matter, and my diplomatic skills to keep the parents at bay until I had concrete suggestions for them. I needed every ounce of my policing skills to keep the kids from hurting each other, and every drop of acting talent to beguile them into wanting to come each day despite the chaos around them. The balancing act was frightful. I came home every night for the first month, had a good cry, kissed my family and went to bed. (God only knows what they had for dinner.)

But as the year continued, *mirabile dictu*, we made progress with these kids. The parents were more responsive and the children more resilient than I could ever have imagined.

This is the story of that remarkable year. But, in a larger sense, it is the story of every year. Parents, as you read this book, I hope you will realize that sooner or later every child has an issue. Has your little girl become withdrawn after the death of a beloved grandparent? Is your son hitting other children in class because he's jealous of his new baby sister? Is your daughter sad because a particular group of girls consistently excludes her? You are not alone: the teacher is there to help you through these difficult passages.

In addition, your child must often deal with troubled classmates: the bully, the angry child or the child who has witnessed a traumatic event, for example. How does the teacher protect all the children in the class—even the difficult ones? It is a time-consuming, exhausting, unnerving and frequently unheralded task. (If we waited for the heralding, we'd be waiting for Godot.) But with dedication and skill, it can be done.

If you are a teacher of young children, you will recognize much of the story that follows as part of your own experience. (I'm just the one who decided to write it down.) If you are a young teacher, or if you're interested in a teacher's work, you may be a little incredulous as you read along. I promise you: everything in this book actually happened. All of it, no matter how unbelievable, is true.

Here, then, is the story of our roller-coaster year.

SEPTEMBER: A ROUGH BEGINNING

It was the second week of school. I'd had tough classes before, but none as hard as this one. My assistant Cathy and I were in a constant state of anxious anticipation. After all, the children outnumbered us twelve to two. Those are not long odds at a racetrack, but you wouldn't have placed any bets on Room 1. It was a teacher's nightmare.

Let me set the scene . . .

The children are just beginning their work period—it's the time we call *free play*. Jenny, Sharon, Cory and Lee are chatting at the playdough table (conversation is the usual by-product of playdough or clay). Jason, Benjamin and David are in the block corner, considering their options. Jeremy is painting at the easel and Amanda is watching him. Mary Ann and Louisa are looking at books.

In walks Harris with his mother in tow. She kisses him good-bye, waves at us and leaves the room faster than I thought was humanly possible. Harris does not kiss her and shows no emotion when she leaves. He doesn't even look in her direction. (Since this is an uncommon way of dealing with separation from a parent, I take notice. It does not augur well.)

Harris immediately runs over to Jason, who is playing quietly. "Let's play house!" he shouts with such enthusiasm that Jason immediately gets up. They go over to the house and loft area, followed by Lee, who knows a good thing when he sees one. Teachers have a sixth sense for disaster: I am not far behind.

The boys begin to take out the dishes and set the table. So far, so good—but so far is only two minutes. Without warning, Harris picks up a piece of plastic fruit and hurls it to the floor. "Ha!" he yells. Lee and Jason immediately follow suit. Lee's banana hits the loft and Jason knocks over a pot with a flying red pepper. I announce the rule—"We do not throw things in class." This stops no one at all. You'd be amazed at the number of objects which can be thrown in the one minute it takes me to move the boys away from the table.

Now, I've got three culprits, all needing discipline, but none needing the same kind. Lee is not yet three (what's he doing in my three-four's class—he's still in Pampers!); he needs to be told the rules. Three-year-old Jason knows the rule but cannot control his impulses. He needs to learn that objects do not exist only for his pleasure—to be thrown or eaten at will. If I didn't know this from their ages, I would know it from their faces: Lee looks perplexed and Jason chagrined. What I see on Harris's face is nothing—none of his past enthusiasm, no anger, just nothing at all. Whatever is making this kid tick is not in good working order.

As these thoughts are running through my mind, the rest of the room suddenly erupts. (Why not? Kids get nervous when there's a lot of *Sturm und Drang*.) Sharon yells "ICK!" She has tasted the playdough. Jeremy has finished his painting and wants to wash his hands. Amanda wants us to take Jeremy's painting off the easel so she can begin. Both are calling our names insistently. In the reading area, Mary Ann and Louisa start to fight over the same book. Louisa shouts over and over, "She isn't sharing!" while Mary Ann starts to cry. At the same instant, Cory falls off her chair and begins to wail.

Cathy looks at me, already busy with the three boys and unable to help her. We both start to laugh, helplessly. "Any suggestions?" she asks, in her wonderful, low-key manner.

I have no choice. "Tell Jeremy and Amanda to wait *one*

minute and go handle Mary Ann and Louisa. I'll take Sharon and Cory."

Leaving the boys with a feeling of trepidation, I hurry to pick up Cory. My first priority is to check for injury, but she's just scared. I walk over to Sharon with Cory in my arms and explain that we don't eat playdough. Even if it looks like a cookie, it's not. I tell her to go get a drink of water. Then I head back to the boys.

Although I've only been gone two minutes, I'm too late. Jason is crying. "Harris bit me!" he sobs, and shows me his hand. There are the teeth marks, sure enough, and there is Harris, impassive as a stone.

Welcome to Pandemonium.

• • •

I hadn't anticipated such a difficult year. I had been given a wonderful assistant and a chance to teach in a new, longer program for three- and four-year-olds. Cathy and I had asked to work together: we liked each other immensely, and knew we'd make a wonderful team. But there were signs of difficulty. Our beloved director of twenty years, Maggie Kaplan, lay dying of cancer. Her replacement, Barbara Gold, was still largely unfamiliar to us. I was determined to lie low and just do my job. But on the first day, our new director changed the method of assigning classrooms to teachers. I received the smallest, dingiest room in the school.

I cried as Cathy and I moved our things. I had been in my classroom for ten years. But it isn't my disposition to be miserable for long. I had a smaller room, but I still had my wonderful assistant. Cathy knew just how to speak to children, and they loved her for it. At twenty-three, she was blessed with a psychological insight that was way beyond her years. And she knew how to talk to parents without saying too much.

I looked around our room. It wasn't so bad—they had installed a loft, which gave the children more room to play. Something was strange about the loft—I couldn't put my finger on it. Never mind—I would figure it out when I saw the children use it.

· · ·

We set to work. Teachers at our school decorate their rooms in a specific motif. It's comforting for the children, impressive for the parents and fun for us. This year we chose underwater life: shiny fish emitting crystal bubbles were swimming on all the bulletin boards. One wall had coral reefs, plants and twelve fish, each labeled with the name and birthday of a particular child. I wanted green background paper for the water, but Cathy insisted on blue.

"These kids aren't from Florida, like you. To them the ocean is blue."

"If we really want to go by their experience, we could make it gray, like the Hudson," I smirked. We settled on a lovely, bright turquoise. By the morning of our parents' orientation meeting, our room had a cheerful, inviting look.

Orientation went smoothly. The parents listened as I explained the process of adjustment. We eased the children into a full day. For the first week, they were split into two groups of six, and went to school for just one hour. The following week, the groups came together. Gradually, we worked up to our full four hours, which included having lunch in school.

The parents seemed relaxed, even as they asked the usual questions.

"Why does it take so long for them to go a full day?"

"Some children need the time to get used to being in a new environment without their parents. Many kids are fine right away. This schedule helps the ones who need the extra time to adjust. If everyone has adjusted well, it helps the group as a whole."

"Can my child come to school even if he's not toilet trained?" (Note the gender. I can count on one hand the number of times a three-year-old girl has come to school untrained. Girls are ready earlier, and are more eager to please.)

"Of course your child can come. If a nursery school teacher can't stand to change a Pamper, he or she needs to get out of the profession and go work at IBM or something. It comes with the territory."

"Are bottles or pacifiers all right for school?"

"No. Leave them home. They're not for school: they get in the way of learning. They remind the child of babyhood, and school is for growing up."

Here's where I do my Ivy League rap. "They don't ask on your application to Harvard when you gave up your bottle, when you were toilet trained or when you learned to read. So don't worry about it. Every child grows at his or her own pace." This usually gets a laugh, but not always. Sometimes the parents are so nervous that they write it down in their notes.

This group laughed, which was a good sign. I fielded only a couple of the inevitable "learning" questions. "Will our children learn to read this year?"

"Probably not. But they'll acquire the tools to be successful readers when they're ready to learn."

"How about math and science?"

"We'll talk about curriculum at Open School Night. First, it's more important that your children adjust to being in school."

We gave out the schedule of home visits and explained what they were. Cathy and I would visit each child. We'd see their rooms, and they'd see our faces. That way, the first day of school wouldn't be so formidable. The visits last "ten minutes door to door." No time to have coffee or to chat with parents. Experience showed that children became exasperated when they were not the center of the visit.

"Any questions?"

The usual. "I work. I can't be home at the time you gave me."

"That's okay. We're visiting your child. Just have him home

with the baby-sitter." This is tough for many parents to accept. It's often the first realization that their child will have a separate life. It is, as one mother told me, "the beginning of the end." I prefer to think of it as "the beginning of the middle"— the child's school years.

I ended the meeting with my usual caveat: "Please remember that a parent *must* accompany his or her child to school on the first day. Otherwise, it's too scary for the child. Baby-sitters are fine afterward." Frankly, I've never been sure this is true. When their parents work all day, children are often just as attached to their baby-sitters. But I do believe that it's a parent's responsibility to be a part of his or her child's first day. That's reason enough to require it.

· · ·

On our home visits we saw eleven children. Our twelfth, Harris, was in London with his parents. He wouldn't be in school until the fourth day. We knew he was coming, though: our secretary said his tuition was paid in full. Seven thousand dollars had been plunked down before the beginning of the year? Sounded as if Harris's parents wanted to make sure we'd keep him. My suspicions rose.

For the most part, the visits went well. As usual, the girls were highly verbal and eager to please. Cory, however, did not speak a word. She buried her face in her mother's neck and barely glanced at us. When we left, Cathy asked me what was wrong.

"She's probably just shy," I told her. "Sometimes it happens." You can rank that prediction right up there with the *Chicago Tribune* headline about Dewey winning the presidency over Truman.

The boys were cute but far more active. One of them fit into the "whirling dervish" category. During our visit, Jason scampered up to his loft bed (five feet high) and swung down on the poles that supported it. When we interested him in his toy cars, he circled around with them until Cathy and I became dizzy just from watching him. It didn't seem to affect Jason, though. I'd been told that he was wild, but not that he was a body in perpetual motion.

"He's adorable!" Cathy said as we left the apartment.

"What you mean is that he's handsome," I replied. Indeed, his entire family was gorgeous—tall, athletic blonds with ice-blue eyes. It was hard to remember they were Orthodox Jews when they so closely resembled the Family Von Trapp. "He *has* got a pretty face, but he's gonna be a handful in the classroom."

"But he's so sweet and so friendly."

"Let's see how you feel about him in a month. All my bells are ringing *'Here comes trouble.'*"

Then there was Lee, best described as the Pillsbury Doughboy type. He was young, pudgy and sweet, with curly brown hair and soft brown eyes. He wore Pampers and walked with the wide-legged gait of a toddler. He showed us his new truck and insisted on turning the lights on and off about thirty times in a row. He cried when we left.

"Lee's just a baby—he's not even three yet. Why is he in our class?" Cathy wondered.

"I really don't know," I replied. "It's a decision that's made by the administration. Sometimes, if a child is mature for his age, he can go into an older class. But Lee seems even *younger* than his years. And he's such a softie—I 'm afraid he's going to be everybody's punching bag. You know, I don't think we have a very easy group."

That prediction you could have taken to the bank.

. . .

Our first day set the tone for the year. Usually, the kids begin to explore the classroom and the parents watch. This time many of the parents simply dropped off their children and waited in the "coffee room" down the hall. Our first group of six had been in the same class last year. They knew each other and were used to the routine of school. They settled down to play with blocks and playdough almost immediately. I was pleased with the lack of separation problems, but not ecstatic. If they don't come at the beginning of the year, they often come later.

I glanced around; everything looked great. *What a terrific beginning!* I thought smugly. Then I noticed that there were only five children. Where was Jeremy Jacobson?

He walked into the classroom five minutes later, brought by his baby-sitter, Falina. She took Jeremy over to the playdough table and got him started, then motioned me over to the side of the room. Looking me straight in the eye, she whispered, "Mr. and Mrs. Jacobson are sorry that they couldn't bring Jeremy today. Their baby died."

I felt as if someone had hit me; I put up my arm to ward off the blow. Their baby died? How could it be? The baby hadn't been born yet. I had seen Carolyn just two days ago at our meeting. She had that heavy, perspiring, I-wish-I'd-delivered-yesterday look typical of women in their last trimester of pregnancy. She had pulled me aside and confided, "I'm so happy I have you. Jeremy's going to need a lot of help. He's very angry about the baby." Now he would need a different kind of help.

I hurriedly asked if Jeremy and his older brother had been told. The answer was no. Carolyn was still in the hospital, where she had gone the night before. Bernard and Carolyn would tell the boys this afternoon, if possible. I scribbled my name and phone number on a napkin and gave it to Falina. If they wanted to talk about what to say, I was available to discuss it at any time.

Only the necessity of teaching stopped me from crying. Like any good actress, I've got to do the show if the audience is out there. I turned my attention to the children.

We all put away the toys; then it was time for snack. I had the kids in stitches as I gave out the napkins. "Now here's a turtle for Jeremy and an elephant for Sharon and a gorilla for Mary Ann . . ." (This stuff is funny to three- and four-year-olds because they get the joke. They don't understand a lot of adult humor, but they know categorically that a napkin is not an animal.)

Afterward, Cathy and I showed the children how to throw their cups and napkins into the large garbage can by the door. Next they sat on the rug by the bookcase and listened to Cathy read a story. And that was it—the hour had flown by. "We'll see you tomorrow," I said as I opened the door to allow the parents in.

"Is that all?" asked Sharon. "It's too short!"

"It is," I agreed. "But school will be longer soon." I smiled. Boy, these kids were a breeze.

Twenty minutes later I discovered the reason: the hurricanes were all in group two. These children didn't want to play with playdough. Jason wanted to throw it at the window. Louisa wanted to hide it in her purse. Lee wanted to feed it to the gerbils. He got his hand in the cage so fast that Cathy had to run to get it out before the gerbils obliged. In a flash like summer lightning, Jason blazed over to the sandbox and began to throw sand at Cory. Caught unawares, she began to cry. While Cathy calmed her down, I turned to discipline Jason. He needed to know that he couldn't hurt other children.

But he was already on the other side of the room. Before I could get to him, he pushed Lee on the chest. Cathy and I held our breath—our little, mushy Lee, not even three years old. What would happen? Was he going to be the perennial victim? He looked the part.

Looks can be deceiving: Jason and I had both guessed wrong. Lee pushed his attacker so hard that Jason fell down on the rug. "Don't do that to me!" hollered Lee, his face red and angry. "Okay," answered Jason, mildly. They were friends for the rest of the year.

Unfortunately, they were comrades-in-mischief. That very

day, they hid under the sandbox at snack time, and ran under the easel at story time. So Cathy read to the other children while I spoke to "the boys." Louisa, who had just turned three, wandered off to the sandbox after only a minute of sitting. That left just two children listening to the book. And we hadn't even met the kid whose tuition was paid in full.

• • •

By the time I got home, I was exhausted. The mental strain of holding the class together was far greater than the physical effort. I turned off the ringer on my phone, climbed into bed and immediately fell into a deep sleep. Usually a parade of garbage trucks couldn't wake me from an afternoon nap. But somewhere in my teacher's brain lay the sad fact of Jeremy's baby. So when the phone rang softly on an extension three rooms away, I was instantly alert. I answered on the second ring.

It was Bernard, Jeremy's father. He thanked me for offering my advice before I had even opened my mouth. His voice was so calm that I wondered if he were still in shock. The delivery was over. Carolyn was "fine, but, you know, sad," and they planned to tell the boys at the four o'clock visiting hour.

I had double-checked with the school psychologist and a friend in the field, in case there was anything different to say for such a special situation. There wasn't. I told Bernard to tell the children two things: they hadn't caused the baby's death and it wasn't going to happen to them.

Bernard didn't speak for a minute. "I wouldn't have thought of that."

"It's important. But most important is that Jeremy, who spent the summer wishing the baby away, be assured that he didn't accomplish his goal. He isn't responsible for what happened."

"I know, I know. It was nobody's fault."

"That's a good thing to say for six-year-old Evan. But three-year-old Jeremy needs to hear the words 'you didn't do it.' And he'll need to hear them frequently."

This was standard child development. Children under six are so egocentric that they believe they cause everything. It was important for Jeremy to be reassured that he had nothing to do with the baby's death.

"Well, uh, thanks."

"If I can be of any help, please let me know."

"Sure. It will be okay. Jeremy will be in school tomorrow and for the rest of the week. The funeral is Thursday, but it's just for Carolyn and me."

Again, I expressed my sympathy, and we ended the conversation. I wondered if he would follow my suggestions. He sounded so sad that I couldn't even be sure he had really heard me. I tried to finish my nap, but sleep was impossible.

· · ·

The next day, I wondered how Jeremy would behave. Faced with a trauma, children sometimes act out their anger or guilt in class by being hostile or destructive. Sometimes they are so sad that they withdraw for a while. Often, they use the classroom therapeutically, making pictures about the event or reenacting their story as they build with blocks or Lego.

Frequently, the classroom is an oasis. The child drops his trouble at the door, and plays contentedly. It is good to have a place where he or she doesn't have to think about the trouble. I didn't know Jeremy very well; which way would he choose?

He certainly seemed comfortable as he walked through the classroom door. Jeremy was a small child with curly blond hair, a winning smile and sparkling blue eyes set in a perfectly round face. His babyish speech and toddler's walk camouflaged a high intelligence and a quirky sense of humor that would be any mother's pride. His cheerful demeanor worked against his being miserable for any length of time.

Sure enough, he walked right over to the playdough table as jaunty and chipper as he had been the day before. He entered into the conversation—about making playdough pizza—with ease. I'd seen the oasis type before, but this was amazing. I asked Falina if he had been told, and she nodded. I walked over to the table to eavesdrop on the conversation. Jeremy didn't know me, but the children were his friends from last year. Maybe he'd tell them.

Jeremy talked about the pizza that Mary Ann was making. He made eleven balls of playdough and counted them correctly (a remarkable feat for a three-year-old). But he didn't utter a word about the baby.

My hands were tied. I couldn't bring up the subject or say anything to help him if he didn't want to talk about it. It was Jeremy's choice: if he wanted school to be his safe place for the moment, then so be it. When he chose to speak, I would be here for him. It was frustrating because I couldn't be sure that his parents had followed my advice. The child needed to be told that it wasn't his fault that his baby had died. But in my profession, one has to *wait* for the right opportunity to act.

Our second and third days were the same as the first. Jeremy's group was easy; the second group barely controllable. We waited for the addition of Harris White, Jr., with a feeling of trepidation. This was a Jewish school. Why wasn't this Christian kid with high-powered parents attending one of our city's fine nonsectarian nursery schools?

"Oh, I *know* he's coming," said his mother's secretary when we had called to inquire. "I'm the one who typed up the twenty-five applications last year. I know Mrs. White thought your school was best for Harris." Twenty-five applications? Our feelings of foreboding intensified.

On Thursday, Harris arrived with his mother. With his piercing green eyes, intelligent face, ivory skin and jet-black hair, he certainly was a presence. His mother walked him over to the playdough table. She looked at the cookie cutters our children were using and said in a voice loud enough to be heard in China: "Oh, Harris, look! Here are cookie cutters just like the ones we use at *Christmas*!"

Harris sat down at the table, but only for a minute. Then he bolted over to the Lego corner. Now his mother could be heard on some parts of the moon: "Great, Harris! We didn't have time to build our *church* this morning, but you can do it now!" We got the general idea.

After a short discussion with me, explaining that they had actually arrived from London very late last night and Harris might be just a wee bit tired, Mrs. White kissed her child, waved a cheery good-bye and hurried out the door. The effect on Harris was immediate. He jumped up, raced over to the block area and stomped on a building that two children had been constructing. He jumped as if he wanted to reduce the blocks to dust. I reached him just as he was beginning to throw toys down from a nearby shelf.

I picked Harris up and carried him across the room to the stairs of the loft. I sat him on my lap, looked into his face and spoke softly. "Harris, in this school we have rules. We don't break up other children's work. We don't jump on blocks. We are careful with our toys. Do you understand?"

His response was frightening. He looked past me with a blank stare. His face held no sorrow, remorse or anger. But when I looked more closely into his eyes, I saw that he was scared to death.

"Do you understand, Harris?" I repeated. "I need to know that you understand before I can let you play." When he realized that I wouldn't let him go unless he responded, he nodded very slowly, without looking at me. I put him down. He returned to the blocks and began to move them around, every so often glancing my way. If I was *always* looking at him, he was controllable. Otherwise, he would shout, "Let's be bad guys!" and begin to throw the object nearest him.

This kind of behavior is often attractive to other kids who don't have the nerve to do it. Harris and Jason and Lee were soon friends. Together, they ran around the room trying to commit mayhem. They wanted to jump in the sandbox (which is on legs). They tried to kick down the easel. They attempted to stick their hands in the paint. Need I go on? They required the full-time attention of one teacher, and that teacher had to be me. Cathy just didn't have the experience to deal with this trio. In fact, the look of shock on her face told me that she had never seen anything like them before.

So I watched the boys, and Cathy ran the room, taking paintings off the easel, answering all the questions and handling any minor disputes that arose ("That girl took my black Magic Marker!"). She did a wonderful job, but it wasn't easy.

At snack, Harris smashed his cup on the table and hooted raucously. Jason and Lee followed suit. Although reading a story was out of the question, we managed to get all the children onto the rug for a short song. "Open Shut Them" is a cute little number about hands that every kid already knows. With its familiarity and silly ending (hands in the mouth), it is a sure-fire attention getter. And it worked again: everyone but Harris sang. He listened expressionlessly—but he didn't try to disrupt. *Good,* I thought. *He must like music.* I filed that idea away for future use.

Dismissal time arrived like the cavalry—not a moment too soon. Cathy and I were sweaty and exhausted. But the hardest part of the day was yet to come. We opened the door and let the parents in.

First, they asked their children if school had been fun. Everyone nodded. Then they asked us. We smiled away our nervousness and lied through our teeth. "Oh, it was fine. The children had a wonderful time."

One mother had been observing through the window in our door. She took me aside. "That boy Harris seems a little active," she commented dryly.

"Well, he just got off a plane from London and he's a bit tired. Let's see how it goes tomorrow." I distinctly remember thinking, *We should be so lucky that his behavior is strictly a matter of fatigue. Not much chance of it.* But, of course, I didn't say that. What good would it have done?

Our week ended as it had begun, with an hour of easy kids followed by an hour of terror. Once again, we handed over the children with false assurances of a good time had by all.

"Why don't we just tell parents the truth?" Cathy asked after everyone had left.

"Because we don't know what the truth is yet," I replied. "We haven't had time to zero in on any problems. When we know what the issues are for each child, we can speak to parents individually. Meanwhile, to tell them that the class as a whole is difficult will just make them nervous. And nervous parents make nervous children. Let's not add any more stress to the situation."

Cathy understood immediately, as she always did. It was a blessing to have an assistant so quick on the uptake. "Speaking of stress," she inquired, "what do you think is going on with Harris?"

It was a difficult, unappealing question, which I tackled at 4 A.M., my usual time for thinking about children. What did we know about Harris so far? He could play intensely with other children, but could not talk to us. He never smiled or laughed or frowned or whined. He was capable of biting or kicking another child without warning and without apparent provocation. He did not like to be touched. He looked frightened whenever I had to discipline him, which, unfortunately, was most of the time.

I had expected him to be difficult, and the kid was as tough as they come. What I had not expected was to love him the minute I set eyes on him. Any teacher will tell you, if she's being candid, that it just happens this way. Sometimes there's a child who goes directly into your heart and nestles there for the duration. You can't get rid of the feeling—all you can do is try not to play favorites. I have no evidence, but I'd swear that it's a chemical reaction.

Okay, so I loved the child. Now, how was I going to help him? I wished that I could talk to Maggie, my former director. She would always ask the questions that inspired the right answers in me. I had actually called her a few days ago, but she was too weak to talk much. She needed all her strength to stay alive until January, when her first grandchild would be born. Maggie was such a beloved figure in our community that parents continually inquired about her health. This made school even more stressful for the teachers. Parents missed her warmth and her graciousness; we missed her insight and her sound guidance.

I thought about the questions that Maggie would have asked me. What is Harris's home life like? What do you know about his parents? On Friday, I had summoned my courage and asked Mrs. White if she knew that this was a Jewish school. Her answer was disarming: "Oh yes, we know. Of course, Harris couldn't go here all the way through the sixth grade because he needs to learn about his own heritage. But I looked at a lot of schools, and this place is the most nurturing one I saw. I'm sure it's the right school for Harris." I was immediately on her side.

As I continued thinking, I realized that the Whites had never filled out one of our questionnaires. The other parents had completed them at our orientation. We had learned some important facts about our students: Benjamin Tyne, for example, had inherited a cholesterol problem and needed to watch his diet. Sharon would have surgery on her ear the second week of school. Lee was allergic to chocolate, and Cory had never attended school before. We learned about the children's sleep habits and "elimination practices." (David, already four years old, wet himself almost every day.) But we had none of these details for Harris. This, then, is what Maggie would have told me: you need to know more.

On Monday, Harris's father brought him to school. A handsome man with an open, friendly face, he introduced himself and shook hands all around. He was quite pleasant, but he had "busy daddy syndrome." That's my name for the fathers who are so anxious to rush off to work that they don't set one foot in the classroom. Any business with the teacher is done at the door. Sometimes a father is eager to get rid of his child. Sometimes he is just genuinely uncomfortable around a classroom. (I suspected that Harris White, Sr., was the former; mercifully, I was wrong.)

Before he dashed completely out of my sight, I thrust one of our questionnaires in his direction. Since they had been in London, I explained, they had never filled one out. Harris Senior's answer surprised me: "Sure. We'll do it tonight and get it back to you tomorrow." Most people with difficult children aren't too happy about putting personal information down on paper.

Tomorrow arrived, and with it came the questionnaire. What it divulged was painful to read. Mr. and Mrs. White had adopted Harris at birth, and hired a baby-sitter who was unable to deal with him. In Mrs. White's words, this "previous Nanny . . . was loving but inarticulate and weak and not at all up to Harris's challenge. In discipline, she knew no middle ground between beating (which I prohibited) and nothing. As a consequence she gave in to Harris, rewarded negative behavior and he basically controlled her instead of the other way around. We should have dealt with the problem a year ago, but this is hindsight."

The questionnaire raised more questions than it answered. My detective's intuition came into play. Over the years, I'd seen at least three hundred of these documents. Not one of them had ever mentioned that the parents had forbidden their nanny to hit their child. It was a given. No one would feel the need to bring it up on a questionnaire.

Was hitting mentioned because it had been recently forbidden? Had the nanny been hitting Harris for years before the Whites found out? Did they actually continue to employ her when they realized what was happening? It seemed to be the case. She had worked for them until last month, according to the questionnaire.

I looked once again at all my facts. Harris was definitely hand-shy (our term for a kid who flinches when he's touched accidentally by a grown-up). He disliked being touched by us in any way. He hit other children indiscriminately and without warning. These were all symptoms of a child who was being hit at home. I wondered why I hadn't seen it before.

I communicated my fears to Cathy. We realized that I was going to have to ask these two very nice people if they had retained a baby-sitter in the face of direct evidence that she had been abusive to their child. The problem was how to ask such a question while retaining any sort of composure. Nursery school teachers are child advocates; stories like this one make the bile rise.

I spoke to Mrs. White the next day. I kept my voice calm and my face as neutral as possible.

"Your questionnaire left me with some questions, Joanna—do you have a moment?"

Once again, I was impressed by her immediate and honest answers. Yes, Harris had been hit by Lonnie, their housekeeper. Yes, his parents had continued to employ her, with the added prohibition of hitting. Since Lonnie was unable to control him in any other way, Harris was totally undisciplined for months. He refused to toilet train. He refused to do anything at all if he didn't want to. His behavior in London was so terrible that his parents were overwhelmed. Their fervent hope was that their "strong" new housekeeper, Opal, their own firmer stance on discipline and a new school experience would begin the process of healing their child. The director of Harris's last school had told them that their son was very disturbed and needed immediate therapy, Joanna confided.

I'll bet that assessment didn't make its way onto any of the twenty-five nursery school applications, was what I thought.

What I said was, "Oh. I'm sorry. That must have been very difficult for you to hear." I did not say the director's opinion was untrue.

The situation was clear. Harris's parents had to deal with their guilt and anxiety, and we had to deal with a frightened child who, having often been hit, had no reason to trust grown-ups. I relayed the conversation to Cathy, adding my suspicion that Harris would more than likely need outside help. We could teach him to behave in school, but we couldn't take away the pain of what had come before. Meanwhile, it was our job to formulate a game plan.

"A game plan?" asked Cathy, obviously not a big sports fan.

"Yes. A strategy for dealing with Harris, so that we can both handle him consistently. This child has been hit and probably screamed at a lot. Our policy will be to touch him and speak to him as gently as possible, while continuing to enforce the rules each and every time he breaks them. He needs to know that we won't hurt him, but also that we won't let him hurt anyone else. That's the only way he's going to feel safe."

"How does that differ from the way we treat every kid?"

"Some kids need to hear a strong, authoritative voice to calm down. Some kids need to be jollied along, with an appeal to their sense of humor. Sometimes a kid needs you to look the other way—if he's finally standing up for himself by pushing a bully, for example. Although the class rules apply to every child, we can't enforce them in the same way at the beginning of the year. Later, when the children come together as a group, we can be more consistent in discipline."

"Gotcha."

• • •

While we were implementing our game plan for Harris, we had another situation to consider: Sharon was having an operation on Friday. A large child with hazel eyes and short, blond hair, Sharon was as sturdy as she looked. Her expressive face was not classically beautiful, but the longer you knew her, the prettier she became. With her perky personality and slightly babyish lisp, she was an instant favorite with the other children. Cathy and I were crazy about her.

Sharon's family was unusually close. Her father, John, had just opened his own employment agency. Her mother, Karen, was a high school teacher. Both were astute observers of their children (their other daughter, Lilia, was nine) and truly concerned with their emotional well-being.

Karen and John asked me when they should tell Sharon about the surgery. They felt that the best time would be the night before she was to enter the hospital. I had to agree. Sharon would be well aware of the pain and difficulty involved. She had undergone a similar operation in the spring, to remove a cyst in her inner ear. The cyst was benign, but the doctor hadn't been able to take it all out. This operation was needed to remove the rest of it.

Being in the hospital hadn't bothered Sharon, her mother told me. Karen knew that her daughter's first question would be about the needles, especially the intravenous one. There would be needles again, and her parents wanted her to have the least possible time to worry about them. I certainly agreed with that decision!

Frequently, children will sense that their parents are uneasy; not knowing what it is about, they will begin to be uneasy themselves. Observing Sharon in the classroom, however, I could see no sign of anxiety. She was her cheerful, chatty self. She sat at the art table with her friends, complimenting their work ("I like your painting, Jenny") and enjoying her own efforts to produce a watercolor ("Mine is blue"). I did notice that she spoke very loudly, almost at a shout. I often had to ask her to lower her voice during our play period. At snack, a time for quiet conversation, her voice was louder even than Harris's. I asked Karen if there was a disturbance in her hearing from the cyst. "No," she told me. "It's probably just that she has to speak up to be heard in our noisy house." (I suppose that was a possibility. Also, there was the fact of school adjustment and maybe of unconscious nervousness. Take your pick. I can tell you, though, that once the operation was over, she never shouted in the classroom again.)

Sharon's parents had good reason to be worried. This operation could be a relatively simple one, lasting about two hours. If the cyst was deeper than expected, however, the surgeon would have to go more slowly to avoid damage to the facial nerve. There was a slim chance that the nerve would be damaged anyway. At three and a half years old, Sharon could awaken with a partially paralyzed face.

Friday morning promised to be a difficult one for us all. Karen would call as soon as Sharon was out of surgery, so we would know the results right after they did. Cathy and I were tense: the thought of dealing with our tough trio of boys was overwhelming. But just when we needed it, a small miracle occurred: Jason discovered the shape pegs.

This activity, called a manipulative because it requires hand-eye coordination and manual dexterity, was sitting on the table nearest the front door. As Jason walked in with his usual bombast, the bright colors of the shapes caught his eye. He went over to the table to investigate, and liked what he saw. He sat down and began to place the pegs in a grid, one by one, creating a beautiful design of shape and color.

We had never seen Jason sit still for one minute, and now he was not only sitting but concentrating on a task. Harris arrived, and went directly to his friend. When he couldn't entice

Jason over to the block area, he sat down at the table. He, too, began to work with the shapes. This was a stroke of good fortune for which I was totally unprepared. The two boys sat and worked quietly for nearly half our play period. Lee, unable to concentrate for more than a moment, could not join them. He just wandered around the room, occasionally calling out, "Jason! Come play in the blocks now!" in a wistful voice. The classroom had twenty minutes of relative peace.

For the first time, I was really able to observe all the children in the room. They seemed to be enjoying their first week together as a whole group. Jenny and Cory had moved from the playdough table to the library area, and were looking at books together. When she was there, Sharon was part of this group. They did everything together. Although there was a lot of conversation, I noticed that Cory spoke only three or four words at a time. Often, even those few words were hard to understand. Also, she had difficulty getting into a chair without falling off it. I'd have to keep an eye on her. Speech and balance problems were often related to hearing.

David was trying to break into the Jeremy–Benjamin friendship. The two boys knew each other from school last year, and were best of friends. David played wherever they did, nearby. I hoped that it wouldn't be long until he got up the courage to join them. It wasn't time for my intervention yet. First, I had to give the children a chance to work it out themselves.

I watched Jeremy with fascination: he was so carefree that I never could have guessed that a trauma had just occurred in his life. Something told me that this was not the end of the story.

Louisa and Mary Ann had begun to play together, but one observation was sufficient to see there were problems. Mary Ann was nearly four, while Louisa had just turned three. Their games consisted of Louisa doing whatever Mary Ann wanted. Young as she was, however, Louisa was a smart kid with strong opinions. She wouldn't play this role for long.

Amanda, pretty as a china doll, was keeping mostly to herself. She wasn't unhappy; she was just watching. Some children like to size up a situation before they jump in and begin to make friends. The best thing a teacher can do is let the child decide when the time is right.

It was an easier morning than usual. By the time the three amigos had revved up to high gear, we were ready for cleanup and snack. Next week, we would add bathroom time to our schedule. I wasn't in a hurry to take these twelve kids out of the room at the same time, but it had to be done. Today, we managed to get them all on the rug. While I read the shortest story in our classroom, *Goodnight, Moon,* Louisa held on to my leg, Harris turned his back and played with a truck and Lee and Jason sat (forcibly) on Cathy's lap. It was a day of small miracles indeed.

After dismissal, Cathy and I learned of the large miracle which had occurred at New York Hospital. Sharon's operation had been short and successful. The cyst had been shallow, and there was no damage to the facial nerve. She would be just fine.

• • •

Sharon walked in on Monday with her cheerful smile and a dressing behind her ear. Since school lasted only an hour and a half today, her parents explained, the doctor said it was all right for her to come, as long as there would be no active play in a gym setting. I assured them that gym didn't start until the end of the week. (I shuddered inwardly at the thought of this group unleashed in a large play area. Would they all survive? Would the teachers?)

Sharon acted as if nothing unusual had happened to her over the weekend. She went right over to Cory and Jenny at the peg table and began to construct a design of her own. She was her usual chatty self. Her parents reported that she had gone through the operation, and even the needles, like a trouper. It was positively amazing. "Even a little scary," said Karen. "Anyone else in our family would have emoted like crazy."

The emotions came on Tuesday. Sharon and her parents were half an hour late. When they arrived, it looked as if everyone had been crying. John explained that they had taken Sharon out to breakfast, where she had accidentally bumped her head on the back of the booth. The possibility of injury had frightened everyone.

I bent down to talk to Sharon. "What's the matter, sweetie?"

"I hit my ear on the back of the seat."

"That must have hurt."

She nodded.

"Does it still hurt now?"

She shook her head.

"Oh good. Then you can come right in and play. Cathy, could you take Sharon over to the art table and show her how to make a collage?"

Cathy had been watching the three dynamos in the block area. Leaving them was a calculated risk, but we had to take it. Both Sharon and her parents needed care at the moment. Cathy came right over.

Taking Sharon by the hand, she said, "Good morning, honey. Come and see what's at the art table." In only a minute, Sharon changed from a crying child to an interested student, as Cathy showed her how to dip small pieces of shiny, colored paper into glue and stick them onto a larger piece of construction paper.

"You mean that's all you have to do to get her to stop crying?" her father asked incredulously.

"Isn't distraction wonderful?" I answered with a smile.

"But she cried all the way from the restaurant."

"Has she cried at all about the operation, the hospital, the anesthesia, the needles?"

"No."

"Then perhaps that's what you're getting now. Even 'good little girls' are entitled to a reaction."

Karen spoke up. "I guess that goes for me, too. I really over-reacted at the restaurant when Sharon hit her head. I've been so upset, and I haven't let myself feel it at all." Her eyes filled with tears.

I put my hand on her shoulder. "It's okay. You've been through a terrible time. You're entitled to be upset."

She nodded and smiled, knowing I was right. Then she and John waved good-bye to Sharon from the door, and left.

I turned my attention to the class. Everything looked pretty good. No one was crying or throwing any sharp object or taking a chunk out of anyone else's hand with their teeth. I sat for a moment to think.

There was Sharon, acting perfectly normal, talking to her friends at the art table. In the book area was Jeremy, smiling at Benjamin as they turned the pages of *Are You My Mother?* Harris was in the block corner trying to build a house with Lee and Jason. What was with these children? Two had been through harrowing experiences in the last few weeks and one had a history of being battered. But none of the three had a word to say about how they were feeling.

Maybe they didn't know their teachers well enough to say anything yet. Maybe it was the school-as-oasis attitude. Maybe they needed to feel more comfortable in the classroom (adjusted to the routine, trusting of their friends, etc.). My instincts, however, told me it was more. What we had here was a group of children unwilling to talk about their emotions. And if preschool children don't talk about their "hard" feelings, such as anger, sorrow or fear, they are condemned to act them out.

We have a lot of work to do, I thought, as I got up and ran across the room. But first I had to grab the huge block that Harris was aiming at Jason's head.

OCTOBER:
THE WITCHES AND THE BOX

The first week of October was our first full-time school week. The children would be staying from 8:45 A.M. until 1 P.M. They would have lunch in school. They would play in the gym or on the roof playground each day. There was no getting around it—now we *had* to take the children out of the classroom as a group.

Our initial trip would be to the bathroom. For some reason, I felt like Wyatt Earp steeling himself before the gunfight at the O.K. Corral. The bathroom was just around two corners, about thirty feet away. Each day for many years, I had taken my students there after playtime and so had every teacher of my acquaintance. What was so threatening about this group that I had a feeling of impending disaster before we even walked out the door?

Perhaps the fact that they wouldn't stay *in* the classroom made me concerned about taking them *out* of it. Louisa ran out so often that it was hard to catch her every time. When I did, she'd look up at me innocently with those big blue eyes, bat her thick, black lashes and say, "I was going to my cubby." Although the cubbies were right outside the classroom, they were out of our line of vision.

"Louisa, you must ask Cathy or me if you want to leave the classroom. We'll tell you if it's okay."

She cocked her head, looking for all the world like a little bird.

"But—my cubby—see, I have to get this to show my friends."
She held up a strand of plastic beads.

"That's fine," I said. "It's a nice idea to bring them in and
show your friends. But you have to ask us first. We always need
to know where you are."

Louisa nodded, but she didn't remember. This is common for
children who have just turned three. They have selective memories—what's really important is what sticks. Naturally, my
other baby, Lee, began to follow Louisa. He thought it was fun
to run in and out of the room. We tried closing the door, but
Cory began to cry. (Some children feel cut off from home with
the door closed in the beginning of school.) So we opened the
door and stood guard, as much as we could.

This, then, was the group we were going to move down the
hall: two kids who squirted out of the room whenever possible;
two who were completely unpredictable (Jason and Harris);
one with poor balance (Cory); and seven variables. No wonder
I was girding my loins.

Normally, I would have had everyone sit on the rug and
called their names one by one to go stand by the door next to
Cathy. Children love to hear their names mentioned, and will
listen very well to any instruction that includes this process.
This group was too antsy. They couldn't sit on the rug for more
than thirty seconds. We still had no formal story time. Cathy
read during playtime to the three or four children who could sit
and listen. Beginning the trip to the bathroom with the calling
of names was out of the question. In educational lingo, it was
"too much structure" for these kids.

Cathy went to the door and closed it most of the way to pre-
vent the children from running out before we were ready. I explained what we were about to do, and asked the children to go
over to Cathy. She took the hands of Louisa and Lee. The other
children were in the middle, and I followed in the rear, holding
the hands of Jason and Harris. (Harris was not too thrilled with

this, but when he saw it was all right with Jason, he submitted.) My final warning to the children was, "Remember: Cathy is in the front and I am in the back. You guys are in the middle." Several of them nodded, which I took as an encouraging sign. We started out.

We had traveled about ten feet when Benjamin and David decided to have a race. They ran in front of Cathy, knocking Cory down along the way. She began to cry. Cathy and the other children sped up to catch the boys. I went over to help Cory up. This, naturally, required the use of my hands. But the minute— nay, the nanosecond—I let go of Jason's hand, he took off in the other direction. Leaving the sobbing Cory and the surprised Harris, I ran after Jason.

He sped with aerodynamic ease around the far corner, where I could no longer see him. To this day, I don't know how I managed to run so fast (thank heavens for adrenaline). I caught up to him in the teachers' room. He was lifting the blade of our paper cutter, which had carelessly been left unlocked. His other hand was placed directly underneath. I stopped him just as he was about to sever his own fingers.

Holding Jason's hand, I began to explain why he shouldn't run away. In response, he twisted out of my grasp and ran over to touch the stove, which happened to be hot. I grabbed him just before he got there. No more explanations now, other than a loudly shouted, "JASON! YOU MUST *NOT* RUN AWAY ANYMORE! YOU COULD GET HURT! IT IS *NOT* OKAY!"

Hannibal Lecter's mask didn't fit any tighter than my grip around Jason's wrist as we headed back to the bathroom. Cathy was faring well there. Cory and Harris had joined the group, and the children were in various stages of using the facilities. As Jason joined his friends, I felt suddenly weak. Was saving kids from major injury in my job description? If so, I needed combat pay.

Cathy was horrified when I related the incident. Clearly, we needed a Strategy for Leaving the Room. I thought of it on the spot. (It's amazing what a traumatic experience will do for clarity of mind.)

As the children milled around, I asked Cathy in a stage voice who had done the best job of walking to the bathroom. She replied that Mary Ann had followed instructions just perfectly. "Good. Then Mary Ann will be the leader back to the classroom." Naturally, everyone else clamored for the honor.

"Whoever does a very good job of walking *behind* Mary Ann and Cathy will be the leader next time. But remember—you have to do a *very* good job."

The effect was immediate. They weren't perfect, but they did a lot better. Lee in particular was intent on being the next leader. He strained to control his impulse to run. Jason was naturally out of the competition by virtue of having his hand held tightly enough to cut off the circulation. (Better the circulation than the fingers was my point of view.) Louisa and Harris did as well as could be expected. We returned to the room without incident, if you don't count twenty cries of, "Is this good? Do I get to be the leader?" from Lee.

I do not actually believe in having leaders for children of this age. They're too young to understand that everyone will get a turn eventually. One leader means eleven disappointed children. But there are exceptions to every rule and this was one of them. We had leaders to and from the classroom all year. Ultimately, it did the trick. Flexibility is a requirement of preschool teaching—and just about everything else in life, I guess.

. . .

The following morning I was in my room early, setting up a special art project. The school was eerily quiet, as it always was when the children weren't around. They weren't due for half an hour, so I had plenty of time. Unexpectedly, my friend Hope appeared at my door. "Patti, I need to tell you something."

I walked over. I assumed it was news of the summer camp at Beth-El, which I helped her administrate. "What's up?" I asked.

"Maggie died this morning. I'm sorry."

I fell to my knees. "No! It's just not possible! She was going to live until her grandchild was born. I know she was. She would never let herself die first. It's just not true!" I sobbed.

"I'm sorry. Her husband called the temple early this morning. I wanted to tell you myself." She helped me to my feet.

I clung to my friend and cried for several minutes. I didn't know how grateful I was that Hope had been the one to tell me until I heard a voice at my back. It was my director.

"She already knows," Barbara hollered over her shoulder; her words rang down the empty hall. To me, she said, "Stop crying so loudly. The children will hear you."

As she closed my door, there wasn't a child in sight.

• • •

Maggie had died, but we were not allowed to cry. Word had come from the Fourth Floor (our name for the administration office): the temple wanted to send out a letter to inform all the parents at the same time. The teachers would hand it out at the beginning of school tomorrow; meanwhile, we were to tell no one. "Just go back into the classroom and do your work" was the message.

I remembered reading that Vivien Leigh had never missed a performance even though she was manic-depressive. She just shoved aside her illness and went on. I took a page from her book that day. I stuffed all my grief into a corner as best I could, smiled at the children and did my job. Whenever we could, though, little groups of teachers huddled in unseen corners and mourned together. Maggie had been seriously ill, but none of us had expected her death so soon.

In the classroom, the atmosphere was somber. Cathy's

grandfather had just died, so she was already in terrible shape. I could barely speak. The children did not know what was happening, but they caught the mood immediately. No child hit, and no one got bitten.

In the block corner, Jeremy and Benjamin were playing with the toy animals. They knocked all of them down, one by one. Then Jeremy picked up a horse, and began to move it through the air as if it were flying. Benjamin imitated him. Suddenly, Jeremy began to chant, "They're alive again! They're alive again!" Benjamin joined him, and the game continued for many minutes. Cathy and I were stunned. "If wishes were horses," then Maggie, Cathy's grandfather and Jeremy's baby would all be alive again.

The next morning, we took the children to the gym for the first time. Our gym was actually an auditorium, carpeted, with many large pieces of indoor play equipment. There were large metal triangles connected by wooden boards for balance work and for jumping. There were structures called "houses" for climbing, sliding and just hanging out on the bottom level. A giant slide with chain-link stairs stood in a corner. Around the room, we had two wooden rowboats, which each seated four, and three yellow plastic, curved pieces we called "bananas," for rocking and seesawing. The children could just run around freely, if they chose. We shared our forty minutes there each day with another group of three- and four-year-olds, so there was also the opportunity to make new friends. The place was a child's idea of a smashingly good time.

The gym was the same distance from the classroom as the bathroom, but also up a flight of stairs. With our "leader" routine in place, we walked to the staircase in fairly decent order (translation: no one was injured). As we began to climb, Cathy went first, most of the children followed her, and I lagged behind with the stragglers. As a reminder of how to walk upstairs, we sang a little ditty: "Hands on the railing, up the stairs we go—o . . ." You'd be amazed at the number of children who forget to hold on, lose their balance and fall. An adult would probably be hospitalized with a broken whatever, but a kid is usually just "shaken up on the play." Nevertheless, we sing, operating under the general principle of "who needs an accident?"

Our children walked into the gym, gasped with delight (even the ones who had played in it last year) and began to run around. It was, I must admit, a pretty sight. For thirty seconds or so. That was the amount of time we spent there without an injury. A child from the other class suddenly bit Benjamin on the back with such ferocity that Benjamin screamed in horror. I deposited the perpetrator on the nearest chair (with a little more force than necessary, I'm afraid), picked up Benjamin and rushed down to the teachers' room.

Benjamin was crying as if both his legs had been broken. When I tried to lift his shirt to assess the damage, he screamed "NO! Don't look at it! It's okay—IT'S OKAY!" After much cajoling on my part, and much screaming, "No! Don't TOUCH it!" on his part, Benjamin let me take a look.

This was unusual behavior for a child with a bite. There generally wasn't much pain involved after the first minute. By now, most children would have stopped crying, even if they were still upset by the idea of the bite. My detective's antennae were up: either the wound was terrible, or there was a problem with Benjamin Tyne.

I looked at the bite. It was strong enough to have gone through Benjamin's shirt and leave a deep red mark, but it hadn't broken the skin. I needed to wash it and apply a first-aid cream, but Benjamin wouldn't have to go to the doctor. (All our students have tetanus shots in order to come to school, but a human bite that breaks the skin should be seen by a doctor anyway.)

It took ten minutes to convince Benjamin to let me clean and medicate the bite. He was practically hysterical with fright. To calm him, I started making jokes.

"Did you see that I put the boy who bit you on a chair?" I asked. Benjamin nodded.

"I was pretty angry, wasn't I? That kid's probably going to have to sit there for a week! Maybe even a month!"

Benjamin began to laugh through his tears. "Yeah, maybe even a year!" he added.

"Maybe his mom will have to come to the gym to give him breakfast every day while he's sitting on the chair!"

I worked swiftly while we exchanged jokes. Benjamin's wonderful sense of the ridiculous was an asset which I would use frequently in the months to come. I had found the key to dealing with this kid: make him laugh. But I didn't know why it was so necessary. What was he frightened of?

I could barely coax Benjamin back into the gym. He asked me the name of the other child (Geoffrey), and whether he would still be there.

"Yes, but Geoffrey's teachers and Cathy and I will make sure that he never bites you again. I promise."

If a teacher makes a promise like that, she'd better make sure she keeps it. I followed Benjamin around for the rest of the period. Any time Geoffrey came near him, I stepped in. But I didn't have much to do, because Benjamin himself ran, terror-stricken, the minute he sighted the enemy. This behavior would continue for several weeks, until Benjamin was sure that Geoffrey would no longer bother him.

Geoffrey was no bigger than a thumbtack and equally benign: he could hurt you, but he never meant to. He ran everywhere and anywhere, as if propelled by some inner, random force. During gym time, his talented teacher, Becky, would be doubly watchful from now on. Geoffrey, thank God, was not my problem—but Benjamin was. I spoke to his mother at dismissal.

Obviously, she was concerned about the bite, but less so when she saw it. (All bites must be reported to the parents of the biter and the victim. But it's a lot easier on the victim's parents if they can see the evidence directly after they've heard the news.) I was interested to see that Benjamin was equally reluctant about having his mother look at his injury.

"Does Benjamin often get very upset when he's been hurt?" I asked.

Francine replied that he did, and that it was frequently difficult to calm him down. She didn't know why it was so. She thanked me for taking such good care of Benjamin, took her son by the hand and left the school. I noticed that he was talking a blue streak as they departed. His mother would know every detail of the day before they had crossed the street.

That was just like Benjamin. A handsome boy with strong verbal skills, he could talk a mile a minute. His straight black hair, always cut short, emphasized his expressive, near-black eyes. With his olive complexion, he could easily have been mistaken for an Israeli.

Benjamin was tall for his age, and this fact had illuminated the problem of our loft. To make use of the space underneath the loft, we had set up the children's kitchen there. The first time he went to use the stove, Benjamin bumped his head on the loft. So did Cory and Mary Ann. Although they learned to duck, there were still occasional casualties. It didn't take a genius to see that the loft was too low. I reported it immediately to the school office, emphasizing that children were being hurt. I hoped that message would get immediate attention, since it involved the paying customers.

Benjamin came to school the day after the biting incident with two imaginary swords strapped to his back. "See these swords?" he said gleefully. "These will protect me from Geoffrey in the gym. If he comes near me"—he pretended to pull them out of their scabbards—"I'll take out these. Then he'll run away and I'll be okay." Benjamin proceeded to run around the room, showing everyone his fantastical swords and demanding admiration. Like the characters in "The Emperor's New Clothes," our children complied. Three- and four-year-olds slip in and out of fantasy play so easily that I'm sure many of the kids believed in the swords. For them, it was a game, but for Benjamin, it was urgent business.

I called Benjamin over and took one of his hands in mine. I looked directly into his face, speaking slowly and carefully. He needed to know I was completely sincere.

"Benjamin, you don't need those swords to protect you in the gym. It's okay with me if you have them, since they're pretend. But you have Cathy and me to protect you. We didn't know about Geoffrey before, but we do now. So we'll watch him and we'll make sure that you and all the other children are safe. That's our job. Do you understand?"

He nodded. "But can I still take my swords up to the gym? My daddy gave them to me."

"Yes, of course you can. Just remember that we'll be there, too. You'll be safe."

Benjamin nodded again, smiled at me and walked off to play with the other boys. But he wasn't convinced that anything could really help him. Although Geoffrey never got within a yard of him in the gym, Benjamin brought his swords for weeks. He appeared one day in jeans with patches on the knees, which he said were "special to keep him safe." He talked about possible accidents; he saw danger almost everywhere.

Cathy and I discussed his odd behavior. Clearly, Benjamin had a real issue with personal safety. It was our guess that the bite from Geoffrey had only exacerbated an existing problem. We needed to learn about Benjamin's life outside the classroom.

What did we already know? His mother had told us that he had a "cholesterol problem," and had given us a list of foods he couldn't eat. But she had said that it wasn't critical: he could actually have a little bit of anything on the list. Was there more to this story? We would have to find out. Probably, the best setting would be the parent-teacher conferences coming up in the first week of November. Instinct told me that an informal, two-minute conference-by-the-door just wouldn't do it. Benjamin's parents didn't give out information as readily as the Whites did.

Of course, their child wasn't as difficult as Harris. Although we'd put our game plan into effect immediately, we hadn't made much progress with Harris. No matter how gently and firmly we enforced the rules, he was still one tough little character. His play in the room continued at the same fierce, unpredictable level.

One morning, however, there was a subtle but unmistakable change. Lee, Jason and Harris were playing with the dolls on the loft. Harris suddenly shouted out: "Let's throw the babies down!"

"Throw them down!" Lee repeated.

I spoke to them from the floor. "No. Baby dolls are not for throwing, just like babies are not for throwing. Do you throw your baby sister, Jason?"

Lee and Harris, who had no siblings, listened with interest.

"No," Jason answered solemnly. "I only tickle her."

"Sounds like fun. And you can play with these babies, too. Wrap them in their blankets, feed them, take them for a ride in the stroller."

Dead silence ensued.

Without warning, Harris shouted: "On the boat! This is a boat! Let's go for a ride on the boat!"

This idea appealed to his buddies, but the actual game consisted only of standing on the loft and hollering at the top of their lungs:

"All aboard! All aboard the boat!"

They screamed so loudly that they frightened the other children, who stopped in their tracks and looked up at the loft.

It was time for me to regain control of the room. I spoke to the boys in a normal voice. It was important for *all* the children to see I was not frightened by loud noises.

"Pretending that you're on a boat is fine, but shouting is *not* fine. You can yell when we go outside to play. Here, we use classroom voices, like mine."

Jason and Lee repeated "All aboard" more softly.

"Well done," I told them.

But Harris looked at me intently, opened his mouth and shrieked "ALL ABOARD!" even louder than before. For the first time, he was issuing a direct challenge to me: "Okay," he seemed to say, "I yelled again. Now what are you going to do about it?"

Here was a child who was testing to see if there were consistent rules, so he could begin to feel safe. He also wanted to see what he could get away with. It was imperative that I hold my ground.

"Harris, if you cannot speak more softly, you will have to come down from the loft."

"No."

"Try it. Try *saying* 'all aboard.'"

"All aboard," he repeated in a normal but petulant voice.

"Great!" I exclaimed, and stepped back a few paces to let the game continue.

Immediately, Harris began to shriek "ALL ABOARD!" at top pitch.

I intervened. "That's it, Harris. You must come down now."

"No, no!" he yelled, his face a familiar mask of blankness. I climbed up the stairs of the loft, took his hand and began to walk him down. Immediately, he became completely limp—the famous "sack of potatoes" act known to all preschool children (they must pass it around somehow). So I carried him down, and sat him on a nearby chair.

"Harris, you need to sit here and take a little time to think about the rules of this classroom. We don't yell in school."

"No, no!" he protested loudly. "I don't want to sit in a chair!" He squirmed, but he sat. He didn't get up or try to run away. They rarely do. Children need rules, just like the rest of us. The other children, who had been watching intently, went back to their activities. There was no longer a threat to their well-being.

While I sat next to Harris and Cathy ran the room, Lee and Jason decided to have a picnic on the boat. Excitedly, they began to haul all the plastic dishes, fruit, flatware, placemats and cups from the kitchen up to the loft. They were having a wonderful time, constructively, for once.

Harris watched his friends closely. His face betrayed nothing, but I assumed he wanted to be with them. I leaned over and spoke softly to him.

"Harris, do you want to have a picnic on the boat with Lee and Jason?"

Without looking at me, he nodded.

"Can you remember that we don't yell in class?" No answer, no movement, no acknowledgment of my existence.

"When you can tell me that you'll try not to shout, then you can get up. Otherwise, you'll just sit here with me."

(This is an advantage teachers have over parents. When disciplining, we rarely have the constraints of time. We aren't responsible for getting a child ready for school, dropping him off and running to work. We don't have to be at Aunt Bertha's in half an hour. We can just sit with a kid until the rule we're enforcing becomes as clear as spring water.)

Harris got the message: if he did what I said, he could resume playing. Otherwise, I was prepared to sit with him until the proverbial cows came home. Slowly, Harris turned and looked directly into my face.

"I won't shout," he told me.

"Okay," I acknowledged. "Go ahead and play."

He bounded up the stairs to join his friends. "A picnic!" he exclaimed. "Let's eat!" He spoke loudly, but he didn't yell. After a minute, he glanced at me—but not to see if I was checking up on him. The quizzical look on his face told me that *he* was checking to see if he was doing the right thing. We had reached a new stage. Harris cared about the rules; he just wasn't sure he could follow them.

It is common for difficult children to change their behavior in this fashion. They move to a new level, where the teacher is their conscience and their guide (acknowledgments to Jiminy Cricket). Harris began to look over at me every few minutes, trying to gauge my reaction to his behavior. Sometimes my response was just a small nod and an encouraging smile. Often, I spoke to him: "Well done, Harris," if he was sharing, or "Try it this way," if he was banging blocks together instead of placing them on the ground. Of course, this constant attention took up a lot of my time. But if Harris could improve, it was better for the whole group.

For the next few days, I watched him constantly, even if I was working with other children. He seemed to be trying to fit in. I was astonished at how fast this change had occurred: I had expected a longer struggle. "Maybe he's going to be all right," I told myself. "Maybe all he needed was a little consistency in his life."

I looked around the room at the other children. They *all* needed a little help. They were playing in small groups, but they never interacted with the children outside their particular coterie. We needed some sort of unifying activity—something that would bring everyone together.

I wish I could say that I thought of one myself. I didn't: it was simply dropped in my lap. One morning, Mary Ann's mother brought in the perfect gift. She thought we might enjoy playing with the gigantic box in which her new dishes had arrived. She and Mary Ann had lugged it to school that morning.

I folded up our easel, and placed the box in our painting corner. It sat on the floor, on top of the washable tablecloth we used as a dropcloth. I taped the open flaps shut, so we had a large, perfect square. Cathy took the paints from the easel and placed them next to the box. Now we were ready to go to work.

"Hmm. This box is nice and big, but it's not too gorgeous," I said to the few children standing right beside me. "Who wants to paint it so it will look more beautiful?" As I expected, all of them did. I hadn't made a general announcement because we would have had everyone clamoring at once.

The children painted in groups of six, and they had a wonderful time. First, the job was to cover the box completely; then, they added the finishing touches. Young children are often more interested in the *process* of an activity rather than the *product* it produces. They would rather paint, for example, than admire their finished painting. In this respect, our project was tailor-made: the kids could slap on as much paint as they wanted. The box didn't tear or weaken from the ten or twelve extra coats it received.

After the paint dried, we had a pink, turquoise and yellow thing of beauty. Next, it was time for collage. Cathy and I helped our students rip construction paper and roll tissue paper into balls. We had just begun to study shapes, so the teachers cut out squares, triangles and circles. With glee, the children dipped all this paper into platefuls of Elmer's Glue and stuck it on the box. After two more days, we had a Magnificent Work of Art, created by all the children in the class.

Naturally, the commendations flowed in. Our box was admired by all the parents, and also by other teachers and children who walked by our room. The children were justly proud of their work.

The box would have remained a work of art, sitting in the front of the room to be admired, had it not been for Louisa. She exclaimed, "It's the box! 'Down in the Box!'" and proceeded to try to climb in.

A word of explanation is necessary here. I had taught the

children a movement song called "Down in the Box," which they loved to perform. Each child got down on the rug, head down and knees to the chest, forming a little ball. I sang about a jack-in-the-box, waiting for the lid to open. Here are the lyrics:

> Down in the box there lives a little man
> He waits and he waits as quiet as he can
> Until I open the box for him—POP!
> See how I'm jumping, jumping, jumping,
> You never knew I could jump so high!
> See how I'm jumping, jumping, jumping,
> You never knew I could touch the sky!

When the box "opened," the children leaped up and began to jump. Hands held in the air around their faces, they really resembled twelve adorable jumping jacks. At the end, they stretched their hands into the air, trying to "touch the sky."

Louisa had decided that she wanted to perform the song with the box as a prop. So I cut the tape which concealed the opening. Next, I cut off two of the four flaps, to make climbing in and out easier. Then Louisa was on her way, followed by Mary Ann, who scrambled in beside her. "Cover us up!" they shouted. The other children obliged. "Now sing!" was the imperative from within the box. I began, and the children joined in. (By this time, all ten of them had gathered around, as if the headline BIG DOINGS AROUND THE BOX had been telegraphed across the room. Kids have a nose for news.)

When we reached "POP!" the two girls pushed the flaps over and jumped up, beaming with delight. Everybody laughed. "Let's finish the song, and you keep on jumping," I told them. We did and they did, to the great satisfaction of all.

Naturally, everyone wanted to go into the box after Louisa and Mary Ann. We took turns, so each child got a chance. The game lasted all through playtime and, to my surprise, for the next few weeks. The children soon took control, developing their own rules. There were the jumpers, who went into the box, and the singers, who were also responsible for opening the flaps. Sometimes, there were three jumpers, and as many as six singers. Everyone in the class participated.

It was the apex of excitement to go into the box, and the singers formed the waiting list. Anyone who wanted a turn in the box, therefore, had to learn the song. Even Harris, who never sang, could be heard belting out the lyrics in his own, drill-sergeant-like fashion.

So great was the desire to go into the box, that there was rarely any arguing. Kids who normally pushed and shoved were models of courtesy—because they'd miss their turn in the box if they weren't. Cathy and I had established that rule by sitting close to the box and silently supervising. One of us was always nearby. But there were rarely any problems, except that no one wanted to do anything else while the box was in the room. So we kept it outside near our cubbies, and brought it in each day for half the play period.

If her teachers forgot, Louisa always remembered. Toward the middle of the morning, her eyes would widen. "The box!" she'd announce, as if she'd discovered plutonium. Then she'd dash out of the room and return in a matter of seconds, pushing a box twice her size, her face aglow with excitement.

The box became the great leveler. Children from different cliques got to know one another. They played together in a game that required a great degree of cooperation. If the rest of the room was chaotic, I could always count on a little island of musical tranquility around the box. "Well," I said to Cathy, as we watched the game one day. "We're on our way to becoming a group." By chance, we had found a unifying activity that could only be classified as unbeatable.

• • •

During the last ten days of October, however, Harris erupted like a volcano. It was both disturbing and surprising: after all, he had begun to make progress. Now he no longer looked at me for confirmation of his behavior. He lashed out unexpectedly, biting or kicking at random. His face returned to its blankness. The reason for his regression became apparent as he began to talk incessantly about Halloween.

Each morning, Harris went directly over to the house and loft (called the *dramatic play area* in educational jargon). "Let's be Halloween witches!" he hollered, grabbing our child-sized broom. His green eyes shone with intensity, but his little mouth was grim. Frequently, Lee would hop onto our small mop and join him. Together, they would whiz around the area, cackling at the top of their lungs. The sound was horrific, even though I stopped them as quickly as possible. The other children began to cut a wide swath around the dramatic play area, effectively ceding it to Harris and Lee. Even Jason found the game too threatening, and began to play elsewhere.

One morning, Harris decided to be a ghost. He placed a baby blanket over his head, and walked around, intoning "Hooooooooooo." His faithful assistant followed his lead. The blankets muffled the noise, but the activity was dangerous. Both Harris and Lee were bumping into people and furniture. I removed the blankets from their heads and suggested they play a different game, such as making dinner at the play stove or building with Lego (two of their favorite activities). They headed for the stove. I went over to help Jeremy and Benjamin with a puzzle.

In a few minutes, the ghosts had reappeared, with the help of two different blankets. The other children began to take cover; the ghosts moved around the room, moaning as scarily as they could. I removed the boys' "costumes" and had them sit on the rug with all the other children. It was time to talk about Halloween.

At Beth-El Nursery School, Halloween was not celebrated. It was considered a holiday of pagan origin, inappropriate for a Jewish day school. Teachers were not even supposed to discuss it. But nearly all of our children dressed up and went trick-or-treating. They usually had questions about scary costumes or about why some candy was safe and some wasn't. I always preferred to break the "no Halloween" rule and answer the questions. We didn't make costumes or carve jack-o'-lanterns. We talked in order to avoid Halloween nightmares.

I began by asking each of my students which costumes they were going to wear for Halloween. They answered one by one. This group of children, who normally couldn't sit for a minute, didn't move a muscle. Obviously, we were speaking of something very important. I asked them if, when they put on their costumes, they were still themselves. Would Jason turn into a Ninja Turtle if he wore a costume of, say, Michelangelo? Or would he still be Jason underneath the costume?

Silence—the children weren't sure. Benjamin spoke up. "*Of course* I'll still be Benjamin," he announced, rolling his eyes in mock exasperation. (I could always count on this kid for comic relief.)

"Right," I replied.

I repeated the question for every child: "Who will you be underneath your Halloween costume?" Each answered with his or her own name. Even Harris said his name, although he spoke softly and wouldn't look at me. I nodded solemnly after they had finished.

"That's right. Even if you look in the mirror and you see your costume, it's really *you* in there. You'll see yourself again as soon as you take your costume off." After a short discussion on what candy was not okay to eat—"Your mommy and daddy make the rules"—we resumed our play period.

I hoped that our meeting would take some of the pressure off Harris, but it was not to be. He continued to terrorize the class as a "scary ghost" or "bad witch." When I had to put him in "time out," he began to yell "ASSHOLE! ASSHOLE!" at the top of his lungs. This resulted in the immediate removal to the cubbies of Harris, the chair he was sitting in and me.

I told him that "asshole" was not okay to say in school, and asked him where he had heard the word.

"My daddy said it," he replied.

"Well, it's not okay, just like hitting and biting are not okay."

"My mommy and daddy punch me and my Opal hits me," was his defiant response.

I didn't know if any of the charges were true. I had seen no physical evidence, such as a bruise or black eye. But I resolved to keep Harris's words in mind. Something was driving this kid to distraction, and I wasn't sure what it was.

The rest of the week was pandemonium. Harris was nearly uncontrollable: one teacher had to watch him every minute of the day. I could see that he needed an outlet for his anxiety, so I allowed Harris to play "witches and ghosts" with Lee in the gym. There were no blankets in this room and it was so big that no one else was affected. He also began to soil himself. Each day, he'd hide behind a piece of gym equipment and make in his pants. Sometimes he'd let me change him, and sometimes he wouldn't. Our classroom began to smell "like a changing room," as one of my colleagues so delicately commented. (Lee also frequently made in his Pampers and wouldn't let us change him. The "Doodie Brothers" were quite a pair.)

Cathy and I talked about Harris. His anxieties were mounting, but school wasn't the appropriate place to deal with them. His disruptive behavior would eventually alienate all the other children, so he would have no friends. He'd always be in trouble with his teachers, so he would acquire the label of "bad boy." Harris needed a therapeutic environment to work out the bad stuff—the pain and fear and anger. Then in school, he could work on learning the good stuff—the friendship and sharing and joy—which would replace all the hard feelings he carried around inside him.

Sometimes these two processes—the working out and the filling up—can both be done in school. But this case was too difficult. I knew it, and Cathy knew it—now we had to convince Harris's parents that he needed therapy. A parent-teacher conference, with the school's director in attendance, was the appropriate venue. Fortunately, our regular conferences were scheduled for early November. This one would be a doozie.

Meanwhile, we had to cope with Harris in the classroom. It wasn't easy. The morning of Halloween, he picked two fights with Lee and bit Jason during the first hour of school. I was at the end of my rope. While Cathy tended to Jason's bite, I took Harris and left the classroom. He jerked his hand away from me, but came along. His black hair was matted down and his pale face was flushed from the rigors of combat. He walked, however, with his customary energy.

"Where are we going?" he asked me.

"To the office," I replied as evenly as I could.

"Why?"

"Because you've been having a very hard time remembering the rules, so you need to be out of the classroom for a little while."

It had always been standard operating procedure to bring an unruly child to Maggie's office. She would chat with the child about his or her problem and the teacher would get a few minutes of much needed peace. I had never asked Barbara what her policy was, but there wasn't time to inquire now.

We reached the director's office. Barbara was not busy, so I brought Harris in and deposited him unceremoniously on the couch. One look at his face told me he was petrified.

"This is Harris," I informed my director. "He needs to be out of the classroom for a while because he bit and hit. Would you speak to him, please?" Barbara looked up to see a little boy cowering in a corner of the couch. As I left the office, I heard her say to him, "Hi, Harris. Would you like to read a book with me?" There was no response.

As soon as I returned to the classroom, I asked Cathy to go and sit with Harris and Barbara. "He looked so frightened, and you know how he doesn't like strangers." She joined them immediately.

Ten minutes later, Harris raced back into class; Cathy and Barbara were not far behind. Harris's blank face revealed nothing, but Barbara looked cheerful as she made her way over to me.

"Harris and I had a wonderful time," she declared. "We read a book together. And we decided that Harris can visit me when he's being *good* and not just when he's being *bad*. Then he smiled at me and took my hand and we walked back here."

"Thanks, Barbara," I managed to say. She smiled beatifically and left the room. I was mystified. Why would a director tell a child, even obliquely, that he was being *bad*? I never used the word, except to tell my students that there was no such thing as a bad child—only kids who didn't follow the rules and needed to be helped to learn them. And how did she get Harris to smile and hold her hand?

But if I was perplexed, my assistant was in shock. Cathy's eyes were like saucers—the flying kind. She could not say a word. Finally, she blurted out:

"Patti, it didn't happen. I was there *the whole time*. Harris wasn't even listening when she said he could visit her if he was good. He did *not* smile at her. His expression never changed. When she tried to take his hand, he said 'NO!,' pulled away from her and ran back to the classroom. That's why he got here before us."

"I see," I said. But I didn't.

"She's lying, and she knows I was there. How could she do it? She must realize that I know the truth . . ."

"Apparently, she doesn't know what the truth is."

Cathy and I stared at each other in silence. I spoke first.

"I guess we've got a bigger problem than we thought." At that moment, I felt like a trapeze artist, high above the circus crowd, who looks down and discovers to her dismay that she's working without a net.

NOVEMBER CONFERENCES:
THE MISSING PIECE

Parent-teacher conferences were scheduled for the mornings of November 2 and 3. (School was canceled on these days.) Although they were difficult, I usually enjoyed these autumn meetings. We spent five minutes talking about the child in school, and fifteen or twenty minutes finding out about his or her home life. We were often able to learn the answer to a puzzle about a particular child—what I called the missing piece.

The input from parents was crucial. Cathy and I met beforehand to talk about the information we needed to elicit. Why did Cory hug us so hard, as if her very life depended on our response to her? Did her parents notice how often she lost her balance? Did they recognize her speech problem? At my request, they had taken Cory to an audiologist who had found nothing wrong with her hearing. Why, then, did these problems continue?

Why was Benjamin overconcerned with his well-being? Was there an illness we were unaware of? Why did David wet himself every day? Had his parents checked with their pediatrician, as I had recommended, to see if there was a physical problem? Did Lee's parents ever discipline him? Did they realize he was much too young to be in this class, and should probably repeat the year?

"Can we ask all those questions?" Cathy wanted to know. "Will the parents know the answers? Won't they just get scared if they don't?"

"We can't ask any of those questions. The parents would be frightened if they knew the scope of our concerns." I explained the technique we would use to find out what we needed to know.

"First, describe the classroom behavior. Then say, 'What do you see at home?' If it's the same behavior, ask 'How do you handle it?' If it's not the same behavior, we can ask what they *do* see at home. This way, we are comparing notes rather than digging for dirt or making accusations. The main thing is to get across the point that parents and teachers are not adversaries. All of us are working together for the benefit of the child."

"Well, it's the truth."

"I know that, but parents don't always believe it. And not all teachers are good at showing their concern in a nonthreatening manner."

"But you are."

"Usually," I admitted. "But once in a while I'm an abject failure. Sometimes the chemistry between parent and teacher is bad. Sometimes my anger shows through. I try not to let it happen but I'm not perfect. I hope it doesn't occur in any of these conferences. The children are too needy."

The first conference day arrived. Cathy and I were both a bit edgy: conferences are nerve-wracking even for the most seasoned veteran. Fortunately, we began with Jenny.

Her parents, Jonathan and Peggy Kaufman, entered our room the embodiment of New York chic. Handsome, well dressed and articulate, they were eager to talk about their daughter. Jenny's initial shyness had given way to a gentle good humor. Although soft-spoken, she was rapidly making friends. In five minutes, her parents and teachers agreed that Jenny was beautiful, sweet and intelligent—in short, a wonderful child!

The rest of our time was spent discussing Jenny's older brother, Ian, a former student of mine, who was having some difficulties in the fourth grade. (My advice: "I remember him as a wonderful kid. Go back and speak to his teacher.") As the conference ended, we congratulated ourselves for having such a happy, stable child as Jenny.

Louisa's mother was next. Stunning and stylish, Elaine Donner swept into the room wearing a black suede cowboy outfit covered in fringes and metal studs. She looked like she had an attitude, but nothing was further from the truth. What she had was an offbeat sense of humor and a strong understanding of her child.

Elaine came up to us with her hand extended, saying, "I want to shake the hands of the women who got my daughter to sing 'CLEANUP TIME, CLEANUP TIME, IT IS TIME FOR CLEANUP TIME.' She's *never* cleaned up before!" We were not surprised to learn that Louisa was cherished at home. Her parents got the same kick out of her as we did. We also discovered that Louisa had the same short attention span at home as we saw at school. Even when her parents read to her, she sat for no more than two minutes. I felt it was a reflection of her young age (she had just turned three) rather than any difficulty. We spent the next twenty minutes exchanging "cute Louisa" stories.

"So far, so good," Cathy commented, after Elaine had graciously thanked us and departed.

"We haven't had any tough ones yet," I reminded my assistant. "Who's next?"

"Amanda Fisher. This could be difficult—her mother is so nervous."

"Yes, but it's the first thing she tells you. It's part of her charm."

Janet Fisher appeared a moment later. An attractive, well-dressed woman, she sat down and immediately began apologizing. "I know I'm neurotic, but could you just tell me how Amanda is doing?"

To our opening comment that Amanda was very bright, she replied, "Well, in her last school, they told me that. Of course I'm glad to hear it, but how's she doing socially?"

We described Amanda's entry into the social life of our class-room. She had hung back, observing, for the first month of school. When she felt comfortable, she had begun to play with the other children, both boys and girls. In just a few weeks, Amanda had become a leader. Everyone loved her, and listened to what she said.

Janet wanted to know 1) if it was okay to hang back in the beginning (yes, it's the style of many children) and 2) if she was really playing with boys (indeed she was: it was unusual to see a child move between girl groups and boy groups as easily as Amanda did).

This led to the heart of our discussion. Janet had recently re-turned to a full-time job, and was conflicted about it. She was afraid that being away from Amanda from 8:30 A.M. to 6 P.M. would be too difficult for her child. We assured her that Aman-da was doing just fine in school.

That didn't seem to be the answer Janet wanted to hear. It sounded as if she wanted us to give her permission to quit, on the grounds that Amanda wasn't thriving.

"She has terrible separation problems all the way to school," Janet insisted.

"But she does very well once she gets here," I countered. "Look, you need to decide whether it's too difficult for you to work based on your *own* feelings. Amanda is doing well. Your problem is separate from her well-being."

"I really don't have a choice. The income is too important. But I don't want to hurt Amanda."

"You're not. You must be a terrific mother, because you have such a terrific child. Give yourself a break," I said softly, patting her hand.

Janet promised to try and relax. She lingered, thanking us warmly, and then, remembering she had to go back to work, dashed out of the room.

"She's a funny lady," Cathy said. "And she really loves her kid."

"We're very lucky this year. All the parents love their kids. Even when they're not sure how to handle them."

"Isn't that true every year?" Cathy asked.

"I wish it were."

Cathy shuddered. I could see her putting that thought away for another time. "Well, so far, these conferences have been fun."

Just then, Lee's parents walked in. I didn't have time to say what I was thinking: *Fasten your seat belt for this one, Cath.*

Carla and Mike were big, pleasant-looking people. They spoke in a lazy, Texan drawl, which immediately put us at ease. This couple seemed as mellow as they sounded. I noted with interest that Lee had picked up his parents' charm, but not their accent.

We began by mentioning Lee's sociability and fine athletic skills. (First Rule of any conference: always start with the good stuff. Every child has strong points. If a teacher can't find anything good to say about a child, I would question that teacher's objectivity.) Next, I segued into the more difficult part of the conference: we were very happy that Lee had been able to make friends and keep up with them on the roof playground, because so much of what we did in the classroom was too old for him.

We gave examples without waiting for a response. Lee was uninterested in any of our table toys. His attention span was very short, especially at story time.

"He listens when I read to him at home," offered Carla.

I pursued this: sometimes, a discrepancy here is important. (Perhaps the child listens better in a one-to-one situation, for example.) Usually, it's just that the parents don't have the same rules as we do in school. Sure enough, Lee was allowed to interrupt with a question whenever he chose, and decide when story time was over. This was fine—as long as a parent is reading to a child, just about any method is fine. But it was important to learn that our expectations for Lee were different from those at home. If no one had ever asked him to simply sit and listen, we needed to know it.

Next, we mentioned Lee's fierce tantrums, and were greeted with complete understanding. He had them at home, as well. When we asked how his parents handled them, we received a shocking answer. Lee's tantrums were so violent that his parents just gave in and allowed him to do whatever he wanted. Story after story came tumbling out of their mouths. One example stood out: Carla told us that Lee "never let her talk on the phone." Whenever she began to speak to someone, Lee would come over and hit her until she got off.

"What do you do in this situation?" Cathy asked her.

"I just get off the phone. What else can I do?" was Carla's answer.

Cathy was too stunned to reply. She looked at me, as did Carla and Mike.

I thought: No wonder this kid has such terrible tantrums. He gets no discipline at all at home; we're doing the primary limit-setting in school.

I said: "Lee needs to be disciplined at times like these. You should tell him *before* the phone rings what the consequence of hitting you will be. Then, if he hits you, you need to follow through."

"But what can I do? He won't stay on a chair if I put him there."

We discussed other options. It was clear that they would never resort to hitting him. They were gentle people. So we didn't have to worry about that. Taking away a dessert which wasn't going to appear until dinnertime was not immediate enough. A young three-year-old would not be able to make the connection: the "punishment" did not fit the "crime." Taking away a favorite TV program was actually punishing the mother. The only time she had to herself all day was when Lee watched "Sesame Street." (Parents need a breather, too.)

"How about putting him in his room for fifteen minutes?"

"He keeps coming out."

"You're the grown-up, Carla," I told her. "You're bigger than he is. Put him in his room and hold the door closed."

"You mean that's okay to do? I thought that was child abuse or something."

"Child abuse is when you hurt a child. Lee is asking for your help in setting the limits of his behavior. Children get scared if they think they're in charge. If you don't set limits, you're forcing him to learn discipline in the outside world, where it is much more painful. He needs you to be up to the task."

They listened, but I wasn't sure they believed me. We spoke for a few more minutes about Lee's lack of interest in toilet training. I told them not to worry; it would come in time. I used this subject to bring up the idea that Lee was struggling with the issues of a younger child.

"Perhaps this is why he is a little young for our class. There's plenty of time for change, but there is a possibility that he would be better off repeating the three's program next year rather than moving on to the all-day four's. We'll talk about it in the spring."

Mike and Carla were surprised at that comment, but they took it with grace. They thanked us profusely, gave hugs all around and left. The conference had taken forty minutes, using up our break time. I hadn't the heart to stop them from talking.

Cathy looked at me.

"Well, at least we've found the missing piece. These two nice, low-key people have a child with an intense, passionate temperament. They just don't know how to handle him. It's what the experts call a 'poor match' between parent and child. They adore him—they just don't seem to be able to give him what he needs."

"Maybe they'll be better after this conference," Cathy said, with more wistfulness than conviction.

"Hope springs eternal . . ." I didn't have time to finish the quotation, because in walked Cory's mom, Theresa, and the roller-coaster ride began again.

We exchanged the usual pleasantries. Cathy described Cory's wonderful drawing and writing ability. She was a smart, competent little girl despite her problems, and we wanted her mother to know we saw that. How else would she believe the rest?

Now was the time to mention the hugging, and work up to the speech problem. But we never got the chance to say another sentence about school. Theresa took over.

She was glad to know Cory was doing well, because the family was in crisis. The husband of Theresa's closest friend was dying of recently diagnosed cancer. This man was also the father of Cory's best friend, Mary Elizabeth, so Cory was watching her best friend's father die. The man had been given just a few months to live, and Theresa felt it would be even shorter.

She stopped for a moment and cleared her throat. Her eyes welled up with tears. Pushing her long hair away from her face, she continued more hesitantly. She told us that Cory's little brother Edward was going through a crisis of his own.

"Edward was born with only one kidney, and that one is damaged. We thought he was going to die this past summer, when he was one year old, so we spent the whole summer crying."

"All of you?" I asked softly.

She knew what I meant. "Oh yes. Cory knows everything. How could we keep it from her?" Fortunately, Edward had recovered. If he lived until he was five, he could receive a transplant. But his kidney had just begun to fail again.

"It's just . . . all too much . . ." Theresa whispered, waving her hand, as if she could push the troubles away forever.

"If there's anything we can do, please let us know," I said.

"Oh, you're doing it already. Thanks for taking such good care of Cory." Theresa hugged us both quickly, and was gone before we could say anything more.

Cathy and I sat still for a long while. It hurt just to breathe, let alone talk. She broke the silence first.

"Well . . . now we know."

"Yes. We have the missing piece. Cory hugs us so hard because we're her only source of stability right now. She can't hear well and she barely speaks. No wonder she hangs on to us for dear life."

"Patti, we didn't tell Theresa anything we'd planned to discuss."

"We couldn't. She has too much to deal with right now. Cory's problems will have to wait."

"But that's not fair," Cathy practically shouted.

"No. But that's how it is. Cory is basically healthy. Dealing with death takes priority over everything."

Cathy's eyes filled up. "Um . . . was that the last conference? I don't think I can do any more today . . ." Her voice trailed off.

"That's the end, thank God. We need a stiff drink."

Cathy giggled. "You can't drink—you'll get a migraine. How about an ice cream cone?"

"You're on," I replied.

• • •

The second day was easier. Three conferences would not be held today: they were scheduled for early mornings on regular school days. Harris's parents were coming tomorrow and Benjamin's conference was the following week. I hadn't yet been able to pin Mary Ann's parents down. Her father traveled frequently—and I wouldn't do that conference without him. I had the suspicion that he was responsible for much of Mary Ann's increasingly difficult behavior.

That left us a relatively easy morning—just four meetings with a sizable break in the middle. Promptly at 8:30 A.M., Sharon's parents walked in. We had spoken to John and Karen often because of their daughter's hospital stay, so this felt more like a second conference than a first one. We reported that Sharon was doing beautifully. She was a spunky, cheerful kid, with a wonderful ability to express her thoughts and her feelings. Karen asked if Sharon ever talked about the hospital.

"She doesn't mention it, but she doesn't seem to feel any ill effects, either," Cathy told her. This seemed in keeping with her easygoing temperament. John mentioned that Sharon was a lot less easygoing at home, especially when she fought with her big sister Lilia.

"That's as it should be. Home is a child's safest place, so the big feelings should come out there. And all siblings are entitled to fight—actually, it's their job." Everyone laughed.

Karen told us that because Lilia, at nine, was so much older than Sharon, their fights frequently ended in laughter. "Lilia gets such a kick out of the things that Sharon says." Apparently, so did the entire family. Sharon was clearly a cherished child. Our conference ended on that mutually satisfactory note.

We had five minutes before Jason's mother was due. I turned to Cathy:

"You'll have to do most of the talking at this one, Cathy. Jason's been getting on my nerves so much that I don't think I can keep the irritation out of my voice when I talk about him. And you're crazy about him."

"You like him, too," she reminded me.

"I know I do. Just not this week."

Anne Aronson walked in so soon after that remark that I found myself hoping she hadn't overheard me. If she did, she hid it well—her pale blue eyes and chiseled features showed no hint of upset.

I hope I look that calm, I thought.

Cathy did an excellent job of highlighting Jason's strong points.

He was a warm, affectionate child who loved to hug his friends and his teachers. Jason enjoyed building with blocks and Lego, and was skilled with puzzles and shape pegs. He could work for twenty minutes on a project that held his interest.

"Otherwise, it *is* very difficult for Jason to sit." Cathy's transition was as smooth as any I'd made.

"He doesn't sit at all, huh?" said Anne, smiling.

"He's rarely still for more than a minute, even at story time," I interjected.

"Feeling a little frustrated, Patti?" Anne asked with a smile. Stupid she was not.

"I am," I admitted. "He's such a good boy—and so bright. There's so much we can teach him once he wants to pay attention."

"Well, I'm not surprised," Anne replied. "It's the same thing I see at home. And it's the same thing I just heard at his sister's conference."

I thought back to last year, when Jason's big sister Ellyn had been in our school. She was indeed the same kind of kid—always moving, unable to keep still for very long even in group situations.

Anne continued: "They're both exactly like me. My parents got the same reports from my teachers when I was young."

"Do your children get their athleticism from you also?" I asked. "Jason is incredibly agile."

She admitted that they did. Now it was just a question of their attention spans catching up to their abilities. We shared the hope that this would occur in the not-too-distant future. Anne thanked us for our patience with Jason as she left.

"Do you feel better about Jason now?" Cathy asked when we were alone.

"Yes, I do. Lots better. Now that I can see his problems in the context of his development, I won't take his inattention so personally. It isn't that he's not listening to me; he's not ready to listen to anybody yet."

"But, Patti," Cathy protested, "you always knew that. You told it to me just a few days ago."

"I knew it, but I guess I didn't feel it. Speaking to Anne really helped me understand her son better."

"Good!" Cathy answered with a smile. "'Cause he really is delicious."

We had an hour's break before our conference with Jeremy's parents. I mentioned that I hoped both parents would come.

"We still haven't met Jeremy's father," Cathy commented. "I hope we recognize him."

When the Jacobsons walked into the room, we realized that we would have known Bernard anywhere. He was the image of his son, if you didn't count the receding hairline. Charming and cheerful, he also seemed to be the source of Jeremy's whimsical sense of humor.

We sang Jeremy's praises. He was cute, funny and intelligent—and gifted in math. He enjoyed playing with other children, and was doing very well in the classroom.

Bernard voiced his doubts. Jeremy was so small and so immature. "He walks like a baby and talks like a baby. His older brother wasn't like this."

We assured Bernard that the speech and physical skills would improve with time. Jeremy was slower than his friends on the stairs, but he kept up with them in the gym.

"But my older son Evan was so verbal," Bernard countered.

"So is Jeremy," I assured him. His vocabulary was wonderful for his age even if he did have a minor lisp. Cathy related some of Jeremy's clever jokes.

"But when Evan was four I used to play chess with him. Jeremy looks so much more like a baby."

"Don't let his looks deceive you," I cautioned. "Jeremy is no baby. He's way ahead in the brains department."

Bernard seemed reassured. He and Carolyn thanked us as they left. (Carolyn told me later that he turned to her as they walked down the hall and said, "Those two are great." I was happy to hear it. Perhaps it meant that he had accepted our point of view.)

"Interesting conference," said Cathy, as soon as they were out of earshot.

"Yeah. I wonder why he was so concerned about Jeremy's babyish traits?"

"Well," she replied, "maybe it's because he wants to forget anything that has to do with a baby, having just lost one."

"Wow." I whistled softly.

Cathy continued: "Did you notice that they didn't even mention the terrible event which occurred only six weeks ago?"

"I guess they're trying to put it behind them."

"But the only way to do that is to talk about it."

I nodded, and was about to answer when David's mother walked in, effectively cutting off our conversation. There was nothing to do but smile and invite her to sit.

"Samuel will be here shortly," Sabrina said, motioning to the doorway as if she expected to see her husband fill it at any moment. I marveled for the thousandth time at how elegant she was. Even in jeans, she looked as if she had just stepped out of a fashion ad. Sabrina's slight British accent added to the impression of class. She was, in fact, as interesting and articulate as her famous husband—"Samuel Cohen, the novelist," as the other parents referred to him. Facing the two of them across a conference table was slightly intimidating.

Sabrina's friendliness soon put us at ease. She made small talk as we waited for Samuel. Their family was adjusting to New York City after the ease of small town life in New Hampshire. (They had moved here a little less than a year ago.) She felt that the children were finally getting used to not having a lot of outdoor space for play. On the other hand, their living room was a baseball field. They kept it nearly bereft of furniture so that it could function as a playroom. David, his older

brother Eli and Samuel were always having catches and prac-
ticing their hitting. The hitting would have to stop soon, because they were getting too good at it. The ball was landing too
hard, and beginning to do some damage.

We loved that story—what child advocate would not? Samuel
found us smiling at one another when he strode into the room.
"Am I late?" he boomed, as he took a seat next to his wife.

"You're just in time," I assured him. "We've been hearing
about the ball field in your living room."

"Oh, that!" He smiled. "The boys are pretty good athletes.
David's almost as good as his six-year-old brother now."

To my great regret, I didn't pick up on that comment. The
fruitful discussion on sibling rivalry that we had with the Cohens in our spring conference might have begun here. Maybe it
would have helped in November as much as it helped in March.
But I was concentrating on my own agenda, so I missed the opportunity.

"David's a super athlete," I agreed, "but then again, he's
wonderful at everything." Cathy and I went on to describe his
abilities in every facet of the room, from his outstanding work
with building materials to his real talent as an artist.

"Sabrina's the artist in the family," said Samuel, beaming at
his wife. "David gets his artistic talent from her. I've been encouraging her to go back to her painting, but . . ."

"There's no time right now, with two young kids," his wife
interjected. "Samuel's away a lot, and then I have complete responsibility for them. I'll get back to it when they're older."

We got a glimpse into the difficulties of being a mother, a
"Great Man's Wife" and trying to be a person as well.

"But we *love* looking at David's work," Sabrina continued.
"He seems so much happier this year."

The Cohens had moved to New York in the middle of a school
year, and it had been difficult for their boys to adjust. Because
of this, and the fact that David's birthday was "on the cusp," in

September, it had been suggested that he repeat the year. It had obviously been the right decision.

"He's having a very good time," I told her. "He's adjusted beautifully, and the children in this class happen to be old enough for him." Many of our students would be four by the end of January.

"He's still wetting his pants in school every day, though," said his mother. "I don't know why."

"There are a lot of possibilities," I began. "Perhaps he concentrates so hard on what he's doing that he doesn't hear the signal in his head that tells him it's time to go to the bathroom. That's fairly common at this age."

"I've been pretty hard on him at home," Sabrina said. "His adjustment should be over. I think he's just too lazy to get up and pee."

I was surprised at that statement, but tried not to show it. Sabrina was clearly exasperated.

"I don't think it's laziness—he's not that kind of kid. Maybe he needs to get your attention. Or maybe it's a physical problem. Have you seen your pediatrician?"

They had agreed to see him in September, when the subject had first come up. But they hadn't done so yet.

"Our doctor's out of town so much that we haven't had the chance," said Sabrina.

Hmmm, I thought. *This guy is my own children's pediatrician. He's been in town.*

"Well," I said, as nonjudgmentally as possible, "it's a good idea to rule out the physical."

They promised they'd take care of it. They looked sincere. They certainly were genuine in their praise of us. Samuel gave us each a bear hug, and Sabrina shook hands warmly.

"Do you think they'll take David to the doctor?" Cathy asked me after they had gone.

"I hope so—I think so. It was really the only problem we had to discuss with them."

"Speaking of problems, we're done with conferences for to-day."

"Yes, indeedy," I replied. "Now we can go home and gear up for the big one tomorrow with Harris's parents."

"Is that really *tomorrow?*" Cathy groaned.

"Yep."

"*Oy vey.*"

"Precisely."

• • •

Tomorrow came faster than I wanted it to. If this conference went well, a child's life would be changed forever. I brushed the other possibility from my mind as I entered Barbara Gold's office at seven fifty-five. Cathy was already there, and Barbara was coming back shortly. Our director had confessed to Cathy that she was "a little frightened" about this meeting.

I thought: Good. Maybe she won't talk much. We can't have her telling the parents that Harris smiled at her and held her hand, or they'll never believe what I have to say.

I said: "I'm sure it will go well, Cathy. Just follow my lead." (There was no sense in making her more nervous than she already was.)

The Whites joined us a few moments after Barbara returned. They looked as serious as we did. They greeted us with their usual charm, however, and sat on the couch opposite our three chairs.

Cathy and I took turns describing Harris's good points. He was an extremely charismatic child. Everyone liked him. His imagination was so wonderful that children always wanted to join in his "pretend games." His intellectual curiosity knew no bounds. He was always asking "why?" and was not satisfied unless he completely understood an answer.

Joanna and Harris Senior beamed; this was the Harris they saw at home. They told an anecdote or two, but I only half listened. The important part of the meeting had yet to start, and I was anxious to get there. When they finished speaking, I plunged in.

"We do, however, have a lot of difficulty with Harris. He frequently kicks and hits his classmates. He also bites them, and knocks over their block buildings. The most difficult thing about this behavior is that it appears without warning. The children can never tell when Harris is going to lash out, because his actions don't seem to be related to the events at hand."

Joanna nodded. "We know that he's bitten Jason and Lee a few times. And those are his good friends."

"Children often pick on a friend—someone whom they feel is going to like them anyway, even after the bite or punch."

Harris Senior and Joanna nodded, but they didn't say a word. I continued.

"Harris also curses when he's disciplined. He yells "asshole" a great deal, especially when he has to sit in time out."

Here we were met with understanding, and a little embarrassment. Apparently they saw this side of Harris at home, too.

"Harris overheard his father say the word once, when we were in the car. He was angry at another driver, and it just slipped out. Of course, Harris Junior picked it up immediately."

"How did he know it was a bad word?" Cathy asked.

"He said it over and over until we had to stop him," Harris Senior replied.

Cathy and I looked at each other. "He's one smart cookie," I said with a smile. "Unfortunately, he says it over and over in school, too. So he's been spending a lot of time sitting on a chair."

"What can we do about this behavior?" Harris Senior asked.

Now I had to lie, and it was difficult to do. I had about a thousand parenting suggestions for them. They would have helped Harris's behavior, but none of them would have gotten to the root of the problem. They would only have been smokescreens used to delay therapy.

So I put on my best professional face and said, "I don't know. And I think you need to talk to someone who *does* know. I am fairly sure that Harris needs a place that is not school and not home to let his angry feelings out."

"You mean you think he needs therapy," said Harris Senior. It was not a question.

"Yes," I answered. "I think it will help him to work out his aggression, which may stem from his problems with your former housekeeper."

Harris's parents looked at each other: the father spoke first. "All right—if that's what he needs, then that's what we'll do." Joanna looked upset, but said nothing.

Cathy entered the conversation with an important point I had forgotten to mention. "He's really trying to do the right thing. He wants to fit in. He really *wants* to have fun and be good in school. He just needs extra help."

Joanna said, "I know he loves school, especially his Patti and Cathy. He talks about you all the time. He wants you to like him."

"We *do* like him," Cathy assured her. "That's why we want so much for him to succeed."

Here Barbara Gold spoke up. She spoke warmly of our school psychologist, Angela Grossman. She gave the Whites Angela's phone number and office hours, and urged them to call her. The Whites promised that they would.

As the conference ended, Joanna came over to me. Her eyes were filled with tears. "If he doesn't succeed here, I don't know what we'll do. He's the most important thing in the world to us."

I hugged her. "He *will* succeed, Joanna. We all love him. He just needs to get the right kind of help—that's all." She hugged me back, and Harris Senior shook hands all around. Then they were gone.

Barbara asked Cathy if she would go into to the classroom, where the children were beginning to gather.

"I'm so relieved that it's over and that it went so well," I told Barbara. "You were very good."

And it was true. She hadn't said a word until the very end, when she was needed. She had let me do my job without butting in. I was just as relieved about this as I was about the parents' reactions.

Barbara looked at me. "Didn't you think I would be?" she asked.

I answered honestly, shaking my head. "I'm not used to it," I blurted out.

Thank heavens, she smiled. She seemed to think I was implying that my former director wasn't very good at conferences. (But Maggie had taught me all I know.)

"It went very well," Barbara agreed. "Now let's hope they call Angela."

. . .

A few days later, Harris had his birthday party in school. (We held a "school party" for each child on or near the special day. In June, we had the summer birthdays, one by one.) Harris received a "birthday scroll," colored by all his friends. He himself decorated a birthday crown, and we wrote the number "4" on it. He wore it proudly all day.

At snack time, Harris's parents arrived with cupcakes for all the children. I always insisted on at least one parent being present. (My not-so-nice aphorism is "No parent, no party." Translated, it means: "Any time you have twenty free minutes to stop by, we'll have your kid's party. Early morning is just as fine as lunchtime. But your child needs you there.") Harris's parents had both taken time off from work to be with him.

They greeted Harris warmly and helped him give out the cupcakes to all the other children. They hugged him when he blew out his candle, and admired his crown. They were funny and pleasant and wonderful to have in the classroom.

During the party, Harris became angry with a child and reached for his belt (a motion we had never seen). Joanna told Cathy that this had been their first sign that Harris was being hit. Cathy hadn't asked if Harris had actually been hit by a belt, or just threatened with one. I didn't blame my assistant—it was enough to know what we knew.

At the party's end, Harris Senior mentioned that they were going to meet with our psychologist the following day. We were thrilled, and assured them that they would like her. After he and Joanna were gone, however, I began to reflect on their behavior. They had been absolutely charming—perfect in every way. Would Angela be able to break through this attractive shell and get them to speak about their problems?

Fortunately, Angela herself appeared at my door half an hour later. She needed an up-to-date report on Harris for the meeting with his parents.

"Be careful when you meet with them tomorrow," I advised her. "Charm is their defense. They'll unconsciously try to snow you into thinking that everything is really all right. But it's not." Angela thanked me and promised to be on her guard.

The following day, she told us the results of her meeting.

"You were right, Patti. They are the most charming people: warm, funny, intelligent. We danced around for almost half an hour without making any headway. But you had tipped me off, so I kept talking. Finally, we got to the problem. They've agreed to take Harris to a therapist. I gave them some names, and strongly recommended the first on the list. Laura Adler is particularly good with tough kids."

I smiled at Angela. "I assume you didn't tell them that."

"Of course not," she laughed. "But she'd be very good for him."

I relayed the news to Cathy, who was as excited as I was. The Whites were on their way!

Harris's behavior improved over the next few weeks, but it wasn't because of the therapist. Our entire classroom calmed somewhat because of the temporary addition of another teacher. Talia Schein was the school's floater: she substituted for absent teachers and helped out wherever else she was needed. She had been too busy to give us any time in the beginning of the year, but now we had her for our morning play period.

Talia was a gifted teacher whose quiet friendliness put children immediately at their ease. Her assignment in our classroom was to stick to the Three Terrors, and redirect their play. It's what one of us would do all the time if we didn't have nine other children to work with. Talia was a gift.

Each day I could see her stopping activities before they got out of hand. ("We don't throw toys, Lee. Let's pick that one up.") She also helped the boys use their words instead of their fists. ("I know you're angry, Harris; but hitting Jason won't get him to share that toy with you. It will only make him cry, and you'll have to sit on a chair. What words can you say that will help him understand what you want?")

With this kind of 100 percent attention, the children began to improve. Naturally, the room quieted down considerably: our game plan was beginning to work.

"Talia is terrific," Cathy said to me one day. "I wish we could have her all the time."

"In the best of all possible worlds, we would," I replied. "But this student-teacher ratio—four to one—is standard only for special education classes."

Cathy looked around. "Well, we've got a kid who's been hit, a kid with hearing and speech problems, a kid who acts as if he's hyperactive and a kid who has constant tantrums. I'd say we qualify."

"Don't tell the parents!" I laughed.

Talia's presence gave us a chance to concentrate on the other children. What we saw was less than heartening. While most of the children were doing pretty well, there were several problem spots in the room.

Our most troubling development involved Jeremy. His best friend Benjamin had become so close with David that they were excluding Jeremy from play. Rejection was one thing this boy didn't need; his baby's death had been trauma enough. Whenever we insisted, the two friends included Jeremy; but the minute our backs were turned, he was out of the loop. Often, we would find him sitting by himself in the library corner with his finger up his nose, turning the pages of a book but not really looking at it.

"Poor little Jeremy," sighed Cathy. "What can we do for him?"

"We can continue to insist that Benjamin and David let him play. We can redirect him toward his other friends like Sharon and Jenny. We can spend more time with him. But I don't think this sadness is all school-directed."

"What's your reasoning?"

"Because he's not trying hard enough to be with other children. Most of the time he just sits by himself without making any kind of effort. I think he's sad about the baby."

"Have you tried to talk to him about it?" Cathy asked me.

"Yes. I thought it was time. But when I mentioned the baby, he clammed up and walked away. He seems to feel it's not okay to talk about the baby's death. I don't think anyone's talking about it at home, either. We'll ask his mother next time she brings him in."

The following day, I mentioned to Carolyn that Jeremy had been somewhat withdrawn at school. We thought he might be sad about the baby. What did she see at home?

Carolyn assured us that everything was fine at home. No one was talking about the baby anymore—things were "moving on." Jeremy was his "same old self." But two days later, when he had a bowel movement in his pants, Jeremy's baby-sitter told us more of the story.

"He hasn't been able to go for a while now, and he's been taking medicine for it," Falina told us. "He's been trained for over a year, but you might see a few more accidents."

"Why didn't Carolyn tell us this?" wondered Cathy after Falina had left.

"Jeremy is cheerful at home," I reminded her. "I'm sure Carolyn didn't associate the bowel problem with any sadness her son is feeling. But I'll bet there's a connection."

Cathy expressed the pure exasperation which only young people can feel: emotion without thought of the consequence. It was exhilarating but impractical.

"We have to do something!" she practically hollered at me.

I calmed her down as well as I could. "Look, there's not much we *can* do right now. Jeremy's parents are obviously in deep mourning. They probably need to believe that everything else in their life is okay. Remember my favorite saying, Cath: 'Keep your eye on the ball and the ball is the kid.' We have to stow the righteous indignation and wait to see what develops."

"But what about Jeremy?"

"We'll do what we can for him in the classroom. We'll cuddle, and we'll praise and we'll see if we can get the other children to play with him."

I was, in fact, able to raise the latter issue at my conference with Benjamin's parents later that week. (Cathy was unable to be present, but this was Bennett Tyne's only free time, so we held it anyway. This is not generally a great idea. If something goes wrong, you should have your partner there to back you up.) I mentioned that Benjamin was playing almost exclusively with David now, and Jeremy was feeling excluded. I had spoken to both boys about it; would they mind speaking to Benjamin at home?

Benjamin's parents, Francine and Bennett, agreed to do so, but the mother let me know that the problem didn't exist outside of school.

"Benjamin and Jeremy still play beautifully on their playdates," Francine told me.

"I'm so glad to hear that," I replied. "But, of course, David isn't there. It's really a separate issue."

Francine smiled, but there was something about her that was tightly wound. I soon found out what it was.

During the course of the conference, I was told that Benjamin's "cholesterol problem" was, in fact, a potentially serious condition. Francine had inherited it from her father, who had died young. With the medication she took four times daily, she would have a normal life span. But she had passed this condition on to her son.

Benjamin, who was not quite four, couldn't begin to take the medicine until he was five. This was why they watched his diet so carefully. No wonder Francine seemed tense: she carried a never-ending burden. I thought back to her calm manner in dealing with Benjamin after Geoffrey had bitten him our first day in the gym. Her collected behavior was all the more amazing, given the situation.

I explained Benjamin's concerns about his own safety. I suggested that they tell him that he was okay, that he was indeed the "tough kid" he liked to say he was. Bennett promised that they would talk with their son. Now I understood why it was so much easier for him to deal with these difficulties. Francine's load was too heavy already.

I also suggested a positive approach. Benjamin was a fine athlete, graceful and coordinated. The more he exercised his strengths in this area, the better it would be for his self-confidence.

Bennett's reaction: "Well . . . he's not too good at sports . . . you know, like his father."

When I insisted that his son was quite competent, Bennett seemed pleased. He admitted that he "threw a ball around a lot" with Benjamin on weekends. But he also let me know that much of his job involved traveling, so he was away a lot. He felt guilty, and I felt the additional stress laid on the family.

Despite their smooth exteriors, these were people with a lot of bumps in their home life. Fortunately, they seemed to adore each other and their two boys. This was their greatest strength. Benjamin certainly knew he was loved. Now he needed to know he was safe.

Mary Ann's conference was now the only one left. We needed to have it as soon as possible, because Mary Ann was not flourishing. She had become the other problem spot in our room. Other than her faithful friend Louisa, no one would play with her.

It was not really surprising: Mary Ann always wanted to be the center of attention. If the girls were playing "Sleeping Beauty," Mary Ann had to be Aurora or she wouldn't play. It didn't take long for the other girls in the class to rebel:

> SHARON: Let's play "Cinderella."
> MARY ANN: Okay. I'll be Cinderella.
> SHARON: You were Cinderella last time. I'll be Cinderella and you be the Prince.
> MARY ANN: No! I want to be Cinderella!
> SHARON: I know! We can have two Cinderellas. Amanda can be the Prince.
> AMANDA: Okay!
> MARY ANN: NO! I WANT TO BE THE ONLY CINDERELLA!
> SHARON: Then we're not playing.

And off they'd go, leaving Mary Ann to cry. She wouldn't *ever* give in. Even Louisa sometimes got tired of being bossed around, and began to play with Harris and Jason. Mary Ann was spending more and more time by herself.

Cathy and I both tried to explain to Mary Ann that she had to share the star roles with the other children. She just couldn't understand why; she was genuinely puzzled.

"Why doesn't she get it?" Cathy asked me one day, after a particularly long crying jag on the part of Mary Ann.

"I think it's because she always gets to be the star at home. But I'm not sure. We'll find out at the conference—if we ever have one. Meanwhile, Mary Ann's going to learn the hard way how it feels to have no friends."

. . .

Thanksgiving was approaching. We were busy teaching the children songs, making decorations and preparing the food for our Thanksgiving feast. The children enjoyed cooking, and they did very well pouring, measuring and stirring. Even Jason and Harris were willing to wait their turns to help prepare corn muffins, cranberry sauce and butter.

Harris, lately, was eager to do whatever Jason did. He walked the same way and frequently made the same comments as his friend. When Jason sneaked playdough into the house area, in order to "cook" it on the stove, Harris was his partner in crime. When Jason threw all the clothes out of the dress-up bin so he could sit in it, his faithful companion joined him. They both hid pieces of a toy in one of our play purses. They climbed on our shelves to see out the window. They were a demonic pair.

We were hoping, however, that this development would result in progress, too. Jason was so affectionate: he loved to hug and to sit on his teachers' laps. He leaned against us when he spoke. And—he was toilet trained!

"If Harris wants to do everything that Jason does, maybe he'll want to make his 'doodies' on the toilet," Cathy said hopefully.

"Devoutly to be wished," I replied. "Maybe I'll pray to St. Jude."

"Who's he?"

"Saint of the Impossible. My friend Evelyn, who's Irish, told me about him. I talk to him a lot."

"But you're so Jewish."

"I don't think that bothers St. Jude. It doesn't bother me."

I'm afraid St. Jude was busy that day. This vignette is my evidence:

The Doodie Ball in the Gym

Cathy and I were watching the kids play at gym time. Suddenly, I noticed seven children gathered in a circle, looking down. I went over to see what was commanding their attention.

On the rug was a small, round piece of excrement. "What's that?" one of the kids asked me. I didn't want to embarrass anyone, so I stupidly said, "I don't know."

Don't ever try to fool a kid on this subject. Benjamin rolled his eyes in exasperation. "It's a doodie ball!" he said, looking at me as if I were a moron.

Harris, the probable culprit, was the only one to issue a disclaimer: "Not me, I didn't do it." But the other children were more interested in what I was going to do with the doodie ball than where it had originated.

I took a piece of tissue out of the ready supply in my pocket (a preschool teacher's necessity). "I'll just pick it up and flush it down the toilet," I announced.

All seven of them looked up at me, screwed up their faces and emitted a loud "EEEEEEWWWWW!" As if I'd catch leprosy. But I bravely carried out my task, and that was the end of the doodie ball in the gym.

• • •

The day before Thanksgiving we were granted a portion of our wish that Harris learn from Jason. The class was preparing to go to the bathroom to wash up for snack.

"I want to be the leader today," announced Jason.

"I want to be the leader today," echoed his faithful friend.

Generally, I let the leader pick the "method of transportation"—skipping, galloping, jumping (but no running). Clearly, this rule would never work with these two. They'd race off like white water through a mountain river. I spoke to them casually.

"Well, boys, we're *walking* to the bathroom today. Do you still want to be the leaders?"

Jason nodded and Harris followed suit.

"Okay," I told the class. "We have two leaders, Jason and Harris, and we are *walking* today."

As we set out, Jason took my left hand. Much to my surprise, Harris came around and took my right hand. It was the first time he had touched either Cathy or myself voluntarily. He didn't look at me, and he didn't smile. But, in imitating Jason, he allowed himself to trust a grown-up.

It was a beginning, and a lot to be thankful for.

DECEMBER: DIFFICULTIES

Returning from Thanksgiving vacation, I felt strong and rested. I had greatly enjoyed the four days away from the classroom—sleeping, relaxing, hanging out with my children and husband, visiting with his sister's wonderful family in from Toronto. Even so, I couldn't wait to get back to the kids. Call it a teacher's liability: whether I like it or not, I lead two lives.

Ten minutes after school began, my newfound stamina was tested. Jenny and her father walked into the classroom, looking miserable. They came directly to me.

Jenny's father had a tale to tell. When the Kaufmans had returned home from their vacation last night, they learned of a flood in the laundry room above their apartment. Their ceiling had collapsed—but only the part directly under the flood. It was in Jenny's bedroom. If she'd been sleeping there, she could have been injured or killed.

Both Jenny and her brother had seen the bedroom covered with rubble. Jonathan and Peggy had explained the situation to their children as well as they could; would I mind talking a little more with Jenny? Jonathan hugged his daughter and left the room quickly.

I sat down in a chair so my face would be close to Jenny's and put my arm around her. She began to speak immediately.

"Know what, Patti?"

"What, honey?"

"When we came home, there was my ceiling all in my room."

"Was it on your bed?"

"I don't know. I couldn't see it."

"Were you scared?"

"Uh-huh."

"I don't blame you. I would have been also."

Jenny wasn't ready to say *why* she had been scared—that she might have been hurt. I didn't press her. I hoped it would come in time. But she *was* interested in telling the other children what had happened. So, after snack, when they were all gathered on the rug to hear a story, I asked Jenny to stand next to me.

I was sitting in a chair that faced the children. When she walked over to me, I put my arm around her, and turned Jenny toward her classmates. For the rest of the year, this would be our method of helping a child to deliver bad news.

She spoke again, in a soft, small voice, about the ceiling which had fallen in her room. The children were horrified: eleven pairs of eyes opened wide in disbelief. And—God bless the healing power of language—they had a lot to say.

"Where are you sleeping now?" was the first question, from Amanda.

She was sleeping in her brother Ian's room, in his extra bed.

"Are your toys still there?" Harris wanted to know.

Jenny nodded. "Especially my dolls are okay."

"Where are your mommy and daddy?" Sharon asked.

Jenny looked at me.

I interpreted the question. "Are they still in the apartment with you, in their regular room?"

"Yes."

"Yes, Jenny's mommy and daddy and brother are all with her. So she is *safe.*"

No one asked if the rest of the ceiling would fall in. Kids don't ask for more information than they can handle. I simply mentioned that the rest of the apartment would be okay.

Then came the stories. Amanda had seen a fire develop in her kitchen. It was so large that her mother had called the fire department and taken her to the lobby. Now the kitchen was "broken" but they would have a new one soon. Another child had seen a flood in his basement. A third had seen a hot iron fall to the floor.

Each tale of accident and survival made Jenny feel better. She calmed down and brightened up as the children spoke. She was learning the value of group support: your friends care about you, and they too have endured tough times.

After this discussion no one had the patience for a story, so we took the children to the bathroom. Another class was using it, so we sat just outside the room and sang songs until it was our turn to go in. In the middle of a cute little ditty called "Grandma's Spectacles," Cory crawled over to give me a hug. Unfortunately, she wrapped her arms around my neck in an awkward way, and wound up pulling my hair. It was one of her hold-on-for-dear-life hugs; she just would not let go. My eyes began to water, I screamed out in pain and I shoved her away roughly.

I know I reacted naturally. No matter how empathetic you are, your first instinct is to protect yourself. But the children looked so frightened that I immediately felt guilty. I reached out to Cory, who was huddled face down on the floor, and brought her back onto my lap.

Then I spoke to the other children.

"I hollered at Cory because she was hurting me so badly. See my tears? I'm sorry I frightened you all. It's important to remember not to hurt anyone else. Also, when you want to hug someone, you must *first* ask if it's okay."

I looked down at Cory as I stroked her hair. "Okay, Cory? Can you remember that? I didn't mean to hurt you, and I know you didn't mean to hurt me. I'm not angry. I just want you to remember the rule."

Cory kept her head in my lap. No matter what I said, she wouldn't look at me. When I lifted up her face, she pulled herself back down, but I got a peek at her angry expression. I realized abruptly that Cory wasn't ashamed. She was angry that I had pushed her away. So she was blocking me out by removing the one sense that never failed her—sight.

An idea hit me with the sudden immensity of an exploding star: Cory had the behaviors of a handicapped child. The hugging, the hiding of her face during discipline, the extreme reactions when frustrated (she stamped her foot, yelled and sulked for many minutes)—they all reminded me of Helen Keller in *The Miracle Worker.* Until we could figure out the problem, she needed me to be her Annie Sullivan. I picked Cory up and carried her to the gym in my arms.

The week continued at the same high pitch. In the gym, Lee encroached on a piece of equipment that Harris was using, so Harris bit him—hard. But he had chosen the wrong victim. Lee was too tough not to respond and too young to know better. He bit Harris right back.

Harris was more surprised than injured. "Lee *bit* me!" he hollered.

"It hurts, doesn't it?" I asked rhetorically.

"YYYEEESSS!" was his emphatic reply.

"That's one reason why it's not okay—for *either* of you. Now, I'm sure you remember the rule: YOU BIT, YOU SIT. Come over here and sit by me."

They sat on the rug next to my chair. I could see the wheels turning in Harris's head: it was quite a while before he bit again. Lee, however, was oblivious and unmoved.

After gym, we took the children to a little room which was set up with chairs and a blackboard. Hebrew school classes met there on Monday and Wednesday afternoons. Our three- and four-year-olds loved to sit in the chairs and "do work" like the big kids. On this day, we played a game called "Aiken Drum."

Cathy and I drew shapes on a blackboard and asked for their names. Then we constructed a man by asking the children to name a shape for each body part. During the game, we sang these lyrics:

> There was a man lived on the moon
> And his name was Aiken Drum,
> And his head was made out of a . . . (the child named
> a shape)
> And his eyes were made out of a . . .
> And his mouth was made out of a . . . (until the whole
> body appeared)
> And his name was Aiken Drum

Many educators feel that very young children shouldn't play games where so much "knowledge" is required to participate. Some feel that children should play more of them. Teachers have to make up their own minds, depending on the kind of group they have each year.

This game may, in fact, sound too sophisticated for three- and four-year-olds, but we arranged it to promote success.

As we drew the shapes on the board, we never called on anybody. We just asked the question, "What shape is this?" and let the kids shout out their answers. We never acknowledged the wrong answers—we just picked out the right ones. No child should be penalized for guessing.

Once the shapes were on the board, we talked about them. "Look," I said. "An oval is really a stretched-out circle."

"And a rectangle is really a stretched-out square!" exclaimed Benjamin.

"You've got it, Benjamin! That's exactly right. Good job!" I replied. I was as excited as he was. We spoke about the properties of the other shapes. I told them they could name any shape for the game, even if it wasn't on the board. Then we began.

We all sang the first lines. "There was a man lived on the moon and his name was Aiken Drum. And his head was made out of a . . ."

Then I gave this instruction: "Raise your hand if you want to name a shape for the head." (This way, no child has to worry about being called on. Not every child wants a turn. Many children learn just by listening.)

Amanda's hand shot up, so I picked her first. She said "Circle!" I drew it on the board. Next, we sang about the eyes, and Jason raised his hand. He took a while to decide. We waited: not all kids can answer immediately.

Jason picked triangles. The class giggled as I drew them in.

"Those are funny eyes," Jason announced proudly.

The nose was next. After we sang the line, Harris cautiously raised his hand. Cathy and I exchanged glances—he so rarely participated!

"Yes, Harris," I said, trying to sound matter-of-fact.

"An eight," he proclaimed with more bravado than assurance.

"An eight is a number with a *wonderful* shape." I smiled encouragingly at him. "We'll just put it in sideways."

"Now he can breathe like us because he has two holes," commented Amanda. Harris beamed at her.

We moved along until we came to the feet. Since this was the final answer, I asked: "Is there anyone who wants a turn and hasn't gotten it?"

Lee, who had been fidgeting in his chair, looked up and yelled, "Coca-Cola!"

"Do you want a turn, Lee?" He was too young to remember to raise his hand, but I wanted to include him.

"Coca-Cola! Coca-Cola," was his loud reply.

"Do you want the Coca-Cola bottle shape, Lee?" I asked, drawing it on the board. "It would make a great foot."

"No, no—Coca-Cola, Coca-Cola," he repeated.

"Coca-Cola isn't a shape," Sharon told him impatiently.

Lee's face turned red, and he began to cry. "Yes it is! Coca-Cola, Coca-Cola, COCA-COLA!" he screamed ferociously, stamping his feet up and down like a drum major moving to a Sousa march. It took about twenty minutes to calm him down. I sat with him while Cathy took the other kids down to lunch.

Lee understood the concept of the "Aiken Drum" game: we had played it many times before. He was young but he was smart. What was the matter? It was no use asking: he was too upset to speak. He may just have wanted to have his way. The game may have lasted longer than his power to sit still did. There was really no way to find the answer.

The following day, I thought I had a clue. Lee did not come to class: he had a high fever which developed into a major cold. It's very common for children who are getting sick to have a difficult day. Their symptoms aren't apparent, but something is wrong on the inside. Often, they can't tell you what it is: they just act out their uncomfortable feelings. I gave Lee the benefit of the doubt and felt sorry for him.

None of us was too healthy at the moment. Cathy had a cold. I felt a stomach virus coming on, and we had to send Sharon home with an ear infection. When she returned two days later, she seemed healthy but tentative. She sat by herself for most of the morning, working on a pegboard, barely answering the questions of her classmates.

"What's the matter with Sharon?" Cathy asked me.

"I think she had a very good time with her mother at home, so it's a little difficult to come back to school. Don't be surprised if she tells us she's too sick to stay in school again."

"Why not?" Cathy laughed. "It worked the first time."

Sure enough, in the gym Sharon shuffled over to us, her head hanging and her hazel eyes mournful, looking just like a chastised puppy.

I nudged Cathy. "Sarah Bernhardt would be proud."

"You know, Patti," our young actress began, "I think I still feel a little sick." She tried to look as pitiful as possible.

"I'm sorry to hear that, Sharon. We'll tell Mommy when she picks you up."

"She isn't picking me up. She has to go to my sister's play."

"Maybe that's why you feel a little sick," I told her. "Well, we'll tell your sitter when *she* comes."

Sharon nodded. "Patti, why are you eating those crackers?"

"Because I'm a little sick today, and I don't feel like eating anything else."

"I'm a little sick, too. Really," Sharon replied.

"I know you are, honey. And we'll tell Eve when she picks you up. But I come to school when I'm a little sick because it's my job. I'm the teacher. And your job is to be the student, even if you're a little sick, too."

"I know that," Sharon nodded. She gave me a hug, then scampered off to play with more good cheer than we had seen all morning.

David was also absent, but not because of illness. At long last, his mother had taken him to the doctor, who had ordered tests to see if David's wetting had any physical cause. They would be conducted in a hospital on an outpatient basis. David had told me he was a little scared, even though the tests wouldn't hurt. I didn't blame him: he would be around strange people and big machines for an entire day.

When David returned to class the following day, he looked fine. Happily, the tests were all negative. They provoked a fascinating result, however: never again did David wet his pants in school.

What had changed? Was David reassured of his parents' love because they spent so much time at the hospital with him? Had he finally been given the extra attention he needed after the move from New Hampshire? Had he been so scared at the hospital that he never wanted to go back again? We never found out. We simply lived with the pleasant result.

The next morning, Harris's mother reported some testing of her own. It seems that Harris was driving her crazy by poking her. "Does this hurt?" he'd ask. When she said, "No," he'd poke a little harder. "Does *this* hurt?" he'd repeat. This would continue until Joanna's answer was yes; then the game would stop.

Although his mother found this disturbing, I was encouraged. (Of course, I wasn't the one being poked.) Harris was trying to determine the boundaries for his actions. He wanted to know just how far he could go without hurting another person. Who better to test than your mother? She will love you even if you go too far. I asked Joanna to tell the therapist about the game. The Whites had begun seeing Laura Adler regularly now and all of us felt encouraged.

Cathy and I felt heartened about the class, as well. Although our days were far from peaceful, we had many moments of enjoyment. At lunch one day, I stopped Jason just as he was about to stuff a raisin in his ear. Instead of lecturing, I asked him why he thought it was a good idea.

"Benjamin told me to," was his response. I applied to Benjamin for an explanation.

His eyes wide with indignation, Benjamin replied, "Well, he was going to put it in *my* ear, so I told him to put it in his *own* ear!"

A rational solution to be sure—but I explained the general unsuitability of raisins as earplugs to the entire class. Cathy did a creditable job of controlling her laughter.

The children were also beginning to take an interest in words, for their sound as well as for their meaning. Three- and four-year-olds love to chant, regardless of whether their words make literal sense. One day, we were making playdough. The dough is very sticky in the beginning, so the kids usually won't touch it. That's teacher territory. As I began to knead, one child commented, "That's yukky. P.U." All the children suddenly began to chant the words "Yukky yukky, P.U." over and over until I had finished mixing the wet ingredients. Then it was their turn to knead. The playdough gleamed in the shiny chrome bowl, purple and gorgeous.

"How about *that*?" I asked them triumphantly.

"Ohhhh—that's not yukky. It's yummy!" one child corrected. Without missing a beat, the chant became "Yummy yummy, P.U." And they went right on chanting as they played. The "P.U." no longer made sense, but they needed it to sustain the rhythm. The children chanted to everyone's satisfaction for at least ten minutes.

At lunch on the same day, one child dropped his yogurt, and blurted out "Oh-oh; NO!" That was picked up by Jason, and became the lunchtime refrain. My favorite chant came at bathroom time, when the children walked (or skipped or toddled) to the gratifying refrain of "I love Patti, I love Cathy." In this profession, small pleasures assume large importance.

Our children were also asking about the sounds of the first letters in their names. (Almost all three- and four-year-olds can say the alphabet, but very few are aware that letters have sounds as well as names. When a child makes that connection, it's a major step toward learning to read.) Cathy and I went through all the initial consonants with them: Harris starts with "huh"; Jenny, Jeremy and Jason begin with "juh," etc. Sadly, we found that two children couldn't pronounce their names correctly. Sharon said "Saron" and Cory said "Tory." I explained that "Sharon" didn't start with an "s" as in "*s*oup," but with a sound like "sh" as in hu*sh*. Sharon could say "Shhh" and "Hush" but she couldn't say her name. Cory couldn't even come close to making the "k" sound for her name. This upset both children as well as their classmates. I was trying to think of a way to change the subject (not always an easy task with persistent three- and four-year-olds). All of a sudden, Louisa stood up and announced in her charming, theatrical way:

> "P is for Patti and Pete also
> P is for peepee and I gotta go!"

She raised her eyebrows, bestowed her million-dollar smile upon us and was out of the room in a flash. We all laughed uproariously, and the gloom was lifted.

Naturally, with things going moderately well, there had to be a Friday the thirteenth. Cathy was out sick, and her substitute had failed to show. It is dangerous for just one teacher to be with twelve three- and four-year-olds. I worked alone for most of the day in a room with children so volatile that there could have been an injury at any moment. If I'd had time, I would have been truly frightened.

But I didn't have a chance. The joint was jumpin' from the minute they walked in the door. Lee was back. He looked healthy, but somewhat tentative. It was understandable: he'd only been in school for two days in the last three weeks. The group had raced along, developing a fairly sustained work pace. As a very young three-year-old, he just wasn't up to it.

Lee went over to David and Benjamin, who were building an elaborate Lego castle. "Let's play, guys," he said, putting a piece of Lego on top of a tower, which immediately came crashing down.

David turned to me. "Lee broke our tower! We want to play by ourselves." There were times when I would have insisted that the two other boys include Lee. But he was so much younger that he couldn't have joined in the fantasy play which accompanied the building of the castle. It was a setup for failure. So I encouraged Lee to build something next to David and Benjamin.

He sat down to build by himself, but he lasted only a minute. Then he wandered over to Harris and Jason, who were working with pegs. They had spent ten minutes making "beautiful designs" at their pegboards and wanted to continue their work. Lee took a board, but he wasn't able to sit for very long. He zipped off again after two minutes.

Next, he decided to carry plastic fruit up to the loft for a "picnic." I had to stop him after a few steps up the ladder: our loft had been "fixed" so poorly that it was even more dangerous. The carpenter had raised the loft, but had reattached the same staircase, which was now at a precipitous angle. Children could go up if they held on to the railing. But there was almost no way to get down the slanted steps unless they used two hands. If a child was carrying anything, it was a virtual impossibility. After two accidents, I had declared the loft off limits for toys, and put in another urgent request for repairs.

"Lee, the loft is broken," I told him. "We can't take toys up the ladder until it is fixed." He just looked at me and kept on going. "Nothing goes up there, Lee. Do you understand?" This time he nodded and came down.

I turned away to help another child, but something told me to look back again in a minute. There was Lee on the loft with the basket of food. I went up, and carefully brought him down—basket and all.

"I just told you that you may not go up there with the basket, Lee," I reminded him.

"Yes I can!" he insisted, stamping his foot.

"No. You may *not*," I repeated with exasperation.

"*Yes*. My mommy *said!*" he countered. (This is a favorite ploy of young children—the use of "mommy" as shield and veiled threat.)

"Mommy makes the rules at home," I told him. "And Daddy. Cathy and I make the rules at school. You may not take food on the loft."

"Yes!" he announced, and turned right around to climb the ladder again.

(This is normal behavior for a two-year-old. But here, in a class where almost every child would be four by February, Lee was a fish out of water. I felt sorry for him, but I was exasperated.)

"If you can't remember the rule, then you'll sit on a chair and take some time out to think about it." I pulled over a chair and put him in it. After three and a half months in my class, he knew not to get up. In fact, he never moved. But he began to wail: "I want my mommeeee!"

I bent down and put my arm around him. "Your mommy's not here right now, Lee," I told him as gently as I could. She'll be here later to pick you up. You're in school now and you have to go by school rules."

To my surprise, he quieted down quickly. I praised him for this, and let him off the chair sooner than I expected to. (It's important to emphasize that certain *behavior* is unacceptable—not the *child* who is acting it out. I tell my students often that there are no bad children—only children who sometimes do bad things.)

What had happened? Had Lee merely needed to be reminded of school rules? Had he tested me to make sure he was as safe here as he was at home? Had he simply wanted to have his own way? I didn't know, and I had no time to reflect on the subject. The rest of the children were clamoring for my attention.

Jeremy had accidentally knocked over David and Benjamin's castle, so everyone in the block area was upset. Cory and Jenny were hollering for me to change the easel paper so they could paint. Mary Ann was upset that I couldn't sit with her while she colored. Sharon was whimpering that she missed her mother. Amanda was calling me to admire the paper where she had just written her name. Harris and Jason were beginning to get too loud. And Louisa was tugging at my pants, asking if she could bring in the giant box we had decorated.

In short, it was bedlam. Still, I told myself, it could be worse.

No one's bitten or scratched or punched yet. I plunged in, fixing whatever I could, explaining that I was the only grown-up in the room, so it might take a bit longer for me to help everyone. The time rushed by. I was too busy to go and complain about not having a sub. By ten, when Jenny's mother came as our guest for Shabbat snack, things were pretty much under control—if you don't count my headache.

It was a relief to have another adult in the room. We said the blessings over the candles, challah and grape juice, and gave out the cookies which Peggy had brought. Six kids—an unusually large number—spilled their grape juice, but with Peggy's cheerful efficiency, I felt as if I had an army of helpers.

"Have you been alone all morning?" she asked incredulously.

I nodded. "It's been okay, though." Silently, I wondered how the rest of the day would be. Peggy promised to alert the office on her way out.

Our next activity, gym, was basically uneventful. Harris had a time out for hitting. (My rules rhyme: YOU HIT, YOU SIT; YOU SPIT, YOU SIT; YOU BIT, YOU SIT. They are easy to remember but hard to follow for some children.) At least I had company: I was able to talk to the teachers of the class that shared our gym time. When it was time to go back to the room, however, I was alone again.

I put out a new activity—collaging with materials of just one color. This kept most of them busy for an hour, but when twelve o'clock came, they were on the verge of chaos. (In educational lingo: the kids were "high.")

I announced cleanup time. Mary Ann and Louisa went right on playing "Sleeping Beauty" under the loft. Harris pulled the large wooden refrigerator on top of himself while trying to get behind it. Amanda began a new painting before I had a chance to remove the brushes. Lee was jumping; Sharon was crying for her mother (though she'd been smiling the moment before). Jason began to roll on the rug.

Just as I thought I was going to dissolve on the classroom floor, one of our best assistant teachers, Nina Levine, appeared at the door.

"I heard you were alone and my class has already dismissed. I'm here to help you." I could have sworn she had wings and a halo.

We calmed the kids down and began cleanup. I went to the teachers' room to get milk for Sharon's birthday party, which was next on the agenda. When I returned, the room was straight and nearly all the kids were on the rug, listening to Nina read a story. Harris, however, was sitting at a table.

I glanced at Nina. "He won't move," she told me.

Harris looked just the way he had in September—his pale little face impassive and his eyes staring into space. I sat down and put my arm around his shoulders.

"Were you scared when I left the room, Harris?" I asked.

He looked at me with surprise, then nodded ever so slightly. He didn't know Nina, and I had suddenly disappeared.

"Okay. I won't leave you again today."

He smiled and ran over to sit with his friends. How did I figure out what was wrong? I know the child and I have good instincts. I took a shot at it and guessed right.

During the birthday party, Sharon's mother commented on how much improved Harris's behavior was. I smiled. Her husband commented on how well behaved the class was. I smiled through gritted teeth. After the party, Sharon left with her parents, wearing the biggest grin I had seen all day.

That left eleven of Them and two of Us for dismissal. Two children ran down the hall when we were helping the others on with their coats. Jason hit me when I tried to zip up his jacket. (I sat him on a chair until we were ready to go.) Lee made Louisa cry by sitting in her cubby and refusing to get up. When Nina took him out, he had a tantrum. Somehow, we managed to get them all into the elevator and down to the lobby.

After the final chorus of "Have a nice weekend!" from the un-suspecting mothers and baby-sitters, Nina and I returned to the fifth floor, to unwind in the teachers' room. I could hardly move.

Nina turned to me. "Patti, you haven't complained enough. That's the hardest class I've ever seen. I'm exhausted and I was only with you for an hour."

I managed half a smile. "And they were pretty good today. Nobody broke any bones."

· · ·

Cathy returned on Monday, much to my relief. She was ap-palled to hear of our horrific day, but there was no repetition of it. The children were more comfortable with both of their teachers in the room. (Children are strong proponents of Browning's assertion that "God's in his heaven—All's right with the world." If the usual grown-ups are around, then the kids know they're safe.) For the next few days, everyone seemed involved and happy—except for Mary Ann.

Cathy and I watched her with growing concern. Anybody could see she was no fun to play with; she always had to have her way. I overheard an interaction she had in the block area with Sharon, Jenny and Cory. The four girls built a tall tower, and enjoyed watching it fall when it became top-heavy. Then they built a slanted structure that resembled a railroad track. They each took a block to use as a conveyance.

Sharon said, "It's a water sled."

Mary Ann replied, "No. It's a snow sled."

Sharon, a strong leader, wasn't giving up so easily. "It's a wa-ter sled," she insisted.

"No!" Mary Ann shouted. "It's a SNOW SLED!"

Suddenly Sharon smiled. "I know! It's a water–snow sled!" This was a perfect compromise, allowing play to continue.

But Mary Ann couldn't accept it. "No. It's a snow sled. I

don't want to play." The other girls continued their game as Mary Ann walked over to me.

"Let's play," she said brightly, as if nothing had happened.

I was working with David, making a pattern out of beads so that he could copy it.

"I'm busy now, Mary Ann. Perhaps you can find another child to play with."

"Can I do what you're doing?"

"Sure," I said. "Sit down with David and me."

"Okay, but I have to have all your beads." Without waiting for an answer, she reached over to take my pattern, even though there was a box right in front of her with hundreds of beads.

I stopped her. "You may not have the pattern I am making. But you may use any of these other beads to make your own pattern."

"Okay," she replied—but she wasn't happy about it.

Later, we were in line for the bathroom. Lee was chosen as the leader, and came up to the front of the line to take Cathy's hand. Although she knew he was first, Mary Ann tried to push past him. I took her shoulders gently, to stop her. Turning around, she pushed me away roughly.

The next day, at dismissal, Mary Ann was putting on her coat just as a teacher walked by her in the hall. Mary Ann looked directly at her and said angrily, "Get out of my way!"

The teacher exploded. "*What* did you say? Just who do you think you are, talking to me that way?"

I spoke to my student. "Listen, Mary Ann, you are a *child*. You may *not* talk to grown-ups that way. Don't your mommy and daddy tell you this at home?"

She shook her head, and I believed her.

"Then we all need to have a little chat," I replied. It was no longer important to have her parent-teacher conference. It was urgent.

Max and Nancy Stein came in early a few mornings later. They, too, realized the conference was crucial: Mary Ann had told them that she didn't like coming to school because no one would play with her. All four of us knew we had work to do.

I began by mentioning Mary Ann's high intelligence and her obvious love of learning. It was perfectly clear that she had the makings of a very good student.

Next, we brought up the fact that Mary Ann always wanted to have her own way.

"For example," I mentioned, "if the kids decide to play 'Beauty and the Beast,' she always insists on being Beauty."

"What's wrong with that?" Max inquired.

Trying to keep the surprise off my face, I replied, "Other children like to be Beauty also. But if Mary Ann can't have her own way, she refuses to play."

"Oh, that's understandable," he told us. "She always gets her own way at home. She's an only child. We do whatever she wants."

There was the problem, right out in the open. Now we had to deal with it. I stole a glance at Cathy. She was so surprised that a small puff of wind would have toppled her. It was up to me.

"It's important for Mary Ann to have rules at home as well as in school," I said as nonjudgmentally as possible. "Everything can't be her way because life isn't like that. There are other people to deal with. Mary Ann is a child. She can't have the privileges of an adult."

We spoke about establishing a consistent bedtime for Mary Ann and about not allowing her to have everything she wanted.

Cathy found her voice, and described two incidents. Once, Mary Ann had continually poked me in the back because she wanted my attention even though she could see that I was hanging up a wet painting. It was annoying and painful. Another time, Mary Ann had approached three girls who were already playing house, and become incensed when they wouldn't allow her to be the mother. The fact that there was already a mother was of no interest to her. She cried for ten minutes afterward.

Max was genuinely surprised at these stories. Nancy was upset, but she defended her child: "Mary Ann plays better with older children."

I replied, "In school, it's just the opposite. A three-year-old like Louisa will forgive an assault of that nature and come back to play with a child twenty minutes later. A four-year-old can stay mad all day. And a five-year-old can ostracize a child all year. So let's fix this before she really winds up with no friends."

Nancy's eyes filled with tears. "I just want her to be happy."

"Oh, you want more than that," I assured her. "You want her to have friends, and to be able to deal with frustration and disappointment, too, don't you?"

She nodded.

"For this, Mary Ann needs to understand that there are *rules*. She's learning that here. She needs to learn it at home, too."

Both parents nodded, shook our hands and promised to work on it. They looked so sincere that Cathy and I found ourselves hoping for the rarest effect of a conference: immediate change.

...

As Hanukkah approached, the children were fairly calm. They made menorahs (the candelabra lit for eight nights, one candle at a time) out of wood, paint and metal nuts. They decorated cigar boxes to take home as gifts for their parents. They listened to the story of Hanukkah with more patience and interest than we had seen from them before.

At the time of the Greek Empire, the Syrians had invaded Judea (ancient Israel), and supplanted Jewish culture with their own. They had also desecrated the Jewish Temple. After a time, they were driven out by a small, guerilla-fighting army composed of Hasmonean Jews, most frequently called Maccabees, and their supporters. After their unexpected victory, the Maccabees restored the Temple, and returned Judaism to the land.

Each year, my students truly began to understand the story of Hanukkah when they participated in it. They threw toy fruit and animals into a mock Temple I set up. They were told that they couldn't celebrate Jewish holidays anymore. They participated in "a great battle," using rolled-up construction paper as swords, with half the children as Syrians and half as Maccabees (naturally, we switched sides often). The Maccabees cheered when they won and the Syrians ran home to their mommies. Then all the children participated in cleaning up the Temple and restoring its "everlasting light" (which always burns in a synagogue).

This year, however, I decided not to act out the story. The brief portion which included the battle seemed too stimulating for my students, who were already struggling to control their impulses. They certainly didn't need the mixed message that violence was okay sometimes.

Cathy agreed. "They're doing so nicely. It would be a shame to ruin this calm period."

"It has been quiet," I agreed. "Nobody's died for at least two weeks."

It was a stupid joke. The next day, Jeremy's mother came in to report that her husband's mother had died. (She reminded me that she had mentioned the possibility last week. I had forgotten.) They would be going to North Carolina for the funeral. Should they take their sons along? Jeremy, in particular, seemed very tense.

I felt strongly that the children should go with their parents. This death had a "waiting for the other shoe to drop" quality. It had been expected, and was the second one in just a few months. That creates a lot of stress in children as well as in adults.

"Jeremy is too young to go to the actual funeral. Since Evan is six, you should talk to him about whether he wants to go. But they should both be with you on the trip. They really need you right now."

Carolyn felt I was right and said so. As she thanked me and left with Jeremy, I felt weak in the knees. This job carried so much responsibility. What if I hadn't known the answer? What if I didn't know the answer next time?

The following day, Jeremy told all his classmates that he was going to North Carolina because his grandma had died. Death became the issue of the day. We discussed it at story time. One child asked if she were going to die.

"Well, yes, but not for a *very* long time. First you have to go finish the school year with Cathy and me. *Then,* there's summer vacation. Maybe you go to camp or to the country. That takes a *long* time. Then you come back to your next classroom—Pre-K. That's a lot of fun—you do all kinds of special projects that you're too young for now. Then there's *another* summer vacation. After *that,* you start kindergarten, in another building . . ." By the time I got to second grade, not even the hardiest kid could listen anymore.

"It's too *long!*" shouted Benjamin.

This was exactly the message I had been trying to deliver: it's a long, long time until you die.

"Yes, it *is* very long," I said. "Let's go to the gym instead." Everyone cheered.

Although the discussion had ended, the idea of death was not out of the children's minds. It is a common worry for four-year-olds; we deal with it all year. Sure enough, we had a lot of children playing dead in the gym that morning.

One child would lie down and several others would try to move the body by pulling an arm or a leg. This group was clever.

They figured out that they could roll a dead person, so they proceeded to line them up. It was eerie: the dead ones never smiled or moved or opened their eyes. When the live children began to get anxious, they came over to me.

"David and Amanda and Benjamin are dead," asserted Jenny.

"Oh, really?" I asked in a news-gathering tone. "Let's see if they are. I'll just go over and give them the tickle test."

I walked over to the corpses and made my announcement. "Let's see if David's alive. I'll just tickle him and see if he laughs." Much to the relief of the other children, he giggled immediately. I shouted out "He lives!" and proceeded to tickle all the other dead people as well. It broke the spell, reminding all the children that the game is "just pretend."

Still, death was never far from their thoughts. One day, as we were giving the children snack, Jason made an announcement. "Peter Pan is dead."

The children were stunned into silence. Even the munching stopped. Jason knew he had an audience.

"Yes," he pronounced, with great solemnity. "Dead."

"No," I said, in a "light-but-disparaging" tone. "He's not dead. He was never alive. He's just pretend." From the continuing silence, I could tell that absolutely no one believed me.

I elaborated. "Look, he's from a book, just like this one." I picked up a book with a ridiculous pink, blobby creature on the cover.

"Peter Pan is pretend, just like the Mess Fairy here. Did you ever see the Mess Fairy walking down Broadway?" The children began to giggle.

Cory spoke up. "Yes. I saw her. She was on Eighty-first Street, close to my house." With her speech problem, it sounded like "Yas. I taw her. See wa on aaee fust steet, cose to my houf." But it was clear enough for the children to understand her joke. The question of death was forgotten in the ensuing laughter.

Cathy turned to me. "Did you hear that wonderful sentence come out of Cory? It wasn't perfect, but it was comprehensible. She's made so much progress."

"It's true," I agreed. "Now is the time to begin speech therapy with her. She wants so much to communicate better than she does. I've got to talk to her mother."

"Go ahead. Cory told me this morning that Mary Elizabeth's father died."

It was the right time to speak up—or as close to the right time as I'd ever get before winter vacation, which was just three days away. There was no time to ask for a formal conference. I steeled myself for a short hallway conversation on the following day.

Theresa brought Cory to school the next morning. By a great stroke of luck, they were the last to arrive. This meant our conversation could be private. Cathy helped Cory find something to do, and I took Theresa out into the hall.

"Cory told us that her friend's daddy has died," I began.

Theresa confirmed it. Her friend had died the slow, harrowing death from cancer that is part of our collective nightmare. Now it was over.

"I'm sorry, although it sounds like a relief."

"I'm sure his wife felt that way."

"How's their daughter?"

"Mary Elizabeth? I don't think she really understands what happened yet."

"Makes sense. And how's Cory?"

"She asked me if Mary Elizabeth's daddy is better now. I said 'Yes, finally, he is, but he's somewhere else. Not here. We won't see him again.' So she drew a picture of our family and Mary Elizabeth was in it."

I nodded and forced back tears. It was difficult to speak, but I managed it.

"How's Edward? He looks great." He was holding his mother's hand at the moment—this child with the beautiful face and the sparkling eyes and the terrible illness.

"He's not doing so well, actually. He's out of crisis, but he's not growing. So he's going to have some tests."

How could I go on after receiving that information? How was I to tell a mother whose baby was so ill that she must focus on her other child? It was harder but more necessary than ever. I just plunged in.

"Theresa, I hope you'll be able to find a person to evaluate Cory's speech over the vacation. You remember I mentioned it before?"

She nodded. We had touched on it briefly one day while chatting in the hall.

I continued: "It's hard, I know, but she's made so much progress on her own. She's gone as far as she can go by herself. Now is really the time to move on it."

Theresa looked like I had slapped her. The pain ran across her face.

"I know . . . you're right. I should have done it already . . . but I've just had so much on my mind . . ." She filled up with tears. So did I.

"I know, I know you have. I'm sorry, Theresa. But I have to be Cory's advocate. It's my job. She's such a wonderful child, and she needs you now."

Theresa hugged me. "You're right. We'll get it done. Thanks."

We chatted awhile about the progress being made in our classroom. She was particularly impressed by Harris's improvement.

"You saved that kid," she stated emphatically. "What a wonderful achievement."

I said: "Thanks."

I thought: Now if I can only save yours.

Theresa left. I leaned against the cubbies and began to cry.

Cathy came out of the classroom, and assured me that I had done the right thing. We had to rush back in, however; the children were having an argument.

Louisa was giving out stick-on earrings (paper baubles with adhesive strong enough to hold them on an earlobe all day). The girls had eagerly accepted them, and had rushed to the mirror to put them on. The boys, however, were dubious.

"Boys don't wear earrings," Lee told Louisa. "That's silly."

Louisa looked at her teachers questioningly.

"Oh yes—some of them do," said the teacher who had come of age in the sixties.

"They sure do," added the hip, young teacher of the nineties. "Of course, you don't have to. But many boys wear an earring in one ear now."

That was all the evidence the boys needed; they were delighted to participate. Louisa proudly gave earrings to the boys, helped put them on and hugged herself for thinking of the idea.

Cathy and I hugged her for the same reason.

January: Improvements

For the first few days after winter vacation, the children were As Good As Gold. Louisa was so delighted to see her friends that she hugged all eleven of them. Harris, Jason and Lee worked in the block area without an argument. Jeremy, David and Benjamin were a cheerful threesome as they constructed a football field out of Lego blocks. The other children played happily around the room.

"What happened?" asked Cathy. "They couldn't have grown up this much in two weeks."

"They'll be themselves again any minute now," I assured her. "They just missed being in school. Whether they know it or not, kids do better when they have a structure to their day."

"Their parents know it. They all looked delighted to drop their children off."

"When you're a parent, you'll understand," I laughed.

"I think I understand now. They *are* difficult. But I missed them a lot over vacation," admitted Cathy.

I smiled at her. "I did, too. Next week, when they're running us ragged, I'll remind you of that sentiment. Working with young children is like eating Chinese food: after you're with them for an hour, you need another vacation."

Cathy and I looked around. There seemed to be some real improvement. Benjamin was sturdy and happy: he never mentioned his personal safety. Mary Ann was attempting to compromise with the other children. We even heard her tell

Sharon: "Well, there can be *two* 'Beauties.'" (I wondered if she had visited Lourdes over vacation.)

After a few days, though, we began to see some backsliding. One morning, Harris kicked the refrigerator, yelled a great deal and hit two children. He had to eat snack by himself. Most kids hate eating alone: I could see he was angry about it.

"We've really got to watch Harris in the gym," I told Cathy. "He seems to have forgotten the rules."

"To say the least," she replied. "Today, it seems more like October than January."

"We'll just have to try to be his conscience again. It should be easier this time. He knows the rules in school. He just hasn't needed them for a while."

"Why aren't they similar to the ones at home?"

It was a question I couldn't answer. And it only increased our vigilance. We had been in the gym about ten minutes when Lee ran over to me.

"I'm going to catch Harris!" he shouted happily. He bolted off without waiting for a reply. It was a game they both enjoyed, so there should have been no trouble, but I followed along anyway. Unfortunately, Lee reached his friend just as Harris was about to go down a slide. When Lee yanked on the back of his shirt, Harris turned around and punched him squarely in the nose. Lee was unhurt but stunned; he fell backward off the slide. I was just in time to catch him.

Putting Lee down, I turned my attention to the culprit. "Harris—that's not okay. YOU HIT, YOU SIT." I took him by the hand and led him to a chair. He looked up at me.

"I didn't hit," he insisted. "I didn't!"

"You *did* hit. You punched Lee in the nose."

"I didn't," he whined.

Four-year-olds don't really lie. They usually slip in and out of fantasy play. Often, they think that saying something makes it true. That's why they sound so convincing. But this didn't seem to be the case with Harris. His green eyes glanced up craftily at me. His small mouth suppressed a smile. I had the distinct feeling that he was trying to put one over on me.

"You did *hit,* and now you *sit,*" I said firmly.

"But he pulled my shirt."

I thought: Aha! A new argument—that means he knows he's lost the first point. Maybe arguing works at home. This would explain why the rules are different.

I said: "I know he pulled your shirt. I'm sure you didn't like that. But you have good words. Use them. Next time say 'DON'T DO THAT!' in your big voice."

Harris looked at me seriously and nodded. I let him up a minute later. He returned directly to Lee, and they renewed their game of tag. After a moment, Lee accidentally bumped into his friend. Harris raised his hand to hit Lee but then looked over at me. I shook my head. Harris yelled, "DON'T DO THAT TO ME!" directly into Lee's surprised face and glanced my way again. I smiled and nodded. The boys resumed their game.

Harris continued to use his words for the rest of the day. Cathy was amazed.

"That was a quick change," she commented.

"He seems to have gotten right back into the saddle," I agreed. "Let's hope it lasts for a while."

"But he never seems to behave for more than a few days at a time."

"Difficult kids are like that, Cathy. They gain ground and then slide back a little. You really see progress only on a grand scale—when it's April or May, for instance, and you look back to September."

"By that standard, he's already improved tremendously. He doesn't bite anymore, and he never throws blocks or toys."

"Those are good things to remember when we're mad as hell at him," I said.

Cathy nodded. "I wish we saw as much progress in Cory. After two weeks at home, her speech is so indistinct that none of the children can understand her."

It was true. Perhaps she didn't have to try so hard at home. Her family was probably used to her speech. Whatever the reason, Cory was having a difficult time in school. I wondered aloud if anything had been done to acquire a speech therapist for her.

"We haven't seen Theresa all week. I hope it's not because she hasn't done anything and is afraid to face us."

Cathy reminded me that Theresa usually brought Cory in on Fridays. We decided that if she didn't come, we would ask Cory's father, David, if they had set to work on the problem.

On Friday, Theresa dropped Cory off as usual. We exchanged the customary pleasantries:

"Hi! How was your vacation?" she asked me.

"We had a vacation? Who remembers back that far?"(We'd been back for a week and it seemed a month.)

Theresa laughed. Then she made her announcement. "Cory will be late on Monday because she has her first appointment with the speech therapist."

Her eyes beamed with the glow of accomplishment, but she also seemed tentative. Did she expect me to be annoyed because this goal hadn't been accomplished sooner? I threw both my fists into the air with just as much excitement as if I had seen the Miami Dolphins score a touchdown in the Super Bowl.

"YESSSS!" I shouted. Theresa smiled with equal parts of pleasure, relief and amusement.

"It wasn't easy, you know," she told me. "There are not so many speech therapists who are really good with kids."

I didn't know (aren't children their main clients?), but I was thrilled that Theresa had found one. Cory was on her way to a better life.

I was happy to carry this victory around in my thoughts during the next few weeks of January. I needed it: the weather was awful and the children were worse. Sometimes, they were so difficult that it was funny.

One morning, Harris made a bowel movement in his pants and absolutely refused to let us change him. Lee did the same. Soon the other children began to notice the odor. At story time, no one wanted to sit next to either boy. Lee didn't seem to mind, but Harris set about exacting revenge. He went over to sit next to Jason.

"Harris smells," complained Jason. "And he always bothers me."

"Just let him sit down," I insisted, as I began to read a book to the group.

A minute later, Jason interrupted. "Harris poked me!"

"Okay, Jason, you can move to another seat." I turned to the perpetrator. "You see, Harris, Jason doesn't want to sit next to you because you won't let him listen." I didn't mention the other obvious reason.

Harris fixed his familiar, zero-affect stare on me and moved a little closer to Louisa. I continued reading.

Less than a minute later I heard, "Harris, stop!" Now he was poking Louisa.

"Harris, it is not okay for you to poke Louisa either."

"I didn't. Benjamin did it." Benjamin was five feet away on the other side of the rug.

"*You* did it, and now you're going to have to sit on a chair—*especially* because you didn't tell the truth."

I put him where he could hear, but where he couldn't see the pictures. He didn't listen, but he stayed on the chair, in his fashion. He was actually half-on, half-off, but I attributed that to the contents of his underwear. (The thought suddenly occurred to me that he always acted up at story time; perhaps he was anxious about words, or about learning to read. I filed that idea away for later inspection.)

Lee's behavior, if possible, was even worse. During play time, he was continually getting into trouble. He tried to open the radiator cover. He took toys away from other children. He pushed when he couldn't have his way. Each time Cathy or I disciplined him, he hollered, "You're NOT the boss. I'M the boss!" He didn't even want to sit down at Amanda's birthday party. This was truly unusual: cupcakes were Lee's favorite food. Clearly, something other than school was affecting his behavior.

I didn't know what it was, and I didn't have time to worry about it. Keeping the two kids from hurting anyone else was taking all of my energies. At our final cleanup time, when all the other children were putting the toys away, Harris and Lee went up on the loft and hid under the big pillows there. When Cathy and I asked them to come out, they just giggled. Not a capital offense, to be sure—but it was the proverbial straw for my camel. I lost my control, along with my temper.

With clenched teeth, I marched up angrily onto the loft. Jenny and Mary Ann followed me, eager to witness discipline in action when it didn't concern them. I sent them down, saying, "You don't want to see this, girls." Cathy glanced up at me and laughed, but she was curious also. I cast aside the pillows and looked directly at the two culprits.

"Time to clean up now." I spoke in a low, menacing voice. Harris read the look in my eye and rose quickly. Lee refused to budge.

"No!" he said defiantly. "I *won't* clean up. You go away."

I took both his hands and pulled him to his feet.

"You *will* clean up, Lee. *I* make the rules, not *you*."

I took a doll and put it in his hands. He grabbed it, hard, and wouldn't let go. I moved him over to the doll crib and shook his arms until the doll fell out of his grasp and landed on the bed.

If you are going to get into a power struggle with a child— which is a terrible idea—you'd better make it clear to the entire class that you've won. I did just that.

"Good cleaning up, Lee," I declared loudly. "Let's do it again." We repeated the same odd dance with a second doll, and with a third. They fell accurately on top of their predecessors.

"Well, that's done. Good job. Now you can sit down." I carried him down the treacherous loft stairs and plopped him unceremoniously on a chair. He immediately began to cry. I was too angry to care. Next, I turned my attention to his buddy.

Harris was cleaning like a madman. So were the other children: I had scared them all. They were scurrying around like mice on a cheese hunt. The sight was so amusing that my anger lifted.

"This is the cleanest room *we'll* ever have," laughed Cathy. "Maybe you should lose your temper every day."

"It wouldn't have any effect if I did. It only works because it's out of the ordinary. But it pains me to think I could get so angry at a three-year-old. How can it help Lee? It only teaches him that you can bully people if you're older and stronger than they are."

"Nobody's perfect, kiddo," Cathy reminded me. "You can't do everything right all of the time. Besides, the more often Lee sees that grown-ups are in charge, the better it is for him."

I nodded, appreciating her loyalty. In my heart, however, I knew I had overreacted. Lee was still bawling on his chair, and Harris had finished his cleanup job. I praised him and told both boys to join their friends on the rug. Lee stopped crying instantly and ran over to sit with the other children. The effect was startling—hysterics to smiles in under three seconds. I wondered if even a Ferrari could go so far so fast. Cathy and I couldn't help but laugh at the ease with which Lee threw off a tantrum.

"He can't be too upset if he stops crying in a second," said Cathy.

"No. He must be on edge about something else. Remind me to ask his mother at dismissal."

I mentioned Lee's difficulties to Carla. She told me that his father had just left on an eleven-day business trip, and Lee was upset about it. I explained that it was important for us to know about any major events such as a trip. It could be the key to any behavior change. Carla promised to keep me informed.

For the next few days, Lee's behavior was unchanged. He continually stamped his pudgy little foot and announced that I was not the boss. That honor was shared alternately by his mommy and by him. With other children, to relieve pressure in a confrontational situation, I often say, "You are not the king, so you can't make the rules in school." It usually makes them laugh. It didn't seem to tickle Lee, however:

"*Yes!* I *am* the king!" he announced in all seriousness. "I *do* make the rules!" The children around him began to laugh, but Lee was insistent.

"Well, King Lee, you had better listen to school rules today, or you will find yourself sitting on a chair which is *not* a throne. And tomorrow we will have a little talk with Mommy." I addressed him lightheartedly, but I was as serious as he was.

Our three-way chat occurred the following morning, when Carla brought Lee to school. Before they had even entered the class, I took them to an empty room.

"Carla, Lee is having a little difficulty with the idea that Cathy and I make the rules at school, while you and Mike make the rules at home. Would you say that's correct?"

Carla backed me up immediately. "Yes, I'd say that's right."

I turned to her son. "So, you see, Lee—you aren't *really* the king. It's fun to pretend, but you still have to follow the rules, just like all the other children. Right, Carla?"

I could see from a puckering of her eyebrows that she didn't want to hurt her son's feelings, but she answered gamely:

"Yes, that's right, Lee. Patti's the boss in school."

I appreciated her support all the more because it had been hard for her to give. Lee smiled at us both, nodded and walked into our classroom. I thanked Carla and followed him in.

Fifteen minutes later, Lee wanted a toy that another child

was using: he began to have a tantrum. Before he could rev up into high gear, I knelt down beside him.

"Remember what we talked about with Mommy this morning?" I asked him. Lee nodded.

"This is one of those times to follow Patti and Cathy's rules. In school we share. You may have the toy next, okay?"

Lee didn't answer, or even look my way. He nodded and ran off. When it was his turn to use the toy, I gave it to him.

"Thank you, Patti," he replied sweetly. It was such a surprise that I was rocked back on my feet by the force of the improvement. Later, he came up to me in the gym, climbed on my lap and gave me a hug. "You're a good teacher, Patti. I won't hit today."

For the next few weeks, Lee's behavior continued to improve. Naturally, we couldn't hope for a complete change from so short a conversation; however, any respite was pleasant enough. Now we could concentrate on helping the other children. After four months of simply striving to maintain order and civility, Cathy and I were overjoyed at being able to concentrate on other areas of development.

One of our goals was increasing the children's independence. We began by asking them to pour their own juice at snack time. (We had waited until January to make sure each child was old enough to succeed.) We had always poured it for them; now we put half-full measuring cups with spouts on each table.

My instructions were simple. "When you want more juice, just tell the person next to you to 'Please pass the pitcher.' Then you can pour your own juice."

Cathy and I walked around the room, helping any child who was unsure. There were two hard parts: getting the juice to come out of the spout, and stopping when the cup was full. Most of the children could do both. Lee had a hard time with the latter, but he learned quickly. Benjamin, however, refused to touch the pitcher.

"What? Noooo—you have to do it. I can't pour." He sat, shaking his head in disbelief. "You have to do it for me."

We coaxed him into trying it: of course, he poured perfectly. He was delighted with his newfound skill. I wondered if his feelings about his health prevented him from seeing his own competence. There was nothing to do but wait and watch. Meanwhile, every step in this direction was another support for his emotional well-being.

There were very few spills, even on that first day. Possibly, this was because the children were familiar with my ideas on that subject. "Does a spill hurt the table? Does it hurt the table's feelings? Then a spill is no big deal." They always laughed, but they got the message.

Advice to parents: if your kid knows that spills are no big deal, then he's relaxed and does a better job getting the juice into the cup. When a child spills, give him a sponge and let him clean it up. That's all.

Advice to teachers: if you've got a kid who spills intentionally, tell the child that spilling on purpose is a "yes big deal." It wastes food, which is not okay. Then you can discipline a repeat offender.

The children did so well that we introduced our next project: name cards. We printed each name on three-by-eight-inch strips of oaktag. Next, we sat in a circle, held up one card at a time and talked about how to recognize each name.

Children don't have to read to identify their names. They just have to recognize the particular configuration of squiggles and swirls that spells the name. For example, Benjamin begins with "a letter with two bubbles." In the middle is a letter which "hooks under" the others and at the end is a "letter with a mound." I used these highly intelligent quotes from my former students when I described each name to its owner.

Some children caught on very quickly. David could read all the names by the end of the first lesson. So could Lee (go figure!).

Some kids were not as sure of themselves. But they knew when I was holding their name, because I looked right at them. If you couldn't figure out the name, you could always look at my face. It's a foolproof procedure, and it worked once more. By the end of the week, all the children could identify their own names.

We used the name cards as place holders for lunch. We also held them up one by one at dismissal. "If you *see* your name, *say* your name and go stand at the door by Cathy." The children loved this task. They giggled, they whispered or they shouted, but they got the job done. I overheard Sharon say to Jenny, "We all know our names!" Jenny nodded happily back at her friend.

Only Cory was uncomfortable. She acknowledged her name but she would not say it. For a child who rarely hesitated to use her speech, even when it was unintelligible, this was a surprising development. I mentioned it to Cathy.

"She doesn't seem very happy in general," added my assistant. "Have you seen her drawings lately? The people all have frowns."

I hadn't noticed. When we looked over her work, however, we saw that only the bigger people had sad faces. The following day, Cory told us the reason why.

She was drawing a picture of her family. I asked her to tell me about it. The figure she identified as the mommy was the one with the frown.

"Why is Mommy frowning, Cory?" I asked her.

"Because Mommy is angry with me," was the response I thought I heard.

"Why is she angry?"

Cory did not reply.

Her mother had an idea, though. She mentioned it to us the following morning.

"Cory thinks I'm angry with her because I'm making her go to speech therapy. None of her friends are going. She feels she must have done something wrong."

"But she hasn't—and I'm sure you tell her that."

"I do. Especially now that I know how much she really needs it. The therapist just finished testing Cory for more severe problems, like a learning disability. Cory's speech was so indistinct that the therapist wasn't sure how extensive the problem was."

I thought: Neither was I.

I said: "What was the result?"

"There was no evidence of anything but the speech difficulties. But it was very obvious that she needs help in that area."

"Now that *you're* sure, maybe it will be easier for Cory to be sure as well."

Theresa nodded. We spoke for a moment about the difficulties of being the "healthy child" in a family. Cory had less of her mother's attention than Edward. She had the additional burden of wondering whether her brother would ever get well. It was a sad time for the whole family.

I avoided mentioning my feelings about Cory's speech. It just didn't seem as if the whole problem could be an inability to pronounce the sounds of letters. There had to be something else. An undiscovered hearing problem was my first choice and my best hope. I didn't mention it again because it was important to both parents that at least one of their children be healthy. We would have to wait and see. I was tired of feeling this way, but there was no other choice. If I pushed the parents any further, I would only scare them. Now it was up to the speech therapist.

I was drawn away from these depressing thoughts by Elaine Donner. I greeted her warmly. Louisa took the bus to and from school, so it was unusual to see her mother here. One look at Louisa, however, convinced me that she was out of sorts.

Elaine explained that they had just come from the pediatrician, who had given Louisa medicine for an ear infection.

I thought: If she's got a brand-new ear infection, why is she in school? She should have a day at home to recover.

I said: "She doesn't look like her usual cheerful self. Is it all right for her to be here today?"

Elaine assured me that it was. Louisa's doctor had said that she could come to school, and that her illness was not contagious. (Ah, pediatricians! If only they would consider their patients' well-being, and not just their health!)

Next, Elaine introduced us to her mother, an attractive, well-dressed woman who smiled politely. Cathy and I were delighted to meet her. When grandparents come to school, they often have the time to be truly interested in a child's world. We filled her ears with praise of Louisa.

To our surprise, both mother and daughter countered with unhappy stories of Louisa—they called her Louie—her stubbornness, her inability to share and her general unworthiness at home. I gave them my standard answer.

"That's as it should be. Louisa saves her best stuff for school. She acts out where she feels safest—at home."

This was obviously lost on Grandma. "Louie never gives me *any* trouble. She knows *all* the rules at my house. She doesn't get away with *anything.*"

"Ah, well, you know the joke about why grandparents and grandchildren get along so well, don't you?" I asked her.

Grandma shook her head.

"They have a common enemy," I said calmly.

A tight smile crossed Grandma's lips.

Elaine Donner positively grinned: "Oh, you mean me? Exactly."

I wondered silently why anyone would spend the first three minutes with her granddaughter's teacher complaining about her grandchild. Anybody with eyes could see how superb Louisa was. And what an excellent parent Elaine was—even if she didn't always know when to keep Louisa home.

Cathy and I listened in satisfaction as Elaine asked her daughter to bring out the painting she had made the day before.

"Louie reported that she worked very hard on a picture yesterday," Elaine told her mother. She kindly omitted the fact that Louisa had covered herself with paint, having refused a smock. (I don't insist on them. Some children won't paint if they are forced to wear one.)

"She worked for twenty minutes," Cathy informed both ladies. The painting was truly a thing of beauty—a large mass of pastel colors swirling around each other. Louisa's mother praised it to the hilt. She did not use general compliments; she described what she loved about the painting.

"You used all the colors nicely and you covered all the space." Turning to us, she asked, "May I take this?" When we assented with enthusiasm, she looked back at her daughter.

"Louie, I'm going to put this up on the wall in my office for everyone to see. I'm very proud you." Louisa beamed.

Cathy whispered to me: "Look how happy she's made her kid. If only Elaine could bottle her parenting skills and sell them. She'd make millions."

I nodded. "But she must have learned some of it from *her* mother. Maybe Grandma is just out of sorts today."

Before Cathy had time to agree, our attention was commanded by the Donners' elaborate leave-taking process. Three kisses and hugs from Mommy and Grandma were insufficient to appease Louisa. She ran out into the hallway for more. As Elaine bent to oblige, she looked up at me.

"Louisa usually isn't like this," she reported.

"She doesn't often get the chance to separate from you at school," I told Elaine. "Usually you put her on the bus. It's not surprising that she'd be a bit uncomfortable in a new situation."

Elaine seemed relieved. She hugged her child once more.

"Bye-bye, Louie, I love you. See you tonight!" she sang out as she disappeared down the hall.

I was grateful for Elaine's cheery farewell. Some parents

look so anxious when they leave that their children must wonder if they're being consigned to peewee hell. Why else would Mom or Dad have that worried face and tense body? Somewhat consoled, Louisa entered the classroom holding my hand, a bit teary but ready for school.

To cheer her up, I brought out one of her favorite things—a counting game. I had invented this particular task to help the children learn a math principle called one-to-one correspondence. Ten moderately large rubber cows were the pieces of the game. I put all the cows in my lap, then placed them on the table, one by one, while telling a little story about them. It was the child's job to decide how many cows were on the table by counting them. This task sounds easier than it is for three- and four-year-olds. They don't always understand that one number goes with one object. Practice helps, however; by the end of the year, almost all the children in my class can complete the game successfully.

Even though she was our youngest girl, Louisa was a whiz at math. She followed my instructions like a tail gunner on a bombing raid: with speed, concentration and accuracy. She counted so well that we played the game twice. Then it was time to let the other kids have their chance. That was okay with Louisa. With her customary cheerfulness, she skipped off to play with Mary Ann.

As I worked with Sharon, I noticed my three bandits hovering around our table, trying not to look interested. After Sharon did her usual creditable job, I called Lee over. He was eager to begin, but the game was a bit too advanced for him. He left after counting to three.

Jason was next. He counted up to five cows accurately, and then decided to stop. I congratulated him on his wonderful job of counting, and shook his hand. (The reason I play this game with one child at a time is so they all feel successful. No other child is there to compete with or lose to.)

Harris was curious but hesitant. He had never done any for-

mal work of this kind with me. I remembered his obtrusive behavior at story time. Was there something about formal learning which frightened him? If so, the best way to begin removing
the feeling was to help him succeed at this task.

"Harris, do you want to be next?" I asked as sweetly as possible.

"No. I don't want to play this game," he replied, moving closer to the table.

"Ohhh. Why not?" I cajoled. "Don't you like this nice little
cow?" He nodded as he slipped into the chair beside me.

I continued. "One nice little man cow. And here's a lady cow.
How many is that?"

We answered at the same time: "Two." I placed my finger on
each cow's head as I counted. "One, two. One number for one
head." I added a third, smaller cow.

"And then they got married and had a baby cow. How many
is that?"

Harris put his finger on each cow and counted "One, two,
three." Then he looked up at me questioningly, hopefully.

"Exactly!" I said with excitement. He began to smile. I
went on.

"The mommy and daddy decided to have a birthday party for
the little cow. So they invited his best friend. How many cows
do you see now?"

Harris counted again, perfectly. When he got to four, he
looked at me again.

"Right!" I exclaimed; Harris's smile grew larger. He went all
the way up to eight, counting perfectly and looking at me each
time for reassurance. When he wanted to stop, he got off the
chair. But he had gone a long way with great success. I was
thrilled at his accomplishment and so was he.

I held out my hand, palm up. "Harris—slap me five. You're a
great counter!" He smiled again, hit my hand and ran off. It was
a golden moment for both of us.

As I watched Harris approach his friends easily and enter into their game, I realized that he had a come a long way since November. His therapist, who visited us the following day, agreed. Dr. Laura Adler was the kind of psychologist I wished every child in trouble could have. She understood the problems of childhood and she was filled with compassion for her small patients. I knew about her high intelligence from our previous phone conversations; I was surprised by her tailored good looks and her delicate charm. No wonder Harris blushed to see her, even though he had known she was coming!

As she observed him, I pointed out to Dr. Adler what was typical about Harris's behavior, and what was strictly for her benefit. It was clear that he was trying to impress her. (Who wouldn't?) To my astonishment, however, he made a bowel movement in his pants during gym, just as he often did. He also scratched a child's face when that little boy tried to scare him. Apparently, there were some actions beyond his control.

Dr. Adler and I met after her observation. She explained that Harris really wanted to be a "big boy" but was having trouble making the transition. We all needed to help him. I described the ways in which I felt we were doing exactly that. Her suggestion about toilet training was that he be encouraged to clean himself. He did so at home, she told me. This was important—but heretofore unimparted—news to me. I agreed with alacrity.

What I actually learned from our meeting was this: Dr. Adler was as involved with Harris and as interested in his well-being as I was. This was a major relief. After all, Cathy and I had to give him up in June, but Dr. Adler would continue with his treatment. I was happy to find Harris in the care of such a competent and caring professional. Something inside me relaxed: he would be all right.

• • •

As January progressed, the children seemed to be relaxing, too. Cory stopped drawing pictures with frowns and began to play with her friends again. Harris seemed more in control of himself: he was trying mightily to use his words instead of his fists. Even little Lee seemed to be more connected. He came up to me one day, crawled into my lap and patted my face gently. "You're a very good teacher, Patti," he told me. "I'll be a very good boy today." And he was.

"Things sure seem to be mellowing out around here," remarked Cathy as she watched the kids at play.

"Yup. They're doing very well. They're calmer. They like each other. They can recognize their names, pour their own juice and sit for a story. They can even wait their turn most of the time. I think it's time to start a daily meeting."

"What about Lee?"

I laughed at Cathy's perspicacity. She'd been teaching for one year, but she always got it right.

"He'll be a problem. We'll have to handle him separately. But I don't think we should wait until he's ready to sit and listen. It may not happen this year, and meeting time is too important to leave out of the curriculum." Little did I know how important it would be.

After snack, when the children were sitting on the rug waiting for a story, I pulled up a chair, and put Lee on my lap. Immediately, he asked me if he was in time out.

"No, no," I explained quietly. "I just need you to sit here with me for a minute, okay?"

He nodded. Everyone else was relatively attentive, so I began.

"From now on, this will be our meeting time. If you have something to say, please raise your hand, and wait till I call on you. Then you may speak."

"Who's not here today?" This was a question we asked every day at some time or other.

Sharon called out. "Amanda's not here. She has a ear infection." (Kids never say "an" ear infection, no matter how many times they're corrected. They just grow into it.)

"Thank you, Sharon. But from now on, please raise your hand if you want to speak." She nodded.

Benjamin's hand shot up, so I called on him.

"Benjamin, what would you like to say?"

"I had a ear infection but I just finished taking my pills yesterday."

As he went on to describe the pain of an ear infection, Lee, in my arms, began to babble. "I want to talk, I want to say it."

I spoke softly to him: "Not now, Lee. Benjamin is talking. If you want to speak, you must raise your hand the way Benjamin did."

Lee didn't get it, and kept complaining. I continued to reassure him softly as I ran the meeting. Because he was on my lap, he wasn't too disruptive.

David raised his hand. "I had a ear infection a long time ago, right here." He pointed to the bottom of his left ear. "And it hurt."

"I'm sure it did. But the pain goes away quickly once you start taking the medicine, right?"

The children nodded, and Jason blurted out, "I had to go to the doctor for my ear and he gave me medicine."

"Don't forget to raise your hand, Jason. How did the medicine taste?"

He made a face: "Awful!"

I laughed. "I'll bet!"

Mary Ann had a comment, and raised her hand primly. "I had a ear infection when I went to Disney World and my mommy didn't think we could fly home but we did."

I nodded. "Sometimes when your ear hurts it's not okay to fly on a plane."

Harris was listening intently. Suddenly he stuck up his hand and didn't call out.

I thought: Wow! He's participating!

I said (trying to sound normal): "Yes, Harris?"

"I flied on a plane to Aunt Susan's and my ears hurt and my mommy gave me *Gum! Bubble gum!* And I chewed it and they didn't hurt anymore!" He spoke with such enthusiasm that even Lee stopped to listen.

"Yes!" I smiled at Harris encouragingly. "That's a very good way to help your ears on a plane."

Benjamin spoke up: "Yeah, well, I fell off an airplane." He wasn't kidding; he looked as solemn as an undertaker.

The other children were immediately quiet.

"You can't fall off a plane, Benjamin," I said. "It's all sealed in."

"And there's seat belts," added Sharon and Jenny.

"No," he said simply. "I did."

The class looked at Benjamin. One child said, "He must have forgotten to do the seat belt." Everyone else was silent.

What could I do? He had scared them all. I certainly couldn't say what I was thinking: *If you'd fallen out of a plane, kid, you'd be dead.* But I couldn't end the conversation like this, and send them home to nightmares. I put Lee down, picked up Benjamin and put him in my lap.

"Benjamin," I said calmly. "Your friends and I want to know. Is this a true story or are you making it up?"

He looked at me and smiled. "It's pretend."

The class heaved an audible "Ahhhh!" and I was right in there with them.

"You're a very good actor, Benjamin. You should be in a movie."

Benjamin replied by putting his hands to his face and yelling "AHHHH" like Macaulay Culkin in *Home Alone.* Everyone laughed, and our meeting reached a natural conclusion. It was time to go upstairs for gym.

Ten minutes later I was still shaking my head over our near

disaster. These kids were so smart. What if I couldn't always stay ahead of them? So often there's an ambush behind the next turn in the road. What if I didn't see it coming?

All right, I told myself. *You can't be perfect. You'll just do the best job you can.* At that moment, my great love for Louis L'Amour novels made perfect sense. The main characters always have grit. They may get trapped, but they never die. They can always work their way out of a tight situation. It's the way life should be—but isn't. That night, I dreamt about falling planes.

• • •

During the last ten days of January, Cathy and I paid special attention to Jeremy Jacobson. He had begun to act like a very unhappy little boy. Each day, he would come into class, speak a few words to Benjamin and David and then head for the book corner. He didn't seem to care which story he picked out. He would sit quietly, with his finger up his nose, and turn every page. When he finished, he would repeat the procedure with another book. We were unable to draw him into play, except on rare occasions.

One Friday, Cathy asked me, "What do you think is going on? Jeremy is so withdrawn, it's almost scary."

"And very sad. He's usually so gregarious. My guess is that he's stuck in the middle of the mourning process. I don't think he's ever talked about the baby."

"Have you ever brought it up?"

"I've tried. He just turns away. It must still be a delicate topic in his house. I'm sure he doesn't want to hurt his mom or dad by bringing up a subject so painful to them. But I think I can mention Jeremy's behavior when I ask his mother how his bowel problem is progressing."

"Don't forget—she doesn't really know we're aware of that particular issue."

"I'm sure she must be, even though it was her baby-sitter who told us. She's a very smart lady. She knows that we live with her child too. He's had a few accidents. How *could* we be unaware?"

When I approached Carolyn the following Monday, she wasn't at all surprised. She seemed pleased by our interest. The bowel withholding problem was continuing, so she had consulted her pediatrician again. He had listened to their story, examined Jeremy and recommended a behavior modification specialist.

"Our doctor is convinced that the problem is a physical one," Carolyn finished. She looked as if she agreed with him.

"Does he know what has happened in your family over the last few months?"

Carolyn nodded.

"Do you talk about the baby at home?"

"Not much. Bernard feels we need to move on."

I hardly knew what to say. This was not just a physical but an emotional problem. If ever there was a case of a child needing to get his feelings out, this was it. It made perfect sense that parents in mourning themselves might not see this—but a family doctor who knew their history? Couldn't he see that this child didn't need a chart with a star for every time he went to the bathroom? Could he admit to the possibility that Jeremy needed to talk? It was nearly unbelievable, and bumping right up to incompetent. With misgiving, I asked the name of her doctor.

She responded, and my heart sank. I had heard too many stories to have any faith in this man at all. I couldn't tell Carolyn that, though. Instead, I said that Jeremy seemed sad, and described his recent behavior.

"Really? He's fine at home," was her reply. She was obviously telling the truth.

I thought: This is not a good sign. When a child feels more comfortable in showing his emotions at school than he is at home, then something is wrong. Home is supposed to be his safest place.

I said: "Perhaps we can speak on the phone the night before Jeremy's appointment. I'll describe his behavior during the week, and you can tell the specialist. That way, she'll have some background to work with."

Carolyn agreed. She was, after all, concerned with helping her son. But I saw the doubt in her eyes. The mother sided with the pediatrician; a physical problem was easier to fix.

Thursday night, I called the Jacobson house. Carolyn hadn't remembered that I was going to call, which surprised me. I reported Jeremy's behavior as clearly and briefly as I could. Basically, it was more of the same sadness.

I was totally unprepared for her response: "Look," she told me. "I don't see a sad kid. I see a happy kid who is doing just fine. If you see a sad kid then the problem is at school." She then related a story about David and Benjamin excluding Jeremy from joining them in a game in school. Jeremy had been too upset to fight back. Bernard, who had taken him to school that day, had witnessed the incident. Unfortunately, he had left without informing Cathy or me.

So here it was. Despite the two important deaths in his family, despite the fact that he never wanted to stay home from school ("He always wants to come" was how Carolyn phrased it), despite the fact that he was withholding his bowel movements and despite the *major* fact that he had never spoken about the baby, Jeremy's parents felt his difficulty was school-related. I could see it from their point of view, given the evidence they had. How could I ever convince them that Jeremy needed to talk about his feelings?

I felt like a fish on a hook. Struggling would only make it worse. After a pause to collect my emotions, I answered as calmly as I could. "Okay. Thanks for the input. I'll certainly watch the three boys more carefully. But if you'll tell the doctor about Jeremy's being so sad in school, I'd appreciate it. Just give her all the facts."

Carolyn said she would, and thanked me for my time. But I knew I hadn't convinced her. I hadn't done any good at all. I hung up the phone feeling miserable.

The following Monday, Carolyn brought Jeremy to school. Both of them were smiling. The visit to the specialist had been wonderful. Jeremy had gone right into the office and beaten the specialist at two games of checkers. Carolyn hadn't had the time to tell her about Jeremy's behavior at school. But it didn't seem to matter. The specialist had said, "He doesn't need my help," and told her simply to continue the medication. No wonder Carolyn looked so cheerful; her world had been reconfirmed.

I forced myself to smile, but Cathy could hardly look at her. I thanked her for the information, and made plans for her to come for Shabbat on Friday. After kissing Jeremy, who was actually playing with friends, Carolyn left the room.

I stuck my clenched fists in my pocket, looked down at the floor and kicked at nothing in particular.

Cathy grabbed my arm. "She still doesn't understand! How could you be so nice to her?"

"Practice," I responded grimly. "But the game ain't over yet."

FEBRUARY: DEATH COMES ALIVE

I woke up one morning to discover that *Hook* had invaded my classroom. The movie had been out since December: my students had seen it over winter vacation. Not until February, however, had its themes and difficulties come bubbling up from the children's memories into imaginary play.

As I watched the kids fashion swords out of paper and tape, I silently cursed Steven Spielberg. It was one thing to turn the story of Peter Pan into an ode to parenthood. Why, oh *why* had he felt the need to *invent* a character, a teenager named Rufio, who is actually killed in a sword fight with Captain Hook himself? Where was the slightly sinister, mostly funny pirate of the Broadway play? He had been replaced by a murderer with a strange accent and a five-pound wig. Add an incredibly terrifying scene where the children are stolen from their beds and hung aloft a pirate ship in swaying nets, and you had an authentic recipe for nightmares.

Of course, I reflected, Steven Spielberg wasn't entirely to blame. His movie was rated PG. Several reviewers had cautioned that *Hook* was not for the very young child. Nevertheless, there had been no parental guidance, as far as I could tell. Almost all of the kids had seen the movie; now it was time to deal with the psychological consequences. I wondered how many preschool classrooms across America were dealing with the same problem.

Children will act out a frightening story over and over, until it is too familiar to be scary anymore. Most of the boys and some of the girls were involved in this particular game. In addition to the swords, they made hooks out of aluminum foil and eye patches out of scarves. The designated Captain Hook would tuck his or her hand into a sleeve, so that only the hook would show. The entire game consisted of running around and making noise. Either Hook chased everyone else, or they were all pirates running up and down the loft, which served as their ship. If two children actually engaged in hand-to-hand combat, they were always Rufio and Hook. Rufio died frequently—but not always. As leader of the Lost Boys, he was often more valuable alive. Peter Pan, the most benign figure in the story, was usually relegated to the sidelines. There were no conflicting feelings about his character, so he wasn't as important to portray. There were some Peter impersonators, however—the kids who always liked to be the hero.

In most cases, I would not have allowed such a game to enter my classroom. There was plenty of time during gym to run around and be a pirate. But the feelings were so intense—particularly for my Unholy Three—that I wanted to supervise their play.

First, I attempted to retrieve the gentler figure of Hook by introducing the music from the Broadway show. I began to play the tape of *Peter Pan* starring Mary Martin and Cyril Ritchard. Most of the children were familiar with the songs: they had all seen a Broadway revival in December. Unfortunately, this merely added spice to an overheated stew. Now the kids had something to sing as they played! They marched up and down their pirate ship, shouting, "YO HO! YO HO! THE TERRIBLE CAPTAIN HOOK!" I removed the music posthaste.

After a few days, it became clear that the game had to be stopped. Some of the children were doing little else. Also, they were having difficulty negotiating the stairs of the loft, which had been "fixed" again. The stairs were now attached in the right place, but they were too steep. Our carpenter had decided that "they shouldn't stick out into the room so much," so he had built us a ladder rather than a staircase. It had taken three days just to train everyone to come down backward, using both hands. It was especially difficult wearing a hook.

When I overheard a comment about "just flying off the ship like Peter Pan," I knew it was time for a meeting. I asked the children to come to the rug. As soon as they were settled, I made the announcement.

"There will be no more 'Captain Hook' games in the classroom."

A chorus of kids shouted, "Why not?"

"Because you don't use the other toys in the room, and you scare the other children when you shout so loudly. But you can still play it on the roof or in the gym, with all the other superhero games."

"Peter Pan isn't a superhero," cried one hair-splitter.

"Close enough," I replied in my best I-have-spoken tone.

"Peter Pan is *real,*" Jason declared.

Hadn't we dealt with this problem already?

"He's not any realer than Batman or Superman. Remember the play you saw in December with Peter Pan?"

They all nodded.

"Well, that Peter Pan was a *lady* named Cathy Rigby. She has children as old as you are. And she didn't fly. She was carried on a wire which was attached to her belt."

I asked if anyone had seen the wire that held her up. All of them said they had spotted it. I mentioned that she needed it because "people can't fly." The children nodded, but they weren't sure.

"What about the movie?" asked Jason. "Peter Pan flies in the movie and there's no wire."

I did my best to explain that the moviemakers can photograph someone in front of a blue screen and then use any background they want to make it look like he's flying. It wasn't an easy concept. I made more of a dent by telling the kids that all the people in the movie and the show were actors.

"When Rufio got 'pretend killed' by Captain Hook, the actor who *played* Rufio was so happy. The people making the movie gave him a lot of money. Then he got up and went home and bought his mommy a big house, which she had always wanted. Isn't that nice?" Thank goodness for *People* magazine.

The children listened intently, trying to put the pieces together. Then I told them that Max, who played the young Peter Pan in the movie, was really Captain Hook's *son*!

"Not Captain Hook, of course. The man who *plays* Captain Hook—Dustin Hoffman."

I knew I could not hope to convince them. Four-year-olds believe just as strongly in fantasy as they do in reality. That's why their play is so passionate. I just wanted to make sure that no one decided to "fly" from the loft or from the top of a climbing toy on the roof. If I succeeded, it was probably by default. No one "flew," but during roof time, the game continued as ferociously as ever.

Even with Peter Pan out of the classroom, we continued to deal with the question of what constitutes reality. When was something real, and when was it pretend? What was the difference between lying and telling the truth? These are hard questions for a four-year-old—and not exactly easy for the rest of us.

Amanda's mother had a related problem which she discussed with me one morning. Janet Fisher was concerned that Amanda did not really like Billie, their new sitter. Amanda claimed that she did, but it seemed to Janet that Amanda was saying whatever she thought her mother wanted to hear. Janet asked me to see if I could discover the truth.

I had a chat with Amanda at lunchtime. It began as a tête-à-tête, but several girls came over to listen, as is often the case when a teacher has a prolonged conversation with one child. If the topic is interesting, the observers stay to put their two cents in.

"So, Amanda, how do you like your new baby-sitter?" I asked casually, as I sat down at the table where she was finishing her lunch.

"She's nice. She's okay. I didn't like Ruth." This was her former sitter, whom she had always greeted warmly at dismissal.

"No?" I asked. "I always thought you did."

"No. She had pimples and moles on her face and that's not nice." Amanda laughed nervously.

It was an odd comment. At this time, Amanda was experiencing an allergic reaction to an antibiotic. Her face was swollen, and covered with red and white blotches. She had been concerned enough to mention it when she arrived that morning; she had come directly over to me and said, "My face."

I hugged her and said, "You're still beautiful, isn't she, Cathy?"

Cathy assented, for it was true.

"Does it hurt?" I asked.

"No," she replied.

"Then it doesn't matter."

Apparently, Amanda thought otherwise. Here she was, criticizing Ruth for the same disability. It was a handy excuse.

"I liked Ruth," Amanda continued, "but I didn't know her very well. She wasn't my sitter."

There was no use fooling with that rationale. Amanda had set it up very nicely—to avoid missing Ruth. I went on.

"So how is Billie, your new sitter?"

"Nice." But her face said the opposite.

"It's important to tell the truth about these things, Amanda. No one else can tell how nice Billie really is except you, because she's *your sitter*.

Amanda looked me directly in the eye. "I don't always like to tell the truth."

"Why not?"

"It's too hard," she replied.

Hmmm. Now we were getting somewhere. "What do you think will happen?" I asked her.

Amanda said nothing. By this time, the other girls were ready to talk.

Louisa chimed in. "If you don't tell the truth, your nose will grow and grow."

"Oh, like Pinocchio?" I asked her. She nodded, smiling.

"Well, that's a great story, but it's not true for real people. Watch."

I commenced on a series of obvious lies.

"I am a boy. My name is Mergatroyd. I live on the moon. I eat cardboard for breakfast."

At the next table, Benjamin nearly fell out of his chair from laughing. But the girls took me seriously, as I meant them to. They smiled, but they also watched my face.

"Look at my nose," I said to them.

"It didn't grow," Amanda commented. The rest of the audience agreed.

"Right. So that's not the reason you tell the truth. You do it because you feel better inside."

Amanda had no reply. She was not yet ready to talk about her feelings. But not everyone had that problem.

"I don't like my new baby-sitter," declared Jenny.

"Why not?"

"She picks me up at school too much. It's not ever my mommy or my daddy."

"Let's talk to Mommy about that," I said. "I'll bet we can fix it." Jenny's mother didn't have a full-time job, and would probably be able to come more often. She just had to be made aware of her child's opinion on the subject.

Louisa joined in: "My mommy said I could have a new baby-sitter instead of Corinne, but I said, 'No, no, no—I just want Corinne!'"

"And do you still have Corinne?"

"*Yes!*" Louisa exulted.

"So, then," I said pointedly, "you told your mommy what you wanted and you got it." Louisa nodded. I noticed Amanda listening intently. Perhaps she would be able to speak honestly in the near future. For the thousandth time, I told myself I would just have to wait.

Mary Ann returned from Florida the following day. When it turned out that she was visiting her grandmother in Miami, the children were appalled.

"*You* said she was in Disney World," they told me accusingly.

"Yes. I made a mistake. That happens."

This did not satisfy my bunch. Some continued to jeer; others looked unsettled. I was stumped. Young children usually love it when a teacher makes an error. They feel superior and laugh uproariously.

It was Cathy who came to the rescue. Bending over, she whispered in my ear, "Ask them if they think a mistake is the same as a lie."

I complied. "Who thinks a mistake is the same as a lie?"

All twelve hands shot up in agreement.

"Well, it isn't. A mistake is when you say something that's wrong but you didn't *know* it was wrong. A lie is when you *know* you're not telling the truth."

As an example, I described a short encounter I'd had with Benjamin yesterday morning in the gym. He had sauntered up to me with a twinkle in his eye and said as casually as possible:

"Know what, Patti? This is a story and it's all true. Really." He nodded for effect.

"I was swimming in the ocean with my daddy and a shark came and bit my foot. But my daddy brought me back and put on a Band-Aid and it was fine. Really."

"Benjamin," I responded, trying to keep a straight face, "*that* is a whopper. Know what a whopper is?"

He didn't, but he was interested, since it obviously had nothing to do with Burger King.

"It's a big, *big* lie," I informed him. "Do you know how I know?"

Benjamin shook his head. "How?"

"Because if a shark had bitten your foot, he would have bitten it *off.*"

Benjamin's eyes widened into two beacons of astonishment. "Oh," was his hushed reply.

His classmates heard the story with fascination; Benjamin confirmed its accuracy with a smile. The word "whopper" gave us power to deal with Benjamin's fibs, which were becoming more commonplace as well as more outlandish. From this point, whenever he told a lie, one of his friends or teachers would say, "Oh, that's a whopper!" It was a signpost that we had left the world of reality and moved into the world of fantasy.

But Benjamin was not alone: many of the children were becoming interested in the emotional and psychological power of words. Four-year-olds are able to recognize, for example, that words can often hurt people more than pushing or shoving. Once they learn this truth, they experiment with it—sometimes with results that are amusing to grown-ups. (Woe be it to you if you show it, though.)

One rainy day, when Cathy and I had taken the children to the gym, Sharon approached us with an unusually pitiful demeanor. Her faithful friend Jenny was at her side.

Remembering that Sharon could have a great career in drama, I kept my tone lighthearted.

"What happened, Sharon?"

Sharon's head drooped and her lower lip began to tremble. "David called me a name."

I thought: As they say in show business, this kid milks it.

Cathy asked, "What did he say?"

"It's so bad I can't even say it."

"We can't talk to David unless we know what he said," Cathy told her.

Jenny piped up: "He called her a baby."

"No." Sharon shook her head sorrowfully. "It was worse than that. He said 'wet baby.'"

Cathy turned her head away to hide her smile, but I could read her thoughts. Imagine the kid who had wet his pants every day for three months calling anybody a "wet baby"? It was nothing short of hilarious. But it was quite serious to Sharon, who truly needed our help. It was time to show her that words could work both ways.

I leaned over and spoke softly to Sharon. "Well then you go right over and tell him that he's a soggy pizza."

Sharon's face brightened immediately. "Yeah!" she cried out. Followed by Jenny, she went right over to the culprit and hurled her message directly into his startled face.

David hated it. As a gesture of disapproval, he stuck his fist in front of Sharon's nose. Sharon was thrilled at having provoked a reaction. Excited by her victory, she and Jenny ran away laughing.

The power of suggestion, however, can be very strong. Later that day, Sharon wet her pants for the first time ever in school. Was it just a coincidence? We didn't know at the time, but later evidence indicated that it was not. Words are powerful weapons.

That same week, we had another example. Lee hit another child, and needed to be in time out. I went over to him and took his hand.

"You know the rule, Lee. YOU HIT, YOU SIT." As I was leading him to a chair, he called over his shoulder: "Harris, kill Patti." His voice was insistent and his grin malicious. (For this, he did heavy seat time. He cried, he said he wouldn't sit, he said he was going to get up, but he didn't. He sat, complaining vociferously, for ten full minutes.)

Jenny, who had observed the entire situation, approached me anxiously.

"Harris shot you and you're dead," she told me. She looked very concerned.

I hadn't seen Harris commit the offense; knowing the penalty, he'd been too careful for that. But I knew that Jenny would never lie. Harris had pretended to kill me, and now she was worried that I was actually dead.

I pulled myself up to my full height, and gave her my best Moses-on-Mount-Sinai stare.

"Do I look dead to you?"

"No," she admitted.

"Then I'm not." I never cracked a smile.

"Oh." She smiled with relief, and ran back to play.

When I related the story to Cathy, she was incredulous.

"Did she really think you were dead?"

"She was just checking to make sure I wasn't."

"Isn't that, well, odd?"

"When it comes to word power, four-year-olds are just learning that saying something doesn't make it so."

Often, it's a hard lesson to learn. One day, Harris ran out of the gym with my permission to get a drink of water from the fountain. No grown-ups were watching the water fountain, but he had been very good. I thought he deserved a chance to try something on his own. A minute later, another teacher brought him back, along with an older girl who was crying.

The teacher's eyes were rolling in disbelief. "This kid spit a whole mouthful of water at my Jessica. Look at her!" Sure enough, Jessica's head and shoulders were glistening with water. Harris apologized when he saw how angry we were, but it was not enough. I took him by the hand and led him to a chair on the side of the gym.

"All right, Harris, you know the rules. YOU SPIT, YOU SIT."

"But I didn't spit," he protested.

"You didn't?" I looked at him incredulously.

"No. I spit water." His ingeniousness did not save him from a time out, but I couldn't help being impressed. This kid was smart: now if we could only harness it.

I told the story to my mother on the phone that evening. Her reply: "Oh—a hair-spitter!" An interest in words never leaves you once you've got it down.

Meanwhile, Cory's words were improving slightly. She was enjoying her speech therapy now. All of the frowns on her drawings had disappeared. She was able to say more words in a sentence and to pronounce them more distinctly. Still . . . there was something getting in her way. Something else . . . and if it wasn't her hearing, the alternatives were disconcerting.

Just as I was thinking about the problem, Cory's father told me that he would be picking his daughter up early. The therapist had recommended that Cory's hearing be checked again, by another specialist. I was so happy that I could barely sleep that night.

But I must have slept, because I certainly dreamt. In the middle of the night, I sat up in bed and spoke in a loud, clear voice: "Please, God, let her be normal." When my husband told me of the incident in the morning, I knew who I had been praying for.

That morning, Theresa brought Cory to school. As Cory greeted her friends, her mother pulled me aside.

"Well, you were right. The specialist found temporary hearing loss from fluid in the inner ear. The audiologist and our pediatrician missed it. I don't know how they could have . . ." She shook her head sadly.

"It's worse some days than others," I told her, as calmly as I could. Inside, I was jumping! No brain tumor! No severe depression! No congenital deafness! No major learning disabilities! The best of all possibilities! Of course, I kept these exclamations to myself. Since I hadn't ever mentioned the dire alternatives, I wasn't going to bring them up now.

"But this is really good news," I told Theresa. "Now that

they've found the problem, it can be treated. Are they going to put tubes in her ears?"

"No. The doctor feels it can be treated with aggressive antibiotics."

It was a good idea, if it worked. This family didn't need another trip to the hospital.

Theresa looked directly at me. "My child has been undercared for and my baby has been overcared for by this pediatrician. Just the same as we've been doing at home. And we'd still be doing it if it weren't for you." She began to cry.

I hugged her. "Thanks . . . but it's okay now, Theresa. Don't worry. They're going to finally fix it." Theresa nodded, hugged me and walked slowly down the hall. I was the lucky one: I got to go back to the children.

Sometimes, children know when you need them to behave. For the rest of the morning, my students were as calm and focused as a choir in church. Even Harris behaved well when his parents came for Shabbat.

The Whites were wonderful. We sang our Hebrew prayers and gave out our challah bread, and they appreciated it all. I forgot to serve the grape juice and spilled a lot of it when I remembered, but they didn't mind a bit. They were so pleased to see Harris relaxed and happy.

"Thank goodness we had that conference in the fall," Harris Senior remarked as the Whites were taking their leave.

"I know Harris is doing well with Dr. Adler. She's wonderful," I replied.

"But it's also the work you've done with him here. This classroom is where he's learned that rules apply not just to him but to all children. There's really no way we could have taught him that. You've done wonders."

"Thanks for telling me," I said. But I was more than pleased. The Whites' gratitude reminded me of why I was still in this job after nearly twenty years. It was to help the children.

• • •

This was a good time to remember why I loved to teach, because the following week, I faced one of my profession's toughest challenges: we received a new boy. His first nursery school had closed for lack of funds. In an unusual move, our school had admitted him in the middle of the year and unceremoniously tossed him our way. How, I wondered, was he ever going to fit in with this bunch of adorable but difficult children?

His name was Avi Peled, and he was Israeli. He had been born in "the States" as his parents informed me, so his English was quite good. Small and wiry, he looked like a fighter. His eyes and hair were inky black; his expression was a semipermanent scowl. He was definitely Not Happy to be here.

Avi's mother, Dvora, brought him into the room and set him up at the Lego table. While Cathy worked with him, I spoke to Mrs. Peled. The first thing she needed to tell me was that Avi was play-acting death a lot. He'd lost his grandmother in December and his twenty-six-year-old uncle to cancer the past spring.

"Your brother?" I asked her.

She nodded sadly.

"I know just how you feel. I lost mine when he was twenty-nine." She was too startled to reply. It was an unfortunate but instantaneous bond.

I thought: Isn't that uncanny? Another child grappling with death—and at this age, when it's such an issue anyway. Well, he'll certainly fit right in.

I was proud of my students that morning. We had told them about Avi, and talked about ways we could make him feel welcome. The children tried their best. Cory invited him to play with her, as did several others. But he wouldn't budge from his mother's side.

We had expected her to stay all morning, but she left after

twenty minutes. I was going to object, but Avi certainly wasn't happy with her in the room. Maybe this would be better.

It wasn't. He stood by me for a while, then went up to the loft and hid his eyes in a pillow for the rest of the morning. Nothing we could say or do would entice him to come down.

"Looks like we're in for a long adjustment. Why am I not surprised?" I whispered to Cathy.

"Because everything in this class is done the hard way?" she guessed, laughing.

"You said it, kid," I told her.

After a few days, there was some improvement. Avi still went right to the loft, but he played with the baby dolls that were up there. This made sense: his mother was four months pregnant. Babies would surely have a certain fascination for him. But he wanted to play by himself. He turned his hands into claws and growled like a lion when anyone else tried to join him. The other kids left him alone. I wondered how long his classmates would stand for his sole possession of the loft. He was monopolizing their favorite place to play.

Cory was the first to approach him. One day, she walked up the stairs, put her arms around Avi and said sweetly, "You are my friend." Then she hugged him. Avi allowed this overture: he seemed too surprised to stop it. In a few minutes, they were playing together with the dolls. It was a breakthrough which we could take no credit for promoting. Cory had done it all. (Luckily, Avi could understand her speech.)

Cathy and I were not having the same success with Marsha, the sitter who picked him up every day. For the first few days, she was five minutes late. She had no excuse, saying only, "What time is it? Only five after one? Boy, you people clear out quickly around here."

"We do," I agreed. I didn't want to say anything that sounded as if I were criticizing her. I don't think of baby-sitters (or caregivers, as they are called in New York) as beneath me on the food chain. I'm the mother of two teenagers, and I still remember how much I depended on the people who looked after my children when they were small. We are all in this together: the sitter, the teachers and the parents are a team looking out for the welfare of the child.

Unfortunately, not everyone feels this way. Sometimes, there has to be a power struggle before this message becomes clear. One morning shortly after Avi's arrival, his mother took me aside.

"I have a message from Avi's sitter," she told me.

This tone of voice always makes me want to look around for my hump.

"Yes?" I replied.

"You must remember to bring down Avi's hat and mittens, so he will not be cold on the way home. And you must get him to go to the bathroom before he leaves school. He can't make it all the way home. Yesterday, he made in his pants and he was embarrassed."

Of course I had put the child's hat and gloves on him. I later discovered that when I wasn't looking he had taken them off and hidden them. And we had brought the kids to the bathroom twice. Avi just hadn't felt comfortable enough to use it yet. I would have been happy to give this information if asked. But these were orders.

"If Avi came down without his hat and gloves, it was an oversight. I'll make sure it doesn't happen again. I'll do my best to get him to go to the bathroom as soon as he's comfortable with it. If not, there's a bathroom downstairs which he can use at dismissal."

"Thank you," Dvora said.

"Now I have a message for your sitter."

"What is that?"

"Be on time."

She looked surprised. "Oh. That is a very important message. I'll tell her right away."

Dvora's response reminded me that she hadn't realized how severe she sounded. I was glad I hadn't gotten visibly angry. Still, the subtext of my message to her baby-sitter was a clear one. I preferred the team approach, but if Marsha wanted to play "tattle to the mother," I was a tough opponent. I hoped this small warning would be sufficient. Sure enough, at dismissal, Marsha was as courteous as an employee at Disney World. She remained so throughout the year.

During our week of adjustment with Avi, Cathy and I also had to contend with Janet Fisher's concerns about Amanda's sitter. Janet called the school frequently to check on her daughter's state of mind. She called again after dismissal each day to see if Amanda had cried when she saw Billie. She called me at home to discuss the situation. She even showed up unexpectedly to observe the situation herself. Naturally, Amanda cried even harder when she learned her mother was going back to the office.

"Remember that the problem may not be Billie," I reminded Janet. "Amanda may just be feeling bad about separating from you. She knows how conflicted you are about returning to work full-time. She may just be acting it out."

Cathy became exasperated. "Why do you put up with this?" she asked me. "Janet is really overstepping her bounds."

"I don't exactly know. I think maybe it's because she's so charmingly honest. She may be excessive and also be right. Let's give it a bit more time."

Janet was Shabbat mother on the day before winter vacation. Amanda was quite cheerful, helping to pass out the treats and sitting on her mother's lap for story. But she cried again as soon as we began to get ready to go home. (She was going with Billie and her mother was returning to the office.)

"Is this what you see every day?" Janet asked me.

"Pretty much."

"Well, then I'll have to make a decision about Billie over vacation," she replied.

I thought that was a dandy idea.

As we went down in the elevator, Amanda was crying, Lee was whimpering and several of the children were pouting. Sharon looked around and shook her head.

"Like usual—same old crankies," she remarked. It was the perfect end to a trying week.

The following ten days were designated "winter vacation" on our calendar. For me, they may as well have been called "winter hibernation." Usually I take my family to my mom and dad in Florida. This time I sent the children and slept.

I'm not sure I was refreshed on our first day back, but I know I was rested. I was so glad to see Harris that I swooped him up and carried him around saying, "Look what I got!" He didn't seem to mind: in fact, he beamed.

At dismissal, Benjamin had to carry two heavy bags down to his sitter. He was struggling, so Cathy offered to help him. He pulled away, however, saying, "Nooooo. You can't carry that heavy bag. That's man's stuff."

Cathy smilingly replied, "I think I can manage." She shot me a glance which read, "Boy, that macho stuff starts early." We giggled; Cathy carried the bag.

Amanda's mother had informed me that she had indeed switched sitters. A young woman named Aya would be picking up Amanda today. Cathy and I were curious to see if the change would make a difference. Amazingly, Amanda rushed into Aya's arms with a smile of true delight.

"Imagine that?" Cathy whispered to me. "Janet's suspicions were right all along."

I nodded. "Put it under the heading of 'even a paranoid has real enemies.'" I was joking, of course. Amanda's mother had accurately identified the problem and taken steps to fix it. She may have been excessive, but she was correct.

In the classroom, Avi began to loosen up a bit. His scowl disappeared, revealing a soft expression and a crinkly smile. He also had a wonderful way with words. One day at cleanup time, I was issuing personal reminders to the inevitable shirkers. I reminded Avi as gently as possible that now was the time to do his job. He came over to me, put his head in my lap and said, "You should remember I don't know that, Patti. I'm only the new boy."

"I did remember, Avi. That's why I told you softly instead of saying [I used a loud mock-angry tone] 'Avi, put that book away RIGHT NOW!'" He laughed and sat down next to me.

Cory was his steadfast friend, and Jeremy his occasional playmate. One morning the two boys were playing "baby" on the loft. Avi was the baby and Jeremy the mommy. Jeremy took good care of baby Avi: he fed him, tucked him in with a pillow and blanket and brought him a baby doll to cuddle. Suddenly, Jeremy hit the doll on the head three times—hard. I should have kept my mouth shut, but I was sitting right there.

"Why did you hit the baby, Jeremy?" I asked softly.

"I don't know," he answered, coloring. Apparently, he had not seen me. He immediately retreated to a corner of the loft and stuck his finger up his nose. I had ruined their game. I felt terrible: he was working out his own anger and I had interfered. I would know better next time.

Fortunately, that time came very quickly. In the gym the next morning, Jeremy pretended he was a dog. The other children loved it. They petted him, fed him "biscuits," walked him on a leash made out of a stray ribbon and hugged him frequently. This was a soothing activity for many of the other children, as well. David, who had become very aggressive in the gym, was kind and gentle to Jeremy-as-dog.

Benjamin came over to us with shining eyes.

"We have a dog!" he announced excitedly. "And we're taking care of him!"

For half an hour, Jeremy received the attention and comfort he could not ask of his friends in real life. One of my professors has called this "the push to health": the child's attempt to find a way to heal himself. This remarkable little boy was working on his own recovery.

Cathy and I were unprepared for Jeremy's next step: the following day, he became a dead dog. The children hugged him, stroked him, rolled him and tried to get him up. They all knew the tickle test, and practiced it regularly on their classmates. But no one tickled Jeremy. Uncannily, it was as if they knew just what he needed: he could pretend to be dead when he clearly wasn't going to die. Only after ten or fifteen minutes did the other children come and get me. When I tickled him awake, they all flew off in another direction, laughing. Jeremy was among them, playing the role of Peter Pan.

This game continued for three weeks. Each day, surrounded by friends, Jeremy was a dog, and then a dead dog. Afterward, he began a lighthearted game of Peter Pan with the other children. And he was always Peter, the star. The poignancy was overwhelming.

"Watch, Cathy," I said, grabbing her arm on the third day of the game. "And learn to trust in the recuperative power of children." I was talking to myself as well.

I had a chance to tell Jeremy's mother about his remarkable actions when she brought him to school a few days later.

"Jeremy's cured," Carolyn told me. "His bowel problems are fixed." Chocolate pudding with stool softeners had done the trick.

"That's great," I said.

"He's fine here, isn't he?" she asked.

"As a matter of fact, he's doing very well. He's working very hard." As I described the baby-bashing incident on the loft with Avi, Carolyn looked momentarily shaken. I then told her of Jeremy's extraordinary play in the gym.

Carolyn listened to the details very carefully. When I was completely finished, she responded.

"I've begun to think he's a very special child."

I agreed wholeheartedly. But equally wonderful was the fact that Carolyn had understood.

· · ·

As we moved into late February, the room was humming. Now that individual children had made progress, the tension of earlier months had diminished somewhat. Just as I was beginning to relax, however, we had a morning as bizarre as a Fellini movie. All that was missing was the eerie, jumpy music. (We already had the midgets.)

Our morning began normally enough. The children came into the room and greeted us. Some began to play with the new toy we had set out on one table; others went over to Cathy, who was constructing a new job chart.

Then Louisa and Harris arrived. They always came by bus, a little later than the others. The bus teacher was holding both their hands, which was unusual.

"What's up?" I asked her.

"I just want you to know," she began, "that the bus driver told me that a bomb was planted in Louisa's apartment building. The police evacuated everyone and closed the street to traffic. So if she talks about a bomb, it's real."

I turned to look at Louie. Her expression was blank and her eyes were as large as golf balls. She was going up to each child and relaying the news: "There's a bomb in my house that makes a big noise and then there's fire!" Harris served as her second: "Yes. A bomb! And the police! And police cars!" Harris was excited: for him, this was a juicy tidbit. When I looked at Louisa, however, I could see that she was scared stiff. It was clearly time for a class meeting.

But in order to talk to the children, I needed to have the facts. I took Louisa aside.

"What happened, Louie?"

"There was a bomb and a big noise and fire," she repeated.

"Did you see fire and smoke?"

She shook her head no, but said nothing.

"I'll bet it was very scary."

"I was scared," she admitted.

"I don't blame you. I would have been scared, too." There was no reason to mention that I already *was* scared. Had the bomb actually detonated? Had there been any damage, or any lives lost? I didn't know.

When our music teacher came at nine-fifteen, I went to call Louisa's apartment. Her baby-sitter, Corinne, had the details. The bomb had been planted in a phone booth directly outside the building. The police had evacuated everyone as a precaution. The bomb had been defused a few minutes ago and taken away. It had never exploded.

Louisa's "fire and noise" was apparently the description of a bomb that someone had given her. She had certainly seen neither. Fortunately, no one had told her that bombs can kill people.

I got back to the room just as Avi's mother was bringing him in. I told her of our latest event, and mentioned that we'd have a discussion about it.

"Oh, you can ask Avi about bombs," she said almost casually. "We were in Israel during the last war. We kept waking him up at 2 A.M. to put him into a protective tent for young children. We found out later that it would not actually have kept any poison gas out. We are all furious with the government."

I thought: This poor kid. His uncle's death, his grandmother's death and a war all in one year.

"It was not a very good year for Avi," Dvora said softly.

"It wasn't a very good year for you, either," I replied.

"No. I suppose not." She looked very sad, as if that thought were just dawning on her.

She shook herself out of it, however, kissed her child and left.

I couldn't dwell on our conversation, either. It was time for our meeting.

Cathy and I called the children to the rug. They sat in their usual stages of readiness: some were listening, some were talking, some were tuning out. When they heard the subject matter, however, they perked up quickly. I asked Louisa to stand next to me.

Louisa faced her friends and told her story. She wasn't very coherent, but her passion made up for it.

"This morning there was a bomb. It makes a big noise and then fire. We had to leave and all the policemen came."

I explained that a bomb was a little device that could make a big noise, start a fire and break windows. I didn't mention people.

"Were you scared?" Amanda asked.

"No. I was brave."

I hugged Louisa. "I know you were. You still are. But it's a pretty scary thing to have happen."

Jason piped up: "Did it fire your toys?"

"No," Louisa responded solemnly. "I saved all my toys."

I spoke again. "Well, there was no fire, really. The bomb didn't explode. The police took it apart and took it away. So nothing actually happened. But it was scary anyway."

Harris spoke up for the first time: "Yeah. I was scared. There were police there. All around. And they put these big blue sticks so no one could drive around."

Cathy and I glanced at each other. How wonderful to hear Harris talk about his emotions!

I explained that the blue sticks had a funny name: they were called horses. This is the kind of word play that strikes a four-year-old as hilarious. They laughed a lot. I was grateful for the comic relief.

Mary Ann spoke next. "Well, I know it's not in *my* house because my house is too far away."

I was happy that someone had brought up the fear that it could happen to them. Young kids so often personalize what they hear. If they don't say it, they are usually thinking it. Mary Ann's comment gave me a chance to respond to the hidden fear.

"That's right, Mary Ann," I agreed. "It's not in anyone's house. Not even Louie's because it didn't go off. So everyone's apartment is safe, and their room is safe and their toys are safe, and *of course* all the mommies and daddies and brothers and sisters are safe." The children nodded, relieved.

Amanda spoke next. She talked again about the fire in her kitchen and how the firemen had come. One trauma brings up all the others.

Jenny mentioned that her ceiling had fallen.

Amanda interrupted: "I know how it happened. The pipe!"

Jenny nodded. A burst upstairs water pipe had indeed been the culprit.

"Were you scared?" I asked her.

"No," Jenny replied, as she always did lately. Then came something new. "But only when I thought that it fell on my bed and I sleep there."

It was the first time Jenny had verbalized how frightening it was to have dodged serious injury through luck. Cathy and I were very glad to hear it.

Benjamin announced, "I had a bomb in my house and I hid in the closet and I was fine." I glanced at him. His face was as innocent as an altar boy's. I had allowed his falling-off-a-plane story to scare everyone at first, but I wasn't about to fall into the same trap again.

"Gee, there haven't been any other bombs around for a *long, long* time, Benjamin. It very rarely happens. It must have been a stink bomb."

I explained what that was, and the kids laughed.

"Yeah, that was it!" Benjamin declared, happy for the attention.

"Good," I replied.

I thought: I nailed that one.

This was a good place to end the meeting, so I told the children they could go back to free play in the room. While Cathy watched the rest of the class, I took Louisa to the office. We called her baby-sitter, who was as reassuring to Louie as she had been to me. Louisa skipped happily back to our room as I walked beside her.

Just as I was about to call for cleanup, Harris burst into the classroom. "Come! Come see my doodie!" He was speaking to me, but his eyes included everyone.

So we all filed into the bathroom to view Harris's triumph: his first bowel movement on the toilet in school. The children were merely curious, but Cathy and I were delighted. (If you have kids, then you know why!)

"Harris, this is wonderful!" Cathy told him. "I'm very proud of you—and *you* should be very proud of *yourself*."

He was. He blushed with pride. His chest was puffed up with a sense of true accomplishment. His pale eyes beamed upon us all.

I thought: Ten minutes ago I was dealing with a bomb scare and now I'm admiring someone's bowel movement.

Even Fellini would be impressed.

EARLY MARCH:
SPRING CONFERENCES

March began as February had ended, with bad things happening to good children. Sharon's baby-sitter, Eve, had to return to Grenada for the funeral of her father, who had died suddenly. Sharon was quite sad—Eve was a very important person in her life—but she didn't make a general announcement to her classmates.

That's good, I thought. Maybe we can avoid another therapy session at meeting today. But it didn't work out that way. Ten minutes later, our school secretary, Linda, came in with the news that Jenny wouldn't be in. Her grandmother was very sick, so her mom had rushed out to California with Jenny and her brother. Although Linda spoke softly, she was overheard by Sharon, who was standing beside me. It was a blow, for Jenny was Sharon's best friend.

"Where is Jenny?" she asked me.

"She's going to California. Remember she was going there next week, for a vacation? Well, now she's going a week early."

"Why?" Sharon asked, even though she knew the answer.

"Her grandma is sick."

"Oh . . . Will she come back?" Trust this kid to get right to the heart of the issue. The grandmother's illness wasn't as important to her as the loss of her friend.

"Yes. Not this week . . . not next week . . . but the week after that. Remember, this is also part of her vacation."

"Oh."

That seemed sufficient for Sharon. She was a kid who would ask questions if she weren't satisfied, so we left it at that.

At meeting, I told the other children about Jenny's absence. They asked if Jenny's grandma would die. I said I didn't know. They talked about other grandparents who had died. Cathy talked about her grandfather, who had died in October. Harris spoke up.

"My grandpa is in the hospital but he didn't die. He's coming home *today* in a *wheelchair! And* . . . my daddy was in a taxi accident yesterday. Another taxi bumped him . . . and he had a *big* cut on his head and there was *blood!*"

I was immediately concerned. Harris could not be making this up.

"Did Daddy go to the hospital?" I asked.

"Yes. They fixed him and then he came home. But he bleeded anyway and my mommy gave him ice to hold."

The other children were fascinated.

I explained that Harris's daddy was hurt, but he wasn't going to die. Harris nodded as if he had known all along, and the other children accepted our joint opinion. I ended the meeting and sent the kids to the bathroom.

With all this trauma floating in my head, I went into the office and phoned Jenny's father. Jonathan explained that his wife's mother had been sick for a while, but had just been put on a respirator. He would be joining the rest of his family in a few days.

I hesitated, then asked him to take my phone number with him. I didn't want to sound egotistic, but you never know when a child will need to talk to you. He was perfectly gracious, and thanked me. Still, I hung up with a heavy heart. What a terrible situation for Jenny and her mom.

The tension was high in our classroom. Cathy had to leave for a graduate school interview, so I was alone for the last hour.

It should have been all right with three kids absent, but it wasn't. Just before lunch, Cory had a major fight with David, which ended with her walloping him. David was hysterical. I asked them for the details, but both children were too upset to provide them. I immediately removed Cory, explaining that she could not hit David no matter how angry she was at him.

Cory was uninterested in hearing what I had to say. She did not want to apologize to David. She would not eat. She simply lay on the rug and cried all through lunch.

I tried several times to speak to her, but she drew away from me. She hid her face and would not be comforted. So I stopped trying to pacify her, and simply let her cry. When the other children complained that the noise "was hurting their ears," I put on their favorite tape. That had an additional benefit: Cory stopped crying and listened to the music. But she wouldn't sit up or leave the rug.

At dismissal, I handed her lunch to her baby-sitter and explained the situation.

"Yes, that sounds like Cory," her sitter laughed. "She can be very stubborn sometimes."

I returned to our room. I still wasn't sure I had done the right thing in refusing to humor her. But I knew that it was time for Cory to play by everyone else's rules. She was getting help. She was improving. It was time to stop treating her like a handicapped child.

· · ·

The next morning, Cory was her usual cheerful self. She looked happy and confident as her father brought her into the room. He took her over to David, and she apologized to him. David simply nodded, but his shining eyes revealed his satisfaction. Apparently, Cory's parents had discussed the situation with her, and I had been supported, as usual. When parents and teachers work together, so much is possible!

I thanked Cory's father, and brought her over to Cathy. "See if you can get Cory over to the puzzle table today. I want to see how she'll do with the new, complex puzzles we've just set out."

Cathy nodded. "My guess is that she'll do just fine at any cognitive task where no speaking is involved."

Cathy was right: Cory was terrific at puzzles. When she finished the first one, she called to Cathy.

"*Look!*" she called out, with an emphasis on the "L." It was a letter she had been unable to say until her speech therapy. We were just as excited about the letter as we were about the puzzle!

We had put out the puzzles and other similar games to learn more about the children's spatial abilities before conferences. Jenny, before she left, had proven to be an expert. So was Jason, of all people. This boy who could hardly sit still for a minute at story time or meeting could do three or four puzzles in a row. He also couldn't sit while he was doing them: he was on and off his chair frequently. But he was a genuine puzzle whiz. I was pleased: it gave us something positive to say to his parents.

We had expected Jeremy and Amanda to be good at puzzles also—Jeremy because he did them at home a lot, and Amanda because she was so smart. But it didn't turn out that way. Jeremy gave up too easily, and Amanda's spatial intelligence was far beneath her logical abilities. In fact, she couldn't do even the simplest spatial task, such as moving a figure from one space to another in a board game. Spatial ability is not directly related to other forms of intelligence—I know a lot of smart people who can't do puzzles—but we were surprised anyway.

We mentioned it to our director at the meeting we had with her before parent-teacher conferences. Barbara agreed that it wasn't important enough to mention at the conference. The mother was too easily upset, and might overreact. Amanda had made so much progress: she had begun the year as an observer, and was now often the center of attention. Her affinity for play-

ing the generally unloved role of Captain Hook made her indis-
pensable in imaginary games of Peter Pan! Her mother had definitely relaxed, also. There was no reason to start a brushfire
when the forest was growing so nicely.

As we went down the list of children, we realized that all of
them had made progress. Dealing with the day-to-day hassles
had prevented us from seeing this completely—but it was evi-
dent as we talked about our students one by one. They weren't
perfect, but they were vastly improved.

Jenny was better about making her wants known, especially
to her friends. We needed to help her learn to separate more
easily in the morning, but her parents had already begun to
work on this without a word from us. Jenny had been in good
shape when she left for California.

David was a wonderful boy who had found a good friend in
Benjamin Tyne. Very bright and artistically talented, he was
nevertheless too aggressive in physical situations. We assumed
it was a reflection of how he dealt with his older brother; we
needed to find out if we were right.

Jeremy was doing better than we could ever have hoped. Although Benjamin and David still excluded him frequently, he was
beginning to make other friends. He needed playdates with
these other children, which would help solidify their relationship.

[A digression here: A playdate is time spent with another
child, usually at one child's apartment, but sometimes in the
park. A parent or sitter delivers and picks up the visiting child.
Since we live in a city, there are no backyards, and no casual
way of meeting. Kids do not ride their bicycles from one house
to another. Playdates are arranged by parents, usually at the
request of the children. (But not always. Sometimes it's an "I
know you don't want to go but I bet you'll have fun anyway"
playdate.) This form of getting together persists at least until
the fourth grade. Such is city living.]

Benjamin continued to be marvelous fun. With his great intelligence and adolescent sense of humor, he was a joy to have around. His concerns about his health had diminished. Now we had to work on his fabulous lies.

Harris was a true success story. He was still a tough kid, but he could control his impulses and show his emotions now. Best of all, the fear in his eyes was completely gone. He was happy—and we were happy for him.

Avi was doing well. He had adjusted nicely, and was able to separate from his mother as soon as he came into the classroom. He, too, needed playdates.

Louisa was her usual, joyous, quirky self. If we were having a rotten day, Cathy and I could always take refuge in admiring her perfections. Every class needs at least one kid like this.

Mary Ann had made vast progress. She had learned to share, to wait her turn and to make accommodations. As a result, she now had lots of friends. We were very proud of her.

Sharon was also doing well. Although she still could not pronounce her name properly, she was able to recognize it on her name card. More important, she was learning not to overdramatize every little problem. We saw less histrionics and more reliance on her own sturdy character. Now we just had to convince her parents that she was growing up.

Jason continued to be a mixture of lovableness and exasperation. He enjoyed school, but he couldn't ever sit still. I didn't really understand this child, and I didn't think we were going to change him. The conference was just a matter of telling the parents about his behavior—again.

Two of our most difficult conferences would be Cory's and Lee's. Cory had made wonderful progress, in her speech and in her sociability. But her hearing was still uneven, and she often still tripped. It would be difficult to report this to parents who were already doing the best they could.

Lee needed to repeat the three's program next year. This had become clearer as the months went by. He was just beginning to show interest in our curriculum, and was only now able to focus on any task for more than a minute. He would greatly profit by a year as the oldest child. Now the problem was telling the parents without offending them. It was important to convey the fact that this was not a matter of intelligence but development. We asked Barbara to sit in, and she promised she would. The presence of a director adds weight to a conference: at the very least, the parents realize its importance.

We would have only ten conferences during the next two days. Three of our families were out West—Jenny for her grandmother's illness, and Benjamin and Mary Ann on separate skiing trips. (Perhaps this is the definition of an upscale nursery school?) I hadn't even believed Benjamin until I checked with his mother, but it was true. So the two mornings would not be quite as long.

I was always less nervous about spring conferences: we knew the parents and we already loved the children. Generally, there were few surprises. But you never could tell. Sure enough, our first meeting brought forth an unexpected revelation.

Cathy and I were happy to begin the day with Louisa's conference. Louisa was always a pleasure to talk about, and we had an appreciative audience. Elaine Donner was a woman who cherished her daughter's individuality, and even celebrated it. We began by trading stories about shoes.

One day, Louisa wore a pair of red shoes with beautiful red bows to school. During the morning, one of the bows unraveled. What looked like a beautiful flower had suddenly been transformed into an untidy ball of ribbon. Louisa's reaction was unusual and amusing. She took off her shoes and she hid behind her teacher.

"Cathy," she exclaimed with ever widening eyes, "I'm afraid of my shoe."

Cathy tried to tell her what had happened—that the ribbon had come undone—but Louisa was uninterested in explanations. She recovered only when Cathy put the shoes outside the classroom in a paper bag, and gave Louisa her extra pair of sneakers to wear.

Elaine had a shoe story of her own. "I took Louie shopping for shoes yesterday. She wanted a pair of red, sparkly plastic ones which no one—honestly, *no one*—would ever dream of wearing. They reminded her of Dorothy in *The Wizard of Oz*. Well, I got them for her. For the past twenty-four hours she's been saying, 'Well, now I know you really love me because you got me the red shoes.'"

It was heartwarming to hear: Elaine had the courage to let her child be herself. Once again, we wondered to ourselves if she could patent her parenting techniques. Then the conference took an unexpected turn.

I mentioned that it was a good time for Louisa to receive a special gift, since she missed her father so much. (He was away on a long buying trip.) Elaine disagreed. She didn't think that Louie missed her father much at all. She'd had a great deal of company. Elaine's mother and father, both theater people, had come over often to do skits with her.

"The same grandmother we met?" I inquired.

I thought: The one who was so reserved and critical?

Elaine nodded.

First impressions are often wrong.

We described the change in Louisa's behavior since her father's departure. She was mopey and sad. Rarely did we hear her voice, and when we did, it was often a complaint.

Cathy described one of our recent class meetings. We were talking about parents going away on trips. Louisa admitted that she was worried about whether Daddy would come back. We assured her that he would, and our words seemed to help.

Elaine was genuinely surprised. As our conversation continued, it became apparent that she paid less attention to Louisa's emotions than to her behavior. It didn't seem to matter much, since she was such a good parent. But it did explain how, on the day of the bomb scare, she and her husband had put Louisa on a school bus instead of taking her to school themselves when the child was so upset.

I thought: Well, nobody's perfect. She parents very well from the gut. She has a nonpsychological point of view, but she has a kid who has very few problems. So it's a good match.

As we ended the conference, Elaine repeated how much her daughter loved school, and how she and her husband loved hearing about Louisa's day. She mentioned what a great class it was, how adorable all the kids were, etc. I barely—just barely—kept a straight face. (Adorable, yes; a great class, no. I loved them dearly, but they were the toughest class of my career.) Elaine thanked us warmly and we thanked her for the great pleasure of having Louisa in our class. We parted in mutual satisfaction.

Harris's conference was next. Joanna and Harris Senior walked in, as charming and friendly as ever. They looked genuinely glad to see us. I could see by the large bandage on Harris Senior's head that his son had accurately described his father's taxi injury. We inquired about the details, and they corroborated Harris Junior's account: the taxi behind had run a red light, ramming into the back of Harris Senior's cab and sending him flying. He had sustained bruised ribs and a cut across his forehead which required four stitches.

I asked how Harris Junior had sorted out an accident where there really was no bad guy or good guy. His parents knew just what I was talking about: Harris played "good guy/bad guy" at home constantly. In fact, his father acknowledged, Harris continually asked if the taxi driver was a bad guy. It seemed as if he were trying to divide the world into good guys and bad guys. This was a fine example of the fact that it just wasn't possible. We all agreed that it was important for this kid, who was trying to sort out his world, to understand that not everything can be divided into "good" and "bad."

Next, we brought up the subject of their housekeeper, Opal. We all agreed that as a baby-sitter, she had her strengths. But Cathy told them that Opal needed to watch him better as they walked along. (We had been given several reports of her behavior from other mothers. Cathy, too, had seen her walk several feet ahead of Harris for a whole block on Columbus Avenue. Cathy was understandably concerned. New York is a city where anything can happen; if it does, it happens quickly.) The Whites promised to talk to Opal.

Next, we had a short discussion about the importance of Joanna's getting home in the evening before Harris's bedtime.

Joanna said, "Well, I do the best I can, and I see him on weekends. I can usually get home by 6, be with Harris until 8, talk to my husband until 9 and then work until 1 A.M."

"Now that he's older, he needs you more," I told her.

"He *is* starting to complain more," she admitted. "Yesterday morning he said, 'Mommy, I'm angry at you,' and he had a whole list of things. I felt terrible."

"Look, you could stay home and take care of Harris full-time, but you'd be resentful. You *like* working. But when you go to work, you feel guilty about leaving your child. So pick the emotion you can deal with best—resentment or guilt. Either way, it isn't Nirvana."

Joanna looked a little relieved.

Harris Senior spoke up. "When I know Joanna is going to be late, I try to be home and pick up the slack."

"Good," I replied. "Because children demand your attention. You can pay him now, or you can pay him later—in the principal's office or the police station."

Joanna rolled her eyes. "I'd rather pay him now."

"Wouldn't we all!" I laughingly agreed.

We spent the rest of the conference more enjoyably—trading "how improved Harris is" stories. Cathy related an encounter with a small child who was constantly goading Harris in the gym. This was the same child Harris had scratched on the face several months ago during Laura Adler's observation of him. Last week, however, he turned around, looked the child right in the eye and yelled "DON'T DO THAT!" He had to yell it twice before the child backed off. He didn't resort to fighting: he used his words and he got his way. This was a triumph of large proportions for Harris.

Harris's parents informed us that Dr. Adler was seeing great improvement, as well. Last week, when she asked him, "What would you do if a lion came to school?" he had replied, "Oh, Patti would say *no lions in school!*" In learning to trust adults, he was learning that authority is there for his protection. We congratulated ourselves for having done a good job in helping Harris grow.

The conference reached a natural end. "Well," Harris Senior said as he rose. "What a difference from the last one!"

He shook hands all around and practically bounced down the hall, despite the bruised ribs. Joanna left with her husband, more subdued but equally gracious. She was the one to mention how great the class was, and how adorable the kids were. Gnash, gnash.

Cathy said, "That was a wonderful conference!"

"Highly gratifying," I agreed. "Who's next?"

As if in response, Cory's parents appeared at the door. As they took their seats, they seemed nervous and uncomfortable. I was surprised—they were usually so relaxed. There was no small talk; they waited for us to begin. They looked as if they expected bad news.

Actually, lots of the news was quite good. Cory's speech had improved a great deal; as a result, her confidence had increased. She spoke much more to her friends, and spent much less time hanging around her teachers.

Cathy spoke about Cory's returning cheerfulness. She no longer seemed sad or embarrassed about going to speech therapy. She also seemed less concerned with her friend Mary Elizabeth's father's death. She was "playing dead" in the gym very little these days. Cory's parents agreed: they saw the end of this game at home as well.

David asked if all four-year-olds played dead. I explained that most kids do it at this age; it seems to be the beginning of death anxiety. Then I described the tickle test I used to bring them "back to life." It gives the children who need it the chance to explore the idea of death. And the kids who just want to be tickled have fun, too.

Most of the children had played dead this year. There had been so many accidents and traumas, and we'd been talking about them in class. In a way, they affected all of us.

"Actually, Cory had one on Saturday," Theresa reported.

She proceeded to describe a horrific incident where, due to a superintendent's error, she and Cory were in the elevator when its door closed, stranding little Edward in the hall. Cory became hysterical. Even after she saw that Edward was fine (his father had been just two steps behind), Cory was "inconsolable for hours."

I said: "What an awful story. The kids in this class have had so many hard things happen to them this year."

I thought: I wonder if our kids can stand any more. Cathy and I can hardly sleep at night as it is.

There was certainly no point in saying that, so we spoke about Cory's intelligence. We explained that she could do all our cognitive work with ease. If she ever hesitated, it was due to her reluctance to speak. With her improved speech, even that was changing rapidly.

Theresa told us that the speech therapist saw great progress as well.

"Cory has a speech delay. At first the therapist thought she'd have to come twice a week, but it hasn't been necessary. We do all the exercises at home and she's making real progress."

"Great," I replied. "This was the time to get her there."

"Thanks to you," said Theresa.

I smiled. I was grateful for her praise—but now was the time to move on to the hard part of the conference.

"What's happening with the hearing specialist?"

David answered. "He has her on long-term antibiotics."

"Here's why I'm asking. Cory's hearing is still not consistently good. Her acuity is fine—once she hears me, she can understand me. But on some days, she has a hard time hearing."

Boy, this was hard. I took a breath and continued.

"Also, her balance is still off. She's still falling. Do you see this at home?"

Theresa nodded. "Yes. All the time."

"Have you told the specialist?"

They both shook their heads.

I retreated behind my professional face, and spoke as calmly as possible.

"I think you'd really better tell him. Cory's an agile runner and climber, so it's not as if she's just a clumsy kid. It's a piece of information the doctor needs to have."

They promised to tell him. The reason they hadn't, Theresa said, was that they couldn't face anything else being wrong.

I knew that. But they had made such a good beginning. They just had to keep going; and all I could do was to keep after them.

Our half hour was up. They thanked us, and said how wonderful school was for Cory. And the children were *so* adorable. (Enough!) After they had gone, we had just a minute to catch our breaths.

"That went pretty well, I think," Cathy said.

"I hope so. They're lovely people with enormous burdens. I'm not sure I would cope as well."

Just then, David Cohen's parents entered our classroom. They came on time, and they were ready to talk as well as listen.

Naturally, we began our discussion with David's strengths.

This was an easy topic, for he was a child with many gifts. He was smart, artistic, great at math, a superb athlete and kind to his classmates. He was also quite sensitive, and possessed a passionate nature. (He was sexy, too, but we didn't think it appropriate to mention. It's not a topic often discussed, but some children have sex appeal, even at four. Many adults who visited our classroom—including some of the other parents— commented on David's "animal magnetism.")

David's difficulties, however, seemed to stem from his birth order. He was a second son—younger brother to Eli, a smart, tough aggressive kid who probably wasn't too thrilled with David's existence. ("Do you know when first children get over the birth of their siblings?" my child development teacher once asked. The answer: "Never.") Eli was constantly picking fights, and David was tough enough to fight back. These experiences at home spilled over into school, particularly during gym or roof. David, accustomed to combat, had difficulty controlling his impulse to fight.

Cathy explained how we handled this in school. We sat him in time out, but while he was there we also talked to him.

I added: "It's important to find out how David is feeling. Talking may help dissipate some of the aggression."

Sabrina spoke up. "We separate the boys when they fight. And we talk to David. He talks all the time when his brother's not around."

Samuel interrupted. "But not about his feelings. I don't ask him either . . ." He paused, gulped and revealed that he, too, was a younger brother of an aggressive, brilliant, extremely successful older brother.

"More successful than you?" I could not help inquiring of this famous novelist.

He nodded, and mentioned his brother's name. He was the acclaimed conductor of a major symphony orchestra, who had achieved worldwide fame.

"So I know David's problem. I identify with him. That was my role. I don't ask about his feelings because I'm afraid of what he'll say."

Samuel looked stunned at his own admission. His wife squeezed his hand. It was a time to be silent and let the words sink in.

Sabrina spoke first, changing the subject slightly. "Is there anything we should be doing to help David along?"

I spoke carefully. "Well, there really *is* something you can do, although it's difficult. David has to spend less unsupervised time with his brother right now. When it's possible, make a playdate and get one of them out of the house."

Sabrina said, "But I can't always do that."

"Of course not. But when you can, it will be a welcome relief for both of them."

Sabrina nodded. Then it was her turn to talk.

"I know you shouldn't compare children, but—"

I stopped her right there.

"It's fine to compare. I wish the person who said it's not would break a bone or something. Parents feel so guilty when they compare their kids, but it's natural and normal. It's really how you measure each child's individuality. You just shouldn't *judge*. Don't say 'John hits a ball better than Tom so he's a better person.'"

Sabrina brightened. "Yes, that's it!" She then described the children's favorite math game. She would give Eli an addition problem to solve, and he would answer it, often adding double digits in his head. Next, she would give one to David. Sometimes he would do just fine. At other times he would yell out anything just to beat his brother, who would often say the answer for him.

My suggestion: "Then Eli shouldn't get another problem until he allows David to answer."

Samuel loved that idea.

Sabrina continued: "Oh, I can manage the game. It's just hard sometimes. And David will get the right answer if he has time to think or count on his fingers."

I explained that it's a tough game for a four-year-old. Most couldn't do it.

"Do you think I'm pushing them?" she asked me. "Should I stop?"

I was struck by the power teachers often wield. Would she have stopped if I'd told her to?

"No. David is way ahead in math. It's terrific for him."

"Both boys love it," she agreed. "It's their favorite game."

I could see why: controlled competition, with the participation of a parent, in a game they're both good at. It sounded like heaven to me.

"Great," is what I said.

Sabrina spoke again. "You know, Eli has it hard, too. He watches David hit a baseball and says, 'Isn't there anything I can do better than him anymore?'"

"Read," I answered.

"Well, there's that. But in sports."

"My point is just to use all the strengths a child has when answering that question."

They nodded in agreement.

"Is there anything else we can do for David?" asked Samuel.

Cathy had the best answer. "Ask David. Maybe he just wants playdates and time at home with his family."

We talked about the boys needing to spend private time with their father. The Cohens knew this, and were trying their best to arrange it. But Sabrina said that they often liked to do things as a family.

"I need to see Samuel, too," she added.

I thought: What a hard life. I hope it's worth it.

I said: "Of course. Family time is the most important thing."

I mentioned that our time was up, but that we could have another conference at any time. They were extremely gracious, thanking us for our time and our wisdom. He gave his customary bear hugs and she shook our hands. They left together, speaking of other things.

• • •

We had half an hour before Lee's conference. We ate, drank and talked about the morning. Basically, however, we spent the time mentally preparing for what was sure to be our hardest conference. Would we be able to communicate to Lee's parents that repeating a year was not a sign of weakness or inferiority?

Barbara Gold joined us just as the Newtons arrived. All five of us sat around one of the children's tables, looking like giants at a coffee klatch. We began the conference, as always, by talking about Lee's strengths.

They were easy to enumerate. Lee was cheerful, friendly and very good to his friends. He enjoyed playing with the children in the class, and was liked by them all. He not only recognized his name on our lunch cards, he recognized all the other children's names as well. This was unusual for someone so young. We gave Lee as much credit as we could.

Then I plunged into the difficult part. "But the other children are moving ahead at a much greater pace. Lee can't keep up—not because he's not as *smart* as they are but because he's not as old."

I gave an example. "One day, Harris and Jason sat down at the puzzle table. They were really enjoying the puzzles, so when Lee came over and asked them to get up and play, they refused. Lee's not interested in puzzles yet, so he wouldn't join them. Instead, his feelings were hurt. He couldn't understand why his two friends wouldn't play with him."

I offered a few more illustrations of his unreadiness, not to rub it in but to drive it home. Lee still couldn't ever understand the need to raise his hand at meeting time (although all the other three-and-a-half-year-olds were able to remember now). And he still couldn't remember that actions have consequences—so the YOU HIT, YOU SIT rules merely enraged him.

I closed with the firm conclusion that Lee needed to repeat the three's program. I didn't say the decision was theirs (Barbara had told me that it was). I just gave my own firm opinion. So far, I was the only one who had spoken. We three held our collective breath, and waited for a reply from the Newtons.

Lee's father spoke first. "Well, it isn't as if we hadn't been prepared for this. You mentioned it at the last conference."

I breathed a not really audible sigh of relief.

Mike continued: "But isn't there a chance that he'll develop a lot over the summer and be ready by the fall?"

His wife answered this. "Yes, but these kids will be developing, too. So he'll still be behind."

"But won't he feel bad being split up from his two best pals?" Mike asked.

I said: "They'll be split up in any event."

I thought: No one should ever have to teach the Gruesome Threesome again! (Just yesterday they had sneaked sand into the playdough, ruining both activities and creating havoc.)

Carla must have read my thoughts: "But won't he just team up with other active kids?"

Barbara handled this one. "Yes, but it won't be *these* active kids, with a year's history of 'super-active' behavior." It was a good answer, telling them only as much as they needed to know.

"Won't he be bored?" asked Mike.

I thought: I'm surprised he's not bored now, since there's so little he can do of our classwork.

I said: "No. He'll really just begin the curriculum in earnest. And if he can go ahead, the teacher will work with him separately, just as I did with David Cohen this year." David's success in repeating the grade really impressed them.

Cathy mentioned that Lee still had the tantrums of a much

younger child, which would be greatly frowned upon in the four's program. Then I asked how discipline was going at home.

Carla responded. "Oh, I just put him in a corner. He cries a lot and very loudly, so I go over to sit with him and explain what he's done wrong."

After a few more examples, we learned that discipline in the Newton home was much as it had ever been: Lee was running the show.

I explained, patiently and without the irritation I was feeling, how to discipline more effectively. Then I used a visual aid: I slammed my fist into my open hand. My hand didn't budge. When the authority figure holds firm, the child feels safe. This explained the big hug and kiss I got from Lee after each tantrum, along with the words, "Patti, you're my best teacher." The kid was relieved that someone had taken a stand.

"Carla, Lee needs you and Mike to do this for him, too."

"All right," she replied, nodding slightly. She sounded as if she would try.

The conference ended with the Newtons promising to think seriously about our recommendation for Lee. I hoped they would take our suggestions for disciplining him as well. These were two sweet people who were afraid to lay down the law. Would Lee be able to get them angry enough to do battle? I wasn't sure.

When the Newtons and Barbara had gone, Cathy and I talked about the morning. The first day's conferences had gone as well as possible. There was nothing left to do except to go home, rest and hope as much for the second day.

• • •

Our first conference on the following day was Jeremy Jacobson's. Carolyn came by herself: she looked nervous. Cathy and I had decided that the best way to open this meeting was on a note of conciliation. I got right to it.

You were right, I told Carolyn. Jeremy was not only upset about the baby, but also about the David-Benjamin friendship which consistently excluded him. We had been focusing a lot of attention on the triangle since she had brought it to our attention.

Carolyn seemed to relax. She wanted to know how this had happened. Was it something the two other boys had against Jeremy?

We assured her that it was not. David and Benjamin were just more interested in each other than in anyone else. They always included Jeremy when we insisted. But Jeremy was much less eager to play with them now.

"He has so many other friends that he could be elected mayor," I assured her.

We talked about Jeremy's pace—his slow, deliberate method of doing work. He achieved his goals, but in his own methodical fashion. We told Carolyn that this would probably always be his learning style. We also spoke of his great intelligence, particularly in math.

Cathy mentioned Jeremy's wonderful sense of humor. Carolyn told us a story which perfectly illustrated the point. Jeremy was eager to visit his brother's school on Monday, but it was only Friday. Carolyn told him that he would have to wait for the weekend to pass.

"Tell Patti to cancel the weekend," he told her. "Then we can go right to school."

After this enjoyable exchange, I felt we could move on to a discussion of Jeremy's emotional development.

"He's doing well, Carolyn," I said. "He's working very hard to make himself feel better."

Much to my delight, Carolyn responded, "He must have had a tremendous amount of guilt to work out. He was very verbal about not wanting the baby to come."

I thought: Yes! That's it exactly!

I then explained the steps Jeremy had taken in school. First he had withdrawn: he looked at books with his finger up his nose for quite a while. Then he began to interact in the gym, first as a dog, then a dead dog. I retold the doll-bashing incident, and then added the parenting play we were seeing now. Recently, Jeremy had put a hat from our dress-up corner on another child's head. When the child protested, he'd replied, "Well, we're going out soon and it's a little windy."

Carolyn listened carefully. She seemed aware of the seriousness of his efforts. When I was finished, she mentioned that the behavior specialist had said that Jeremy didn't need her help.

"As it turns out, the specialist was right. He's doing the work himself. It's quite remarkable."

"Jeremy said it would be all right if I had another baby now," she said.

"That's wonderful," I replied.

Our time was up. As she rose to leave, Carolyn joked, "Well, you have my permission to take his finger out of his nose any time."

"I never do it," I explained. "My rule is: 'If it doesn't come off your body, you can put it in your mouth or your nose.' That means the fingers are okay, but nothing else."

I told the story of James, a little boy in our school who had pushed a bead so far into his ear that a doctor had to remove it. When his teacher asked him why he had done it, James replied, "Because I have no pockets."

Carolyn laughed. It was a big, hearty sound that I didn't know she had in her. Perhaps she was healing, too.

Amanda's conference was highly enjoyable—like a slice of a Woody Allen movie. Her parents seemed to be polar opposites: the mother all emotion and the father all rationality. They were united by a good sense of humor, a sincere regard for each other and great affection for their child.

Cathy ran the conference with great skill. It was a pleasure to talk about Amanda, she told them. Her intelligence and great logical thinking made her an asset to the class, especially at meeting time. She got along with everyone, and was in great demand as a playmate. She was a zestful and interesting child. Amanda's mother couldn't believe there were no problems; Amanda's father knew it all along.

When Cathy complimented Janet on figuring out the baby-sitter situation, Elliott demurred.

"Amanda didn't like Billie because she thought Janet didn't like her."

This was a minority opinion: we all disagreed. I felt that Amanda's experience with lying had taught her a lesson. Perhaps it was even the catalyst for her to experiment with "being bad." Cathy told them about Amanda's love for the "bad" characters in the children's imaginary games. She always wanted to be Hook or Haman, the villain in the Purim story. Janet was interested; Elliott pooh-poohed the idea.

"She certainly spends a lot of time playing with the big boys," I told him. "Sometimes she seemed to be trying to get a time out, just to see what it feels like."

Janet said, "Amanda calls them the 'wild boys.' We assumed that was your name for them."

I thought: No, but it will be from now on. It's a perfect fit.

I said: "No, that was her own idea."

The mother was pleased; the father unimpressed.

The conference continued along these lines. Finally, Elliott said, "Well, I'm all logic, and Janet's all feeling. I guess the best way is somewhere in between."

We assured them that, whatever their method, they were doing a terrific job: they had a well-balanced, happy kid. They, in turn, told us how wonderful the class was—arrgh!—and how much they appreciated our work.

We ended the conference without mentioning Amanda's spatial difficulties. The problem could very well improve over the next year. Why upset a worry-prone mother with something that only time could fix? It was a decision we would later regret.

Dvora Peled was waiting, so we began Avi's conference immediately. It was a pleasure to tell her that Avi had made a fine adjustment to his new school. He had friends, he enjoyed the work and he seemed happy in our classroom.

Dvora felt the same way. Avi never complained about having to go to a new school anymore. As she talked about her son, it was clear that Dvora had a very good understanding of him. We were glad to see it: this was not something we had known before the conference.

Next, we spoke of Avi's unusual way with words. Cathy told this story:

"At meeting, one day, Avi called out: 'Patti, you don't have any children!'

"The children corrected him. Cory said, 'She's a mommy *and* a teacher.'"

"We talked about Patti's two children. Avi turned to me. 'Cathy, do you have any children?'

"When I said I didn't, he replied, `Well, we better go out and find you one.'"

Dvora knew exactly what we were talking about. "Last week Avi said to me, '*Ema* [Mommy], you are yelling at me again and it's just not worth it.'"

One story involved the death of Dvora's brother. She had told Avi that Uncle Yoni's soul floated up to the sky where you couldn't see it. On the plane ride home, he looked out the window "to make sure the plane didn't bump into Uncle Yoni."

Dvora added, "My career is very important to me, but since my brother's death, I can see that it's okay if I'm out of work for one year. It's not so terrible. My family is fine. And I have good quality time with them."

I nodded. It was a sad way to find out, but an important lesson to learn while her children were still young. I turned the conversation back to Avi.

"He's a very intelligent child," I told her.

Dvora was glad to hear it. She was worried about the fact that he could not yet count to twelve.

"Are you teaching him in Hebrew and English?"

She said they were.

"When you count with him, you need to stick to one language. Frequently, two languages interfere with each other. I'd recommend English, because he's in America, and he'll be speaking English in school."

To my surprise, Dvora agreed. She seemed pleased with the advice. I had thought she'd be more insistent on using Hebrew. There I was, judging a book by its cover again. I resolved to do better.

Cathy told her not to worry about Avi. "He'll learn his letters and numbers with ease as soon as he's really interested."

How did we know that?

"Because he's such a creative thinker," I said. "When he's working with playdough, he makes an octopus or a dinosaur. When he uses manipulatives, he's always inventing new ways to look at them. He doesn't build a house, but a man on an elephant. It's one signpost of intelligence."

Our time was up. Dvora thanked us warmly. She felt our class provided what Avi's other school had been lacking: Jewish education and a great deal of nurturing. She couldn't believe her good fortune in having found us. She didn't tell us what a wonderful bunch of children we had; she told us how wonderful *we* were. Cathy and I were not just appreciative (unless that's the appropriate word to describe the passengers on the last lifeboat leaving the *Titanic*). We were thrilled and relieved that somebody had noticed. It was nice to end a conference with everybody smiling.

Jason's conference was next. I felt the same way as I did in November. Jason got on my nerves so often that it was difficult for me to see him objectively. Cathy did a much better job of dealing with his inattention and lack of impulse control. So, once again, she would run the conference.

She began by telling Jason's mother about his cheerfulness, his wonderful spatial ability and his genuine concern for other children. As I listened to Cathy, I began to like the kid better myself.

"He hasn't made much progress in sitting, but he *has* learned to raise his hand when he has something to say at meeting time," Cathy added.

It occurred to me that he had, in fact, made progress. I described to both Cathy and Anne how Jason no longer just ran around during meeting or story time. He had various ploys for getting up which he felt were acceptable to his teachers. During story time, he was sure to need a tissue or two. This required walking across the room to the tissue box. He might ask to get something from his cubby, which meant going out of the classroom for a minute. He sometimes even asked to go to the bathroom.

I realized as I talked that this did constitute a change for the better; there was much less rolling around or bouncing on the rug when he was supposed to be sitting. Some part of him was always in motion—his hand or his foot frequently tapped the rug if the rest of his body was still. But when I thought back to the Wild Man of September who had nearly severed his own hand, I was aware of his vast improvement.

Naturally, I didn't say that to Jason's mother. But Anne's reaction to our description of her son was much the same as it had been in November.

"This is the same thing I heard at my daughter's conference: 'Terrific, if only she'd sit.' And my parents heard the same thing about me at every conference when I was young."

Anne's comments showed me that she wasn't worried about Jason; after all, she'd turned out all right. I relaxed. The child didn't seem to have an attention deficit—he sat very well when he was interested in something. It would just be tough on his teachers for the next few years until he developed more self-control. I was more than willing to accept this view of Jason. It meant I hadn't failed in my continuing efforts to tame him. He just wasn't tamable yet.

Anne thanked us for our patience with Jason. We smiled. She commented on how darling all the children were. We smiled through gritted teeth. As she left, I realized I wasn't as exasperated with Jason as I had been. Perhaps it was the result of the conference; however, the fact that I hadn't seen him in forty-eight hours didn't hurt, either.

"You handled that conference beautifully," I told Cathy after Anne's departure. "I could never have done as well, given my mixed feelings."

"It's okay to have mixed feelings," she replied. "It's just not okay to talk about them with the parents. Aren't you the one who's always telling me just to describe the child's behavior without making a judgment?"

"Yup."

"So you did a good job, too." It was nice of Cathy to say so. Even experienced teachers need feedback.

Our last conference of the day presented a different problem. Both of us loved Sharon so much that we wondered if we'd do a good job talking about the areas where she needed help. It was an interesting test: could we apply the corrective as well as lavish the praise?

Cathy began this conference by speaking of Sharon's resilient nature. We were happy to see the parents nod in recognition.

"We've noticed," said John.

"But she sure doesn't get it from either of us," laughed Karen.

I told the "wet baby" story as an example of Sharon's strength. I dwelled particularly on the fun Sharon had in "fighting back" with words. They told us that the name-calling game continued at home, with amusing results.

When Sharon and her sister Lilia fought, Sharon would frequently resort to name-calling of the most absurd kind. All concerned felt that this was preferable to hitting. The fights usually ended in laughter: Lilia was so much older that she found the names—Idiotrathead was one—amusing. We saw their point.

"Lilia thinks it's hysterical and Sharon thinks she's won," was how John put it.

We spoke a little more about Sharon's growing independence. Suddenly, Karen said:

"What you're doing is giving me permission to stop treating her at all like a baby. I've wanted to—it's really time. But with the extra work I've been doing at school, and my longer hours, I've been afraid to do it."

She had understood our message before we had put it clearly on the table.

"That's okay," I answered. "It's time. It will be a help, not a detriment, to Sharon. I know from experience how hard it is to give up the last baby—"

Karen interrupted. "Oh, that's all right. That's why we got a dog!"

"Good move!" Cathy cheered.

Karen told a story about Sharon's jealousy of the dog. When people admired the dog on their walk one day, Sharon said, "That's what they used to say about me!"

I thought: This kid's one sharp cookie.

After mentioning how bright Sharon is, we talked about her speech. The Sonfelds wanted to know if Sharon needed immediate help. I told them I thought we could wait one more year. Minor lisps sometimes cleared up by themselves. It was just more difficult for Sharon because she couldn't say her name. This was a source of embarrassment for her, when she thought about it. Fortunately, that wasn't very often.

Neither of Sharon's parents were aware that she said "Saron." They were surprised, and so were we. It had never occurred to us that they didn't know, or we would have mentioned it sooner. Sometimes, parents miss the things that are most obvious just because they are so daily. We all resolved to help Sharon with the "sh" sound.

After a little small talk, the conference ended on a note of mutual satisfaction. Sharon was a delightful child, and it was our pleasure to have her in our classroom. Her parents thanked us, did us the favor of *not* mentioning how delightful all the other children were, and took their leave.

"A pleasant end to a pleasant morning," remarked Cathy, as we tidied up the room a bit.

"Finishing conferences is always a great relief," I remarked. "It's like taking a fifty-pound weight off my back."

"We do have three more," Cathy reminded me.

"Yes, but they'll be one day at a time. This machine-gun approach—ten in two days—is what really provides the stress."

"Well, they're over. Now the rest of the month should be fun, with Purim coming and all."

"I think so. Getting ready for Purim is hard work, although the holiday itself is fun. But the rest of March should be clear sailing."

It turned out to be just the opposite. Purim was a joy from beginning to end. Afterward, we headed directly into turbulent waters.

Late March:
Costumes and Crises

On our first day back after conferences, Mary Ann returned from vacation. She looked tan and healthy. After hugging her teachers, she ran off to play with her friends. I turned my attention to her mother, who obviously had something to say. One look at Nancy's face convinced me that it was not good news.

She told a harrowing story. Mary Ann, on a ski lift with her mother, was unable to jump off at the proper time. Nancy tugged at her hand, but to no avail. This particular ski lift had no safety bar. As the bucket turned around and rose to return to the base of the mountain, Mary Ann fell. The drop was twelve feet, and she landed head first. Miraculously, she was unhurt. A twelve-inch cushion of new snow prevented any injury. Her parents took her to a doctor, and watched her carefully through the night. But the next day, she was back on skis, fearless as ever.

Nancy, however, was terribly upset, especially when she considered what could have happened. Her distress was severe enough to stifle my first thought: *How could you take a four-year-old on a lift with no safety bar?* I couldn't ask that question, though: she was suffering enough.

"Mary Ann is fine. There seem to be no adverse effects at all. I just thought you should know."

I thanked Nancy sincerely; it was very important that I know. What if the story came bubbling up from Mary Ann one day, and I was unprepared to deal with it? An important opportunity would be lost.

I hugged Nancy, and expressed my great relief that her daughter was unharmed. "That's really something to be grateful for," I told her.

After she had gone, I went directly to Mary Ann.

"Did you have a good time on your vacation, honey?" I asked her.

"Yeah!" she replied happily.

"Tell me about it."

"Well, I went on skis and I skied all over the place. We skied down Fanny Hill but it was too easy."

"Mommy told me you had an accident," I said gently.

"And then we went to Aspen Mountain and I skied on all the moguls . . . and it was so fun!" She continued as if I hadn't said a word.

"It's okay if you don't want to talk about your fall, sweetie. Just remember that I'm here if you ever *want* to talk."

She stared at me blankly, and then walked off. I had never seen Mary Ann at a loss for words before. Obviously, this incident was too frightening to talk about. I could only hope that she would speak up at another time.

Our preparations for Purim were a welcome diversion. Everybody loved this holiday. It celebrates the time when a Persian queen named Esther, who happened to be Jewish, saved her people from destruction at the hands of the evil Haman. On Purim, children and adults dress up in costume and come to the synagogue to listen to the reading of the story. Although it is found in the Bible as the Book of Esther, it is traditionally read from a handwritten scroll, called the megillah. Each time the name of Haman is mentioned, the congregation shakes noisemakers, or groggers, and shouts out loud. The purpose is to blot out the name of wicked Haman; the result is a rollicking good time.

We had to decorate costumes, paint crowns, make groggers and bake little triangular cookies called "hamantaschen" (the translation is "Haman's pockets," but they look like his hat) to send home. (Giving to friends or to charity is a tradition which has grown up around this holiday.) This year, the rabbi requested that each class also construct a large decoration for the auditorium wall where the celebration would be held. I wondered if he knew how much more difficult this made our preparations. I wondered if he wanted to spend a morning here to see just how hard it was to do. I wondered how my children could possibly accomplish it all.

Having no choice, we set to work. Our costumes were made out of pillowcases, with holes cut out for the arms and head. One by one, the children painted them at the easel. We used food coloring instead of the usual tempera paint. The colors were translucent and gloriously bright. Some children loved the activity; others had to be coaxed inch by inch.

Benjamin Tyne was a case in point. On the day he returned from his ski trip to Colorado, I asked him to paint his pillowcase. The other children had finished, and Purim was in a few days. We were almost into Now-or-Never Land.

Because David had not yet arrived, Benjamin acceded to my request. This was a child who was only mildly interested in art, but he had to make his costume anyway. It was "the rule of the school," we told the children, that everyone have a costume on Purim. Benjamin asked me to sit with him while he painted. While he worked at the easel, he talked nonstop.

"When do you think David will get here?" (He made small brushstrokes on the pillowcase.)

"I don't know. Won't it be nice to be finished with your costume, though, so you can play with him when he *does* get here?"

"Oh. Will that be soon?" (He painted over what he had already done.)

"Benjamin, paint on the white part."

"Okay." (He painted two quick strokes.)

Next came a loud gasp and a look of horror. "Oh-oh. It *dripped!*"

"That's what it's supposed to do," I reassured him. "It's not paint—it's food coloring and water. The drips are gorgeous. See?"

I pointed to all the other costumes hanging on the wall.

Benjamin was dubious. He painted a few more strokes in the same garrulous manner. When he noticed David entering the room, however, he flew directly to his friend. The costume-painting was at an end.

I didn't call him back, although less than half the costume was painted. Instead, I felt all the absurdity of making a child do something that he doesn't want to do. I silently cursed Purim, with all its rigid requirements. Not that it was the fault of the holiday. I switched to cursing public relations. All the parents would be at our celebration, so everything had to be "perfect."

The great day arrived. We had finished all the costumes, noisemakers, crowns and the wall hanging. (Tomorrow, we would do the baking. That was bending the rules a bit: the hamantaschen were supposed to go home on Purim itself. But we had accomplished a near-miracle in getting everything else ready, so no one gave me an argument.)

I was more than a little nervous. I've had classes go bananas on the day of the Purim party. I alerted Cathy to the possibility. We wondered what we could do to help them if it turned out to be a bad day.

I had sent home a note requesting that the children wear their regular clothes to school. When they came in party clothes to celebrate the special day, they often refused to put on their costumes. The parents responded beautifully: the kids looked like they were going to a garage sale.

Much to our surprise, they were calm and adorable. During

playtime, they worked quietly with the familiar toys we had set out. We had a short, calm snack and an equally easygoing bathroom time. Then, there was nothing left to do but dress up and have a good time at the party.

We had a little more time to dress than the other classes, as we were going to be the last group to enter the auditorium. (This was a wise choice, given our track record with impulse control.) Cathy and I helped the children slip into their painted pillowcases. We used red ribbon to tie them at the waist. We also made red sashes for everyone. Next, we applied makeup, depending on which character the child wanted to be. The king received a beard (colored in with eyebrow pencil); Queen Esther got red cheeks and blue eye shadow; Haman wore a villain's curly mustache and goatee. Naturally, only Amanda wanted to be Haman—but she was rip-snortingly good at the part. She strode around the room shouting and brandishing her fist. We were all enchanted.

Not everyone was thrilled with the costumes: Benjamin clearly needed encouragement. As Cathy finished tying his sash, she said to him, "Benj, you look *so* cool. Go look in the mirror." He looked, and he was clearly unimpressed.

"Don't you love it?" Cathy asked him.

"No." He shook his head. I could just see what was running through his mind. *What's all this fuss about? It's not a real costume, like Robin Hood or the Ninja Turtles."* I decided not to tackle it unless it was verbalized. But every year I see that look come into some kid's eyes. Call it *mal du siècle,* or "material possession" overload. Our children have so much that sometimes it's hard for them to appreciate simpler things.

Sweet little Sharon came to the rescue.

"Oh, Benjamin . . . you look *sooo* beautiful," she squealed. Although he was not completely convinced, he was mollified. The exclamations of three women (mine included) had softened his feelings.

We handed out the crowns and the noisemakers, and we were ready to roll. Unfortunately, we had been so efficient that we had ten minutes to spare. I decided to keep the kids busy with a moving-around activity, since they'd be sitting for so long during the puppet show. Cathy put on a tape. We marched around a table in full costume, shaking our noisemakers. When Cathy stopped the music, we stopped the moving and shaking.

The music was our liveliest—from the *15 Years of Motown* album. Marvin Gaye was wailing and we were marching. It was a Soul Purim.

Finally, it was time to go. As we walked calmly and cheerfully to the elevator, my colleague Renée came out of her classroom to admire us. She took me aside for a moment.

"Did you ever think you'd get them to this stage? Dressed for Purim, walking quietly, happy?"

I shook my head. "I didn't really think it was possible."

"Bravo," said Renée.

She applauded us all the way down the hall.

• • •

The Purim party was a wonderful success. The children sat well for the puppet show, sang all the songs we had learned and even managed to bear with the constant bombardment of camera flashes as well-meaning parents snapped photos ceaselessly. The parents loved the costumes, thanked us enthusiastically and seemed genuinely glad to be participating. Grandparents, cousins and baby-sitters came. Avi's entire afternoon play group attended. It was truly a "good time was had by all" day.

That night, however, I was jolted back to the other side of real life. I received a phone call from California. Jenny missed me and needed to talk to me, said her mother. She had gone to a Purim party, and that had prompted the call.

"Of course," I told her. That's why I had given them the phone number.

So there was Jenny, a sweet little voice on the other end, saying that she was having a good time, but she missed her friends in school.

I asked her who she was playing with.

She said her brother was there, and a boy cousin who was nine years old. Small wonder she missed school.

"Jenny, the children ask for you every day . . . especially Sharon. We'll all be so happy to see you when you get back. And you *are* coming back, honey. I promise. I know it seems like a long time, but soon you'll be home."

"I miss you," is what Jenny said.

She gave the phone back to her mother. Peggy sounded stressed and distracted. There had been no change in her mother's condition. I told her what I had said to Jenny, and asked her to talk along these lines when she could. Jenny needed the reality fix. (It sounded as if Peggy did, too.) Peggy promised to call next week and let us know their plans.

I hung up with a sigh: another killer situation for the classroom. But our group was skilled at dealing with them by now. Jenny's friends would help her when she finally came home.

· · ·

The day after Purim was one of those mornings a teacher remembers forever: rewarding, a bit crazy and fun. It began with a heartwarming conference. Mary Ann had made so much improvement in social areas that it was a pleasure to speak with her parents.

"I thought she must be doing better," said her mother. "The phone's been ringing off the hook with parents in this class asking for playdates."

We were happy to hear that piece of good news, and eager to discuss what accounted for the change.

"Have you seen improvements at home?" I inquired.

They had indeed made some changes. There was now a consistent bedtime, and much more of an effort to provide appropriate discipline.

As we talked, however, it became apparent that Mary Ann had made most of the changes herself. Realizing that she had few friends, she was able to adapt to the rules of social intercourse. She learned to wait her turn, share and not always insist on having her way. It was an impressive feat for a four-year-old. She had our guidance, but she did the work herself.

The conference ended with all of us thanking each other. Then the children entered the room and our splendid day with them began. The main event was baking hamantaschen.

As we gathered the ingredients on the two tables we had pushed together, I thought: *I'll bet no one has ever tried the complex recipe for these little cookies with so many tough kids before.* I was certainly wrong: there had been other difficult classes in the world before this one. It just seemed like a very large mountain at the start of the climb. We washed our hands, rolled up our sleeves and plunged in.

In a preschool classroom, the best time to bake is during free play. All the children gather around at the start. As we progress, the kids with shorter attention spans can peel off and play in the room, coming back when they want to participate. The only difficulty is that one teacher must watch the room while the other teacher assists the children who are baking.

All of us gathered around the table to begin. The first ingredients were four eggs. I had always done this part in the past, but I had recently attended a cooking-with-kids workshop where the instructor avowed that four-year-olds were good egg crackers. I decided to give it a try.

Hard-won advice to all teachers and parents: if you allow this, have a few extra eggs around. Jason and Benjamin did a fine job of cracking; they just needed help getting the egg out of the shell and into the bowl. Amanda made a good crack, but most of the egg slithered onto the floor.

She looked up at me nervously. "That was all right, wasn't it? It was a mistake."

"It's no big deal," I told her, having no idea if the recipe would still work. "We'll just use more oil."

I turned to Cathy and whispered, "Go see if you can find another egg. There are no more in the fridge, so you'll have to ask around."

She nodded. "Will you be all right here alone?"

"I think so." The answer was so truthful that we both began to laugh.

Off she went on what was sure to be a five- or ten-minute expedition. All the kids were still around the mixing bowl; I figured I could handle things until she got back. Pouring was next (oil, salt, sugar and vanilla), and they all loved that.

Just as we began, in walked our school secretary with a well-dressed man and woman.

"These are the Goldbergs, prospective parents," she announced to me from the doorway. "Barbara would like them to observe your class for a little while."

I grinned. Only God knew what it would be like in our room for the next twenty minutes. I donned my damn-the-torpedoes attitude and my best welcoming smile.

They came over and shook hands. This was a nice but infrequent gesture. Most parents sit right down and start watching, as if they're at a movie. Then they look around as if they're wondering where the popcorn is.

I greeted these folks as politely as possible.

"Hi. As you can see, we're very busy today, making hamantaschen. Please have a seat." They did, smiling. I relaxed.

I turned my attention back to the table, where the kids were doing a good job of pouring. We talked about the colors and smells of the ingredients.

Amanda commented, "Sugar and salt and flour are all white but different."

Jason said, "Ewwwww. Banilla smells yukky."

"It does," I agreed. "But vanilla *tastes* yummy. Want to try?"

I was greeted by a gaggle of Yeahs!

I poured a little vanilla into a cup.

"When I come to you, dip one finger in." The children eagerly participated, but they all thought the vanilla was "disgusting."

"You try it, Patti," said Jason.

I did. To my surprise, it had an acrid, liquorish taste.

"You're all right. It *does* taste disgusting. I must have been confusing it with something else." The kids laughed jovially at my error. By now, they thought it was a hoot when I made a mistake.

Next came the hardest part: mixing in the flour, bit by bit, until it became cookie dough. I had to do this myself, until it was almost dough. I knew they couldn't do it: either the extreme messiness would upset them or so much dough would stick to their hands that there would be nothing left in the bowl.

"Okay. This is the teacher part. I'll do the mixing in the beginning and you all can be next. Right now, though, you have to *wait* and *watch*."

Cathy returned just in time to help (without an egg, however). She poured the flour, I mixed and the children watched. Something about a mixing activity induces children to talk. Like playdough and clay, it's a social proposition. Soon Lee had made up a chant:

> "Yummy in my tummy
> Yummy in my tummy
> Mummy in my bummy
> Zummy in my lummy"

"Don't say that," Amanda told him.

"Yes—that's okay," I interjected as I mixed. "That's how you can play with words. You can't pick them up like blocks or dolls. So you can play by changing them around."

A recalcitrant strand of hair fell into my eyes. I blew on it to no avail. Cathy took pity on me and tucked it back into my scrunchie as well as she could. I went on mixing.

The children picked up Lee's chant. "Sounds nice," I said.

Harris decided to make a change.

"Yummy in my bizaboc."

Benjamin rolled his eyes. "Harris—it has to *rhyme*," he said in his best adolescent sneer.

I continued mixing amid choruses of "*Eeewww*. Look at your hands!" and "When is it going to be our turn?"

It was too long for them to wait, but with one egg less and a cold, dry day outside (the dough changes with the humidity), I had to be careful. Some children grew tired and left the table.

"I'm sorry. I know it's hard to wait. Just another minute, and then it will be your turn."

When I was finally finished, only six children were left. I turned the bowl over to them, saying, "Thank you, children. You waited very patiently." Two at a time, they dug in.

Somehow, I had forgotten to bring in the rolling pins we needed, so Cathy was off on a search again. With my hands free, however, I was able to glance around the room. I immediately noticed that all was not well with Louisa.

Something had upset her before she got to class. (The bus teacher mentioned that she had fought with Harris all the way to school.) Louisa had placed three chairs together, one for herself and one for each of the books she had brought to school. There she sat, resisting all the entreaties of her classmates to play.

As I was trying to figure out what I could do to help, Harris decided that the time was right to tease his friend. He sat in one of Louisa's chairs, directly on top of her book, and flashed her a wicked smile.

Louisa exploded. "GET OFF MY BOOK . . . GET OFF MY BOOK!" she screamed, stamping her feet and turning red. Then she began to cry.

I left the cooking table, praying that our hard-won dough wouldn't fall out of the bowl. (Sometimes you just have to trust to luck.) I spoke sternly to the Offender.

"Harris, you *must* get off Louie's book. It's *not okay* to tease her."

Harris looked up at me and smirked. I could see that he thought I'd be loath to touch him with all the dough on my hands. He figured I was helpless, but he figured wrong.

I picked him up by one arm, getting dough on his shirt, and placed him on a chair by the door.

"You're in time out, kiddo. That's no way to behave toward your good friend." Harris was too surprised to make a peep.

Meanwhile, Louisa was still sobbing, Cathy was still out of the room, the dough was being overmixed by the Conscientious Six and two strangers were watching. What was I to do first?

I turned to the observing parents. "You're getting a dose of everything today," I said, shaking my head in mock exasperation.

They laughed; okay, they were on my side. I brushed off my hands as well as I could and went over to pick up Louisa. She had stopped crying, but I couldn't get her to relax. So I tucked her on one hip and carried her over to the cooking table. At this moment, Cathy returned with two rolling pins. (It was not enough, but it was better than nothing. How *could* I have forgotten them? I chalked it up in the Nobody's Perfect column.)

"Okay," I announced, "everybody with doughy hands go wash them. And bring back a wet paper towel."

They wanted to know why.

"Because we need to clean the table. Cathy, would you please go with them?"

"Sure—come on, kids."

Some of the children spoke to Harris on their way out.

"NOOOO!" he yelled at them. Then he spoke more quietly to Jason. "Don't talk to me when I'm in time out."

"Harris is right," I told Jason. It represented a big step for Harris, in fact.

"I really like the way you said that so nicely, Harris," I said. "You may get up now." He dashed out the door after Jason, paper towel bound.

I removed everything from the cooking table so it could be washed. About ten seconds later the brigade arrived. They scrubbed away with enthusiasm: kids love to clean, if it doesn't involve their own toys. After about two minutes, the job was done. I told them to throw away their towels and get a napkin to dry the table.

As the dryers were working, Jeremy strolled in from the bathroom with Cathy at his side. His usual snail's pace had worked against him. He wanted to be a cleaner when the other kids were already drying. "I was too slow," he said, dismayed.

"That's okay, Jeremy. That very dirty corner still needs cleaning. Go work on it." He complied happily.

So there we were, five dryers and a toweler wetting whatever they dried. Eventually, the table was dry enough to spread the flour and roll out the dough. Now the cookie-cutting and filling began. Each child pressed a glass down on the dough to make a circle. Next, they put six chocolate chips in the middle, and pinched three corners to make a triangle. Then they placed their triangle on a cookie sheet and began the process again.

All the children joined us eventually. It may have been the lure of cookie-making. It may have been the fact that I didn't mind if a few chocolate chips gotten eaten along the way. Either reason was fine with me—as long as the children participated.

As we worked, someone said, "Now you see this," in a singsong manner. It reminded me of a song from the movie *The Little Mermaid*. I launched right into the first verse of "Kiss the Girl."

Usually, three- and four-year-olds will tell me to stop singing, even though I can carry a tune pretty well. To my surprise, however, everyone at the table began to sway and sing along.

"She don't say a word and she won't say a word until you *kiss* the girl!"

We were rolling the dough, singing the song and swaying to the music: "It's a Calypso Purim," I shouted out as I twirled around with one of the kids.

Benjamin changed the words to fit the activity: "Until you roll the dough."

I sang out, "Until you pinch the dough," as I helped Louie form the corners.

I had no idea what the visiting parents thought of our offbeat activity. Actually, I had forgotten their existence. They must have been pleased, though. They went right into the office and signed up for next year. More important was the fact that the hamantaschen came out of the oven a golden brown and tasted absolutely delicious!

• • •

Trouble next unfolded the following day, when Amanda and her father came to class a little earlier than usual. Although the father looked fine, the child was visibly upset. Elliott stopped to speak to another parent, but Amanda came directly to me.

"Know what? My mommy bumped her head on the closet and there was blood—a lot of blood all the way down her." She drew an imaginary line down the side of her face.

"Were you scared when you saw the blood?"

"Uh-huh—I cried and cried."

"I'll bet. That's a scary thing to see. How is Mommy now?"

"She's better, I think." Amanda paused. "I don't know."

We had gotten to the root of the problem—not just the blood, but also the uncertainty.

Luckily, Amanda's father was still in the room. "Let's ask Daddy," I said, and called him over.

Elliott downplayed the incident. Janet had somehow cut her face on the edge of the closet door. According to him, it was not too big a deal.

"Did she need stitches?" I asked him.

"Uh, we don't know yet," he admitted.

Then it *was* a big deal—the not knowing made it so. No wonder Amanda was frightened. I thanked Elliott and returned to his daughter.

Amanda and I talked about how nicely her own face had healed after the allergic reaction. I called Harris over, and he told Amanda that his daddy's stitches were better. Bodies healed, I told her. Mommy would be fine. She nodded, and went over to work on a puzzle.

Not a minute later, in walked Cory with her dad. He had an unpleasant message for me. Cory's baby-sitter Annie had flown back to Ireland for six weeks. One of her sisters was getting married, and another had just died. Cory had been told about the wedding, but not about the death.

One of our mothers, who had been listening, spoke up. "Of course, Cory's standing right here as you're talking. So she knows now."

Cory's dad didn't reply, but I did.

"That's not necessarily true. Come in, Cory."

Both her father and I were aware that because of her hearing problems, Cory didn't catch everything that was said around her. But it wasn't public knowledge. I would watch her today, and talk to her if she seemed upset. Otherwise, it was best left alone. The kid had enough to contend with this year.

Cory seemed fine. She certainly was not in any obvious pain. Jeremy, however, was a bona fide wreck. His parents had gone to Maine for four days. It was their first vacation alone since the baby's death, and it was a well-deserved one. But Jeremy didn't see it that way. He was distraught: he could barely function. He spent half the morning in Cathy's lap and the other half in mine, complaining that he missed his mommy.

In the gym, he chose to sit on me. "This just isn't my kind of day," he whispered, and burst into tears.

I rubbed his back and spoke softly.

"Jeremy, are you afraid that Mommy won't come back?"

He stopped crying to look at me intently. Then, slowly, he nodded.

I continued: "Remember the last time Mommy went away? To the hospital? The baby died, but Mommy came back. She will this time, too."

Jeremy's whole body stiffened. He refused to look at me. Clearly, this was a terrifying subject—but I pressed on.

"Jeremy, don't you know it's all right to talk about the baby? It is—it's okay. And just like Mommy came back from the hospital, she'll come back from Maine."

Every muscle in his body was tense, but he nodded slowly. I promised to tell his baby-sitter to call Mommy so he could speak to her today. We counted the days until his parents returned on Sunday; there were only two more. Jeremy hugged me, got off my lap and went slowly over to his friends.

I was shaking from tension. Cathy, who had overheard our conversation, put her hand on my shoulder.

"You really went to the heart of the matter."

"Somebody's got to do it," I answered. "And now was the right time."

She nodded in agreement, but we didn't have time for further discussion. It was One of Those Days in the gym. Amanda cut her lip. Harris got a bloody nose. Two other children bumped their heads together very hard. At one point, we had more children crying than playing. Fortunately, it was Friday.

Trouble can find a teacher, however—even if it's a weekend. On Saturday, my phone rang at 9:15 P.M. It was Jenny's father, calling from California. Peggy's mother was being taken off the respirator and would die some time that night. Jenny was very sad about her grandmother. When her father asked her what he could do to make it better for her, Jenny said that she wanted to speak to me.

I thought she just wanted to hear my voice, to touch base with reality. But it was not so. Jenny had a message for me.

"My grandma's dead," she said. "You could tell the children for me."

"You don't want to wait until you get back? Then you can tell them yourself."

"No. You tell them for me." The small voice on the other end was firm and clear. I promised to do what she asked.

We talked awhile longer about what she'd be glad to see when she came home. She missed her dress-up clothes and her friends at school the most.

"Are you sad, Jenny?"

"I just started to be sad when I started to play a game."

"What game?"

"House."

"Sure. That game reminds you of all the people in your house who you love."

"Yes."

"Just remember: no one else in your house is dying. You still have Mommy and Daddy and Ian."

"Yeah. Bye, Patti."

"I love you, honey. Go get your dad for me."

I told Jonathan about the conversation, sent condolences to Peggy and hung up hurt. Well, I told myself, we'll all feel better when Jenny's home.

• • •

On Monday morning, I called a meeting to tell the children about Jenny's grandmother. Immediately upon hearing the news, they began to fidget. Jeremy took a toy car from the shelf behind him. David and Benjamin started to make jokes. Cory began poking Avi. Jason, Harris and Lee were talking. They played, they wiggled, they futzed. And they didn't look at me.

"Wow!" said Cathy. "Look at the big-time anxiety in this room!"

"Exactly. This means that more talk, not less, is required. We'll go on."

I spoke to the children in a louder voice.

"Okay, kids. We're still in meeting. Anyone want to say anything?"

David raised his hand and I called on him.

"My best grandpa died," he said simply.

"Were you sad?"

"Yes."

"Sure. It's sad when someone you love dies because you can't see them again. Jenny will be sad, too, when she gets back to class."

Now we had the children's attention.

Benjamin spoke up. "My mommy's best grandpa died."

"Yes. That was in November."

Cory said something nearly unintelligible about one of her grandparents dying while she was in her mommy's tummy.

I nodded. "That can happen. Anyone else?" Jeremy's hand wasn't raised but I called on him anyway.

"My best grandma Sarah died. My daddy was sad."

"That was when you went to North Carolina in the fall. I remember. Cathy?"

"My grandpa died in the fall and I was very sad."

"I know you were. But sometimes people we love—grandmas and grandpas and parents—get sick, and then they get better. Harris's grandpa was in the hospital but he's better now."

Harris's eyes narrowed. "How did you know that?"

"You told me, Harris. [It wasn't like him to forget, but this was a frightening subject.] Then I spoke to your dad."

Harris nodded. "Pa's coming home and he's going to be in a wheelchair," he told us for the second time in as many weeks.

"Have you seen him yet?" I asked. Harris shook his head.

"I see." Tough stuff.

Jason joined in. "My great big grandma fell down and hurt her hip." He was speaking of his great-grandmother.

"Is she better now?" He nodded.

"Good."

David chimed in. "My best cousin Noah hurt his hip and he was in the hospital."

"Oh, I'm sorry to hear that. Is *he* better now?"

David nodded.

"I'm glad. See, children? People get sick or hurt, but they often get better."

Then Jeremy raised his hand. When I called on him, he came up to my chair, put his hand on my leg and turned to face his friends. I put my hand on his lower back for support, and held my breath.

Jeremy spoke to the children: "My mommy went to the hospital to have a baby but the baby couldn't make it and it died."

I was stunned.

The room was as silent as the bottom of a well.

I raised my fist in an involuntary gesture of victory, then glanced at Cathy. She was smiling, but her eyes were filled with tears.

I noticed that I was crying, too. *Stow it,* I told myself sternly. *You've got work to do. You can cry later.* I wiped away the tears as quickly as I could and listened to Amanda.

"What?" she was asking. She was appalled. "What happened to the baby?"

Benjamin saved me and his friend from having to answer.

"It couldn't make it," he declared.

I found my voice, thanked Benjamin and turned back to Jeremy.

"Did the baby's dying make you sad?"

"Yes. And it made my mommy very sad."

"Are you feeling better now?"

"I'm still sad. I want to have another baby so my mommy won't be sad anymore."

With that comment, Jeremy felt he was finished; he sat down in his original spot. The satisfied look on his face showed his relief as well as his pleasure. He had begun to let his burden go by talking about it. It was a shining moment for us all.

I was too overwhelmed to talk, so Cathy called on the next few children. Avi was next.

"No one in my family ever died," was his contribution.

The child had lost a grandmother and an uncle to cancer in the past year. Cathy and I looked at each other.

"I'm not touching that one," she whispered.

"No. We'll just mention it to his mother, so he knows it's okay to talk about it."

Cory raised her hand. Out poured the story of the big death in her life.

"Mary Elizabeth's daddy died. Because he was very old and very sad."

"And very sick," I added. (The man had died of stomach cancer.)

"No. Not sick. And Mary Elizabeth was so sad."

"Is she feeling better now?"

"No, she's sad again."

"Well, it's good that she has you to help her feel better. And that's what we have to do for Jenny."

I asked if the children had ideas for helping Jenny. They decided that we could hug her, kiss her, play with her and make her laugh.

"But Jenny's shy," said Amanda.

"So we have to work a little harder. But we can do it because we all love Jenny, right?"

Everyone nodded. It was time for gym, and I said so. I couldn't handle any more, even if they could.

As we went upstairs, I looked at my watch. The entire discussion—momentous and magnificent—had taken just seven minutes.

• • •

At dismissal that day, Sharon asked Cory who was picking her up.

Cory replied, "A new sitter—a friend of Annie's. She had to go away because her sister died. But she's coming back."

So much for secrets.

• • •

Later that week, I was able to talk to Jeremy's mother. We hadn't seen her since she returned from Maine. After exchanging pleasantries, Carolyn said, "I understand Jeremy had a hard time while I was gone."

"Yes," I answered. "He spent a lot of time on our laps. He was afraid you wouldn't come back. But I told him that you would, just like you did from the hospital."

Carolyn nodded. "He told me, 'Patti said mommies and daddies always come back. And she was right.'"

I thought: That must be why he talked about the baby. I said it was okay. If I was right once, I was probably right twice.

I went a bit further.

"Carolyn, Jeremy mentioned the baby on Monday."

Carolyn was genuinely surprised. "He did? In what context?"

I explained the subject of our class meeting. Then I told her exactly what Jeremy had said, closing with the idea of her having another baby so she'd be happy again.

"But he knows I'm better," she said.

"I'm sure. I just thought you should have this information."

She paused. "Remember what he said to me last month. That it would be okay if I had another baby?"

I nodded. "Now we know why."

I refrained from giving advice. I just hoped that she'd be able to talk to him on her own. At any rate, Jeremy had taken a great leap; now his family knew about it, too.

We received further evidence that our discussions were beginning to take hold in the minds and hearts of the children. David's mother approached me at dismissal.

"David is very concerned about Jenny," she told me.

"We all are," I agreed.

"He told me about Jenny's grandmother. I guess you talked about it in class?"

"Along with everything else that's happened this year. Does David have a cousin Noah who hurt his hip?"

She nodded in amazement. "David told me that it's good to talk about your problems. It makes you feel better. I asked if his teachers told him that and he said yes. That's a very important lesson to learn."

I smiled at Sabrina. It was good to know our message was sinking in.

APRIL: FLOWERS AND SHOWERS

The following Monday, Jenny returned. It was a holiday in our classroom: we hugged and kissed her; everyone smiled and laughed. No hero ever received a finer welcome.

Cathy and I gave Jenny all the kudos of the day: she fed the gerbils, and she was leader all morning. (These were the first things she told her mother at dismissal.) But it was the children who did the best job of making Jenny feel comfortable. They never left her alone. They included her in any game they were playing. They hugged her frequently and said how happy they were to have her back. Even the boys who didn't know her very well tried as hard as the girls to welcome Jenny home.

As we watched the class, Cathy turned to me. "It's just unbelievable how they remembered what we said at meeting last week. They're doing everything we talked about."

I was pleased. "They took our discussion seriously. They've truly learned the importance of taking care of each other."

"They have such big hearts."

"They do. And it's a good thing, given the difficult year we're having."

"Maybe this is the end of all the trouble."

"Maybe. We've got a class that can handle whatever comes up, though."

• • •

What came up next was the issue of Benjamin's lies. That very day, at playtime, he came over to me.

"Harris bit that rubber puzzle and he ripped it," was the complaint.

Harris vehemently denied the accusation.

I looked from one face to the other. No clues there: both boys had their "clear-eyed sincerity" faces on. I decided to use the situation as an object lesson.

"Well, who can *ever* believe you, Benjamin, when you lie so much?" I said to him. "You're the child who said you fell out of a plane, and whose foot was bitten by a shark. If you tell lies all the time, how can I believe you're telling the truth now?"

Benjamin squirmed. He was saved from answering, however, by Cathy.

"Hmmm," she said, holding up the puzzle in question. "It would appear from the puzzle that Benjamin *is* telling the truth this time. It's wet, and it has teeth marks."

We both repressed laughter. Benjamin looked mollified; Harris chagrined.

Our "punishment" for Harris was to help fix the puzzle and then to put all the pieces back in it. To our surprise—and his— he was terrific at it. (He hadn't approached the puzzles after we had set out the more difficult ones.) He stayed at the table enjoying his newfound skill until cleanup.

The following morning, Benjamin's parents came in for their conference. We spoke of their child's extreme intelligence and his unbelievably mature sense of humor. We told them that Benjamin's sense of well-being had improved dramatically: he never seemed overconcerned with his health or his safety anymore. We emphasized his wonderful progress in many areas, especially his new interest in art.

Then we told the story of the puzzle. All four of us laughed, but they were well aware of the problem. Benjamin was lying at home, too.

"You found a good way to handle it," said Benjamin's father, Bennett. "We'll try that at home."

What we really needed to do, I told them, was talk about the reason for the lies.

At this critical juncture, our lack of preparation foiled us. Cathy and I knew Benjamin so well that we had neglected to plan for the conference. We hadn't talked about what we were going to say. It was a mistake with long-lasting consequences.

"Why do you think Benjamin lies so frequently?" I asked his parents.

Cathy interjected, "It's a sort of testing."

Benjamin's mother, Francine, readily agreed.

I was not happy. That wasn't the answer I wanted them to consider. Now I was starting from behind the eight ball. The "testing" theory was wrong, but it had just been sanctioned by one of the teachers.

I thought: What a horrible mistake. This is why you discuss the kid with your colleague before *the conference.*

I said: "There may be some testing involved here. But testing what?"

"The boundaries of acceptable behavior," replied Cathy. (I threw her a warning look, and she stopped talking.)

"My patience," laughed Francine.

I continued: "Umm, it seems to be more of an attention-getting ploy. Here in school, he lies when he wants to be noticed. You've said he's a very good big brother, but somewhere he has got to be jealous and resentful of the new baby. I believe this is how it's coming out."

Francine replied, "He doesn't exhibit any of those feelings."

Something inside me sank. There was no way I was going to reach these people now. I tried again, though.

"But he lies all the time and he gets too angry about other stuff. Those are the feelings coming out in another way. If you talk to him about the fact that it's okay to have negative feelings about the baby, you may find some of the other symptoms alleviated."

I'll give Francine credit. She looked me right in the eye and said, "Okay. We'll try it." But I didn't think either of them believed me. I could barely contain my frustration.

To our mutual relief, Bennett changed the subject: why was Benjamin so much more difficult to handle after Bennett came home from one of his frequent business trips?

I tried to explain the answer. It was psychological in nature, and after my first failure, I wasn't sure I could get my point across.

"Benjamin behaves well when you're away because it's too scary not to. In the magical thinking of young children, if he's bad, you may not come back. Once you're back and it's safe, he can show the anger he feels at your being away."

I suggested a week-by-week chart, so he could have some knowledge (and hence, some *control*) of where his father was and when he'd be back. That idea went over well. I felt a little better.

Bennett had one more question, and it was a terrific one. "Why is it that issues we thought were settled—like separation—keep coming up again?"

I explained the jagged progress of childhood. There are cycles of anxiety-provoking growth followed by relative calm, as the child integrates what he or she has learned. Some researchers say that these cycles are six months in duration. From my experience, they're yearly. You've heard of "the terrible twos"? Four-year-olds are harder, six-year-olds harder still, and by eight, you want to tear out your hair—or theirs. (This is why all third-grade teachers deserve an express train to heaven when they're ready to go.)

The major issues—separation, dealing with death, self-control, learning to become a social being, etc.—come up again and again. But children have better skills for dealing with them as they get older.

"That's good to know," Bennett said. "So Benjamin may have separation problems next year in his new school?"

"Yes," I replied. "And they could come in December or January." Implicit in this discussion were the words *"And it won't be your fault."* I didn't have to say them, but they were there just the same.

The conference ended on a mutually complimentary note. They told us how much Benjamin loved coming to school, and we told them how much we loved Benjamin. Who wouldn't?

As Francine and Bennett left, the children poured in, so I had no chance to talk to Cathy. I was stuck with my feelings of frustration and failure. In a way, it was a blessing; I might have yelled at her for something that was entirely my fault.

I wasn't a very attentive teacher that morning. Luckily, the kids didn't need very much. They were doing splendidly all by themselves. And we did have a golden moment. Amanda walked over to where I was sitting and leaned up against me. She wanted to tell me something important.

"You know the lion in *The Wizard of Oz*?"

I nodded.

"He's lost his luggage."

I had to think about that one for a moment.

"Oh. You mean he's lost his *courage*. The words sound alike, don't they? Yes, and he's very unhappy about it until the Wizard helps him get it back."

I kept talking and I did *not* crack a smile. That way, sensitive little Amanda was not embarrassed. Instead, she nodded, and walked away repeating "Luggage . . . courage . . . luggage . . . courage."

I was pleased that I had not gone for the joke. My first thought had been, *Well, it's not that far to the Emerald City. All he really needs is a toothbrush.*

When the day ended, I was able to have a conversation with Cathy. I wasn't sure how to bring up the subject of the conference without hurting her feelings, but I knew it had to be done.

"Cathy, about Benjamin's conference . . . It didn't go exactly the way I had hoped."

Cathy wanted to know what was wrong. She felt it had gone very well.

"Most of it did. But the part about the lying didn't work so well. You and I were contradicting each other."

I asked if I had ever explained to her my theory about Benjamin's lying being tied into sibling rivalry. She said I hadn't.

I could hardly believe it, yet I knew it was true. It was one of those cases of forgetting to tell an important fact to someone you're very close to. You just assume you've done it.

Cathy was apologetic. "I'm so sorry. I messed up the conference."

"No you didn't. It was my fault for not preparing us adequately. Maybe we'll luck out, and have another chance to discuss the subject during the year."

That chance came much sooner than we expected. A few days later, Benjamin's brother Aaron became ill. His fever went up to one hundred and five and he wasn't breathing well. He was only a year old, so it was very frightening for the entire family. When Francine brought Benjamin to school, she looked frazzled. After a minute, she bent to kiss her son good-bye.

"I have to go now, Benjamin. I must get right back to Aaron."

I knew that she was exhausted and worried. Who wouldn't be? But she had forgotten what I'd said about Benjamin's jealousy of the baby. Benjamin proceeded to prove my point.

He hung on to his mother, wailing, "NO! Please don't go!"

"What's going on here, Benjamin?" asked his mother. "This isn't like you. I *must* get right home to your baby brother. You know how sick he is."

Naturally, this line of reasoning only increased Benjamin's distress. He wailed even louder and clung to his mother's leg. She determinedly walked to the door, dragging Benjamin along.

"Benjamin, I don't understand why you're acting this way. I must get home to Aaron." Each mention of his brother sent Benjamin's cries up a decibel in sound and urgency.

I had to intervene: this could have continued for an hour. I hadn't wished to interfere, but I had to do so for the sake of the child.

I spoke in a low, nonthreatening voice, even though I was across the room.

"Francine. Don't say that again."

"Oh. I see." And she kissed her son. "Benjamin, I have to go, but I'll be back to get you at dismissal. Would you like that?"

Benjamin nodded. I called out: "Benjamin, come finish your placemat with me." He came right over, looking relieved to be out of the struggle. His mother hurried out the door.

While he was working, Benjamin told me how Aaron had been awake all night, and how the baby's crying had disturbed him. He was tired. Anyone could see, however, that he was happy to be in school.

In fact, he was doing very well here. So were all the children. Spring had worked its annual miracle: our students were blooming. Now that they were older and could concentrate for longer periods of time, we were able to put their sprightly intelligence to work. In the small room with a blackboard where we had often played "Aiken Drum," I began more difficult lessons about shapes, numbers and letters. One day we had a glorious experience.

"Draw the train," they shouted, as I began to write on the board.

"Okay." I drew three large rectangles touching each other horizontally. On top of the one to the right, I drew two smaller vertical rectangles.

"What are all these shapes?" I asked.

"Rectangles!" yelled Jason. My "guessing never hurts" system was working well.

"Right!" I said.

"But it can't run without wheels," someone protested.

"Right again," and I added four semicircles to the bottom of the train.

"Those are circles," declared Cory.

"No, they're half-circles," corrected Amanda.

"No, no, they're circles. Just the other part is hidden," explained Benjamin.

That was a very sophisticated answer to come from a child of four. I followed it up by placing another circle on the board, and covering it with my hand to show what Benjamin was talking about. Then I placed an actual semicircle below the circle.

"It looks like a D!" shouted Jason excitedly.

"D is for Donner," said Louisa, referring to her last name.

"D is for Daddy," added Mary Ann.

Their small faces were shining from the intoxication of learning. Cathy and I looked at each other in amazement.

I continued: "The train is starting so I have to put in a driver."

"No—an engineer," said Harris. "He drives a train."

"You're right, Harris. Thanks for reminding me." I drew a little triangle in the engineer's seat. This was Tommy Triangle, their favorite shape in the game. Since he always drove the train, we had given him a name.

"The train is going to the right," announced Amanda.

"How do you know?" Cathy asked her.

"Because right is that way." She pointed correctly.

"Which way would it be going if it went the other way?"

"Oh, then it would drive right into that wall." It was a perfect answer from a child who didn't know the word for "left."

The passengers on the train were different shapes; today we had a square, a trapezoid, an oval and two inverted triangles.

The kids wanted to know why I had drawn the triangles upside down. I explained that triangles could be upside down or "regular, like Tommy." They didn't buy it.

"But why are they standing on their heads?" asked Harris.

"You tell me."

"Because you *drew* them that way," replied Jason with exasperation.

"Okay." The concept was too hard: it was time to move along. So I drew legs on their tops, told the kids they liked to sleep this way, and put a baseball cap on Tommy because he had just been to a Yankee game.

"I want a hot dog," said Lee, with a certain logic.

"Time for lunch then," I replied, and the game was over.

• • •

Despite our difficulties during the year, our children had really learned the power of words, as four-year-olds do. Two short discussions during snack proved the point:

> LEE: Can I have your cracker?
> HARRIS: No.
> LEE: Then I'm not coming to your house.
> HARRIS: That's okay. Snow White is coming.
> LEE (starting to cry): *I want to come!*

One day, I was handing out animal crackers. Harris picked one up and "walked" it over to Sharon.

"Will you marry me? I'm a girl."

"You're a girl?" I asked. "Then I'm a frog."

"I'm a chicken," said Benjamin.

"I'm an egg," added Cory.

"I'm a goat," laughed Jenny.

Harris got the message.

"Will you marry me?" he asked Sharon again. "I'm a boy."

• • •

Meanwhile, Benjamin was using his words to express his continued suffering at home. After a week, his little brother was still sick. The baby's fever continued, and he had developed a terrible cough, which Benjamin claimed kept the whole family up at night. He revealed all this to Cathy at the playdough table. Cathy told him how sorry she was.

"It's really hard for me to be a good big brother all the time," Benjamin told her. "It hurts my bones and my muscles."

"I know exactly how you feel," said Cathy (the oldest of three sisters).

Neither of us had ever mentioned the difficulties associated with big brotherhood to Benjamin. This was a spontaneous outburst. We glanced at each other, relieved to hear this appropriate emotion emerge. Perhaps more truth would mean less lying.

The conversation took an interesting turn. Cathy explained all the fine points of being the big brother. Benjamin could do so much more than Aaron. Benjamin disagreed with her on every point.

"You can eat more foods than Aaron."

"But he doesn't eat baby food anymore. He gets pieces of grown-up food."

"He can't wear the big clothes you wear."

"But they're the same kind now. Aaron has undershirts just like mine but smaller. No snaps anymore."

"He doesn't go to school."

"Yes he does," Benjamin insisted. "One day a week he goes to baby school."

Cathy looked up at me. "Can you believe this?" she mouthed.

I shook my head and came over. This family had done a conscientious job of setting their children up as equals. But it just wasn't so. Benjamin needed to feel the advantages of being the oldest so he wouldn't mind the disadvantages as much.

I leaned over the table where he and Cathy were working.

"Benjamin, can Baby Aaron come to *this* school and be in *this* class?"

"No." He smiled.

"Can he walk?" He smiled more broadly. "No."

"Can he play running games with his friends?" added Cathy.

"No." Now we saw an ear-to-ear grin.

"Can he bake hamantaschen? Can he sing any of our songs? Can he have a conversation with his friends?" I asked.

"No, no!" Benjamin replied excitedly.

"That's right. He'll be able to do these things some day, but not now. You're the big brother and you can do a lot more fun things than Baby Aaron can."

Benjamin gave me a big, hard hug.

...

After a few days, Benjamin's father brought us the news that Aaron had definitely improved. With this in mind, I asked both Bennett and Benjamin to sit down at a table with me. By previous arrangement, Cathy took control of the rest of the class. Now that the baby was out of danger, it was time to tell Bennett what his son had said about how hard it was to be a good big brother all the time.

"Actually, we just bought him a toy yesterday for being so good while Aaron has been sick."

"That's great, because it's a hard thing to do. Benjamin is really entitled to that toy." I mentioned Benjamin's comment about being good really hurting his bones and his muscles.

Benjamin piped up: "I never said that."

I was stunned. Never in all my years of teaching had I seen a child contradict himself with such urgency.

"Yes you did, Benjamin. And do you know how I remember?"

"How?" he asked

"Because I have a big book at home called a journal where I write everything down. And this conversation is in it."

"Oh," he said. But he didn't change his story.

Luckily, Bennett believed me. He had seen Benjamin deny

the truth too often. "What shall we do? Just talk him through it?"

"Yes. He needs acknowledgment that being a good big brother is hard sometimes. Because it is."

"No it's not," insisted Benjamin.

There was no use continuing the conversation. I hoped I'd convinced the father; I certainly hadn't made a dent in Benjamin's armor. I ended the discussion feeling as frustrated as ever.

As Bennett left, he mentioned that Aaron's illness had been diagnosed as asthma. I told him I was sorry, but when I thought about it later, I wasn't. I was glad that Aaron had a chronic illness to match Benjamin's "cholesterol problem." They would both live and be well, with medication. And Aaron wouldn't be the "healthy kid" to Benjamin's "sick kid." For once, it truly *was* a fair deal.

I mentioned my frustration over Benjamin's sibling problem to Barbara Gold in her office one afternoon. I was filling her in on the later conferences, as I was required to do. She gave me some advice that I will never forget:

"Patti, you enjoy helping children with their emotional needs. And you're very good at it. But you must remember that you aren't going to be able to help everyone. It's just not possible. Some of them are going to slip through your fingers. You can't get so upset over 'the ones that got away.'"

It was superb advice. I'd heard variations on the theme before; Maggie used to tell me not to set such high standards for myself. But this time I not only understood the words—I accepted them. It was enough to be the best teacher I could be. Because no matter what I did, no matter how hard I tried, I couldn't save all the children.

• • •

April rolled along. We had our share of difficulties (Cory's brother's condition slipped a bit; Jeremy's cousin was diagnosed with leukemia), but the children in our classroom were flourishing. They were a tight-knit group. Now that they could speak their minds, they were able to handle most of their own disputes. The teachers stepped more into the background: we mediated far more than we disciplined. It was pure joy to watch the children soar off on their own.

At lunch one day, we overheard a delightful conversation which demonstrated their newfound desire to figure out a problem by using their words.

CORY: My mommy says she's fat and she exercises all the time.
AMANDA: My mommy is fat.
MARY ANN: My mommy is skinny.
LEE: My mommy is the fattest in the whole world.
AVI: My mommy is fat because she has a baby in her tummy.
LOUISA: The first thing I did when I got borned was make a peepee on my baby warmer!
AMANDA: When you have a baby, it comes out of your tushy.
MARY ANN: No it doesn't. My mommy says it comes out of your vagina.
CORY: My mommy also says a baby comes out of your tushy.

The kids were at an impasse, so they looked up at Cathy.

CATHY: Mary Ann's right, kids.
BENJAMIN: If a baby comes out of your vagina, it must hurt. Does it bleed?
CATHY: A little. But it stops quickly and you get better right away.

MARY ANN (thinking out loud): Boys can't have babies. They don't have vaginas.
CORY: That's right. They only have penises.
AMANDA (musing): If boys had a baby come out of their penises, it would have to be very skinny.

Cathy couldn't help laughing. Naturally, the children wanted to know what was so funny. They had been hard at work on an important problem. Cathy wisely told them that some things are funny to grown-ups but not to children.

At roof time, we saw the same kind of discussion. Five minutes of negotiating preceded every two minutes of play. Here's a sample:

Six or seven kids gathered on the roof to decide which game to play. They all began talking at once. Sharon called them to order using my technique: "One, two, three, *shhhhh!*" It worked, so she became the leader.

"All right [pronounced "white"], we're playing 'Peter Pan.' I'm Wendy. Who wants to play Peter?"

"I do," said someone. (I wasn't close enough to hear who it was. If I got any closer, they would be too self-conscious to continue.)

"No, I do," insisted Cory.

"There could be two," said Mary Ann graciously. (Hooray!)

"I'm Wendy, too," said Jenny.

"No. You be Tinker Bell," came from Mary Ann.

"Okay," replied Jenny. She looked happy about the shift.

"I'm a pirate!" shouted Harris.

"I'm a pirate, too!" Lee chimed in.

"Who's Hook?" asked Sharon. "Amanda, will you be Hook?"

"Noooo. I'm never going to be a bad guy again. I'm Peter. Let's go!" And the game began.

Nobody bothered to resolve the contradictions inherent in three Wendys, three Pans and no Hook. They all just ran around the roof for a few minutes. Harris, Lee and Jason yelled, "Yo Ho!" as they ran. All the Peters flew by, running with their arms out. The game took less time than the negotiation. Nothing was accomplished; everyone was satisfied.

Amanda's decision to leave the "bad guy" roles to others was the result of a recent experience on the roof. She had finally achieved her first "time out." She and Jason had been pretending to fight as part of a "Peter Pan" game. Harris saw them, and decided to come to Amanda's rescue. (She was doing quite well without him, but he had a wild crush on her.) When Harris entered the fray, the fight became serious. I separated them all, and had them sit on the sidelines ten feet apart.

"You're in time out for fighting," I told them.

Jason and Harris accepted their fate: they were quite familiar with time outs. Amanda, however, began to cry piteously.

"But I didn't hit! He started it, not me!"

"As a matter of fact, that's not true. You started at the same time. And you know the rules: YOU HIT, YOU SIT."

She sat there, hunched over. "Is this what it's like?" she moaned. "How long do I have to stay here?" She was sad, but she was interested, too.

"When do we get up?" she called to Harris.

"I'm going to give her time to really enjoy this," I laughingly told Cathy.

"Yeah," she agreed. "The kid's been wanting to be in time out for so long."

I let her sit long enough to get the flavor of being disciplined. I released Harris and Jason. Then I went over to our little villainess. I gave her the standard line.

"Amanda?"

"Yes?" She looked up at me through teary eyes.

"Can you remember not to fight with anyone else?"

"Yes."

"Then as soon as you've stopped crying *completely,* you may get up."

"Okay."

It took her one second to cheer up. She flew to the other side of the roof with an expression of utter delight. Time out was no longer an object of concern to her: she had met the enemy and it wasn't so terrible after all.

• • •

The coming of spring brought more than the annual blessing of the children's maturity. It also brought our most beautiful holiday, Passover. Each year we told the story of how our ancestors left Egypt, and celebrated the event with a special meal called a Seder. The children would have Seders in their own homes on Passover, and hear the entire story of the Exodus. In school, the story was aimed at their level of understanding. The Egyptian Pharaoh was mean, but he didn't hurt anyone. There were plagues, but no one died. The main thrust of the story was that the Jewish people were in bondage, and they became free, with the help of Moses and God.

Slavery was a difficult concept to convey to a child of three or four. Every year, I refined my story in the attempt to make it clearer.

Once, I began by saying that Passover was a holiday about being free. A child sang out, "Patti—I'm free and a half!" (Referring to her age—three and a half—with her customary lisp.)

The following year I spoke of slavery, using the words to a song we sing. "The Jews had to work every day and every night with their tools. There was hammering and shoveling . . ."

"And screwing!" a boy said brightly.

My assistant doubled over with laughter. I thought for a moment.

"Oh . . . you mean with screwdrivers?"

The child nodded. Bingo.

"No, honey; there were no screwdrivers way back then."

I couldn't imagine anything so funny happening this year. After the first two sentences of the story, our children had become frightened. Cathy and I were pummeled with questions. Were the Jews going to be okay by the end of the story? Was the mean Pharaoh still alive? Could he hurt us?

Never before had a class had so much anxiety over the beginning of the Passover story. They may have been overly worried due to the terrible events of the year. On the other hand, they may just have been better at expressing their fears because they'd had so much experience talking about their emotions.

We answered as reassuringly as we could. Pharaoh had been dead a long, long time and the Jews were happy at the end of the story. (No need to bother with disturbing current events—but the situation in the Middle East did make it harder to answer with a straight face.) I went on to explain exactly what it meant to be a slave.

"You have to work all the time, in the day and in the night. You never get paid for your work. If you want to take a day off, you can't . . ."

"Hmm. Could be a mommy," said Benjamin.

It was too much, and too true.

We discussed the story of the Exodus, and then we acted it out in the classroom. Two rest mats served as the Red Sea. The children were all slaves, and Cathy was Pharaoh in his chariot, chasing them. As the Jews reached the sea, the child appointed as Moses stretched out his staff (a block) and I moved the mats apart. All the children walked between them to the other side of the room. When "Pharaoh" tried to cross, I brought the mats together.

"Pharaoh and his men could not pass, and the Jews were saved!" I told the children. They cheered spontaneously. *It was fun being God,* I thought; usually I'm just the boss.

Walking between the mats clarified the story of the escape for these kids. They acted it out with the mats in the gym over and over. The happy ending seemed to fortify the entire class.

I said as much to Samuel Cohen when he dropped off his son the next day.

"They've had so many hard things happen this year. I think a happy ending is really a help for them."

It was a rare lapse for me. I never discussed how much stress was in the classroom. It would be too frightening for the parents to know the full extent of the children's problems.

Samuel wasn't sure. "Maybe it's just that you're hearing more about it this year."

"No, it's not," I insisted. "It's just a very unusual situation."

"But you give them a chance to deal with it."

"Yes, of course. By now they can almost do it themselves. They really understand that when something bad happens, they need to talk about it."

"That's good," he said. He sounded only half-convinced.

I'll never know what made me bring up the subject with Samuel that day, but I'll always be grateful. At least he was somewhat prepared. Not two hours later, I was holding the bloody face of his son.

David had been running on the carpeted floor of the gym. No other child was anywhere near him. (How could they be? No one could catch him when he turned on the speed.) As he glanced backward at Benjamin, David tripped over his own feet. He landed head first on a perfectly benign piece of plastic gym equipment. Because of his speed and the odd angle of his fall, David broke his nose.

He was only a foot away from me. If I'd known what was going to happen, I could have reached out and grabbed him. I was practically *next* to him, for God's sake. But there was no warning, so there was no chance to intervene.

The crack of David's nose on the equipment was loud enough to be heard across the entire gym. The other kids flocked to us. As I bent to pick David up, blood gushed out of his nose. There is a lot of blood with any injury to the head, but this was unusual: somewhere between a nosebleed and a major injury. It poured over David's hands and clothes, and over mine as well.

The children gathered around us, too frightened to make noise. I held David's head straight up while Cathy ran to get the tissue box. She wiped away the first blood from David's face, then gave me a new batch of tissues to catch the rest. We couldn't apply direct pressure as well as we wished: there was a large piece of bone where none had been before. It hadn't broken the skin, but we were afraid to touch it. We just caught whatever blood came out.

When the other children could no longer see the blood gushing, they found their voices.

"What happened to David?" they asked in concert.

"He banged his nose," I said calmly. (I'm very good in a crisis; I fall apart later.)

"How did he do it?"

"He fell on that banana." I pointed to the yellow, curved piece of equipment we called by that nickname. It had been in the gym for as long as I had worked here, and had never given us any trouble. I felt bad to see its reputation ruined on a fluke. People have crazy thoughts during a crisis.

Harris looked at my hand and David's shirt.

"What's *that*?" He pointed. "Is it *blood*?"

I said: "Yes. When you get any cut on your face or head, it always bleeds a lot."

I thought: Not this much, though. We were on our third batch of tissues.

Cathy had gone down to call David's parents. She returned with an ice pop wrapped in cellophane to hold on David's nose. This was our standard procedure, to bring down the swelling.

It clearly wasn't going to do the trick in this case. The bleeding slowed down to a trickle but the bump remained. It was beginning to turn black and blue.

"His nose is broken," Cathy whispered to me.

I'd never seen it happen to a four-year-old: their noses were almost all cartilage. But it certainly *looked* broken.

Amanda noticed. "What's wrong with him?" she asked, genuinely frightened. "Is he going to be all right?"

I looked into nine pairs of eyes filled with rising panic.

"Look," I said lightly. "Is David going to die?"

"Nooooo." They giggled at the question.

"Is he going to have to stay in the hospital?"

"Nooooo."

"Right. The most he'll do is go and see the doctor. He'll be okay. And now he is going to eat his ice pop."

As David munched, the children talked about the ice pops they'd eaten when they'd gotten hurt. Lee had hurt his lip. Jason couldn't remember what he'd hurt.

"It was your chin," Amanda told him. She forgot nothing.

In a few minutes, we returned to the classroom, to be met by David's parents. They gathered up their son, thanked us for our care and left the room in a hurry. They had an appointment with a surgeon.

David, in remarkably good spirits, waved good-bye to his friends. We took the class to the bathroom, and they emerged looking very worried. I sat them down in a row just outside the bathroom door.

Benjamin was hunched up by the door with his arms around his knees. "Are you upset about David?" I asked him. He nodded tightly.

"Well, I don't blame you. He's one of your best friends. Is anyone else worried about David?"

Amanda responded: "I'm sad about David"—she held up two fingers an inch apart—"just this little bit."

Others nodded.

"He's going to the doctor now," I told them. "He'll be okay." That was the best I could do for them.

No one mentioned David again that day. It was all any of us could take. It was enough.

• • •

That night, I called the Cohen home. Sabrina answered. They had seen the surgeon; the injury was worse than they thought. David had broken a bone, deviated his septum and incurred a hematoma. He was scheduled for outpatient surgery—under general anesthesia—the following day at noon.

My heart froze. *Surgery. Some kids don't even survive the anesthesia.*

"I'm so sorry, Sabrina," was all I could say.

"Don't be sorry. No one blames you. David told me what happened. It couldn't be helped."

"I know it wasn't my fault, but it was on my watch."

Sabrina told me of a freak accident with her elder son which had happened while she was standing right next to him. Eli had needed seventy stitches in his forehead. Then, as if she had read my mind, she told me that David had already undergone general anesthesia when he had tubes placed in his ears to improve his hearing. She said everything would be all right.

She was comforting *me*.

I thanked her, and asked her to let us know when David was out of surgery. She promised to call the school as soon as possible. I wished her good luck and hung up.

In bed that night, I tossed and turned. The last thing I saw before I finally fell asleep was a small, dark-haired boy falling past me. I tried to grab him—he was tantalizingly near. I touched him, but I couldn't manage to hold on. He slipped through my fingers and continued to fall down, down toward a destination I could not see.

• • •

I awoke the next morning with a pit in my stomach which was roughly the size of a grapefruit. I had no room for breakfast. *This is how you're gonna feel until the kid is out of surgery,* I told myself. *So pull yourself together and go help his classmates.*

Cathy and I met for a few minutes before school to discuss what to tell the children. David would be an outpatient, so we decided not to use the words "operation," "surgery" or "hospital." David was having his nosed fixed by a doctor today. He would be back in school soon. Cathy suggested that we make get-well cards for David. It was a great idea—a therapeutic activity for us all.

As the children filed into our room, Cathy took them to the art table while I told the parents what had occurred. Most of them hadn't heard; all of them were distressed.

"How are you going to handle it?" was a common question.

I explained, and promised to send a note home if anything changed. I don't know if I succeeded in appearing calm: I certainly wasn't.

But the day went well. The children had no questions about our explanation. When Benjamin mentioned that David would be in the hospital, I said that he was only visiting the hospital. He'd be home later. I told them that they could call David's house tonight to see how he was.

We all enjoyed making the cards. Mary Ann drew a funny picture of David with a smokestack on his head. Each child dictated a message. Lee's was "Have a nice picture!" Most kids said, "I love you" or "Please get better." I punched holes in all the pictures and bound them into a book, using yarn. Then we read the book to the children. They thought it was funny and beautiful—and they were right. Later, I gave it to David's baby-sitter when she came to pick up his brother, who was in another class. It would be there when he came home.

Sabrina called the school at three o'clock to say that David was in recovery. The operation had gone well. They had repaired the septum, straightened the bone as well as they could and left the hematoma untouched. David's nose would look a little different, but he would be fine.

I went home and took a long nap—the sleep of the grateful and relieved. At 7 P.M., when I thought it was decent, I called the Cohen household. Lo and behold, David answered the phone! He sounded fine, and was in no pain. He just wasn't happy with the big bandage on his nose.

Sabrina spoke next. David would be unable to come to school for ten days, while the bone was setting. (This was okay, as we had a ten-day vacation coming up at the end of the week.) He could join our Seder on Friday, but only if a parent came along. The hardest thing was keeping him apart from his brother at the moment. David felt so good that he wanted to play! I was relieved beyond description.

Sabrina then thanked me for our book. Their housekeeper had handed it to David as soon as he walked in the door. His brother had read it to him, and "they had laughed and laughed at the smokestack part." It was the first thing he showed any visitors. I promised I'd tell the children, and hung up feeling lighter than air. It was over.

The next morning I learned that there wasn't much to tell. Most of the kids had spoken to David just as I had. We concentrated instead on finishing our preparations for the Seder meal.

On Friday, we were disappointed to learn that David would not be joining us: he was too embarrassed by the big bandage. The children would have to wait until after vacation to see for themselves that he was truly recovered.

Sharon was particularly disappointed. She asked if we could send some of our Passover food home to David "so he wouldn't miss anything." At our beautiful Seder, she reminded us to fill up a plate for her friend. She and her baby-sitter dropped it off at David's house on their way home from school.

This was an unusual reaction from a child who was not particularly close to David. But I didn't wonder about it then. I was busy with Passover preparations in my own home, as well. The first three days of my vacation were devoted to cooking and cleaning for the holiday. During the next week I relaxed, and tried my best not to think about school at all.

• • •

We returned to class near the end of April. Cathy, who had been away, looked tan and healthy. The children looked terrific; they all seemed to have grown at least an inch. David, perfectly recovered, was as handsome as ever. The difference in his nose was imperceptible.

This, unfortunately, was not the case with Sharon. She came in walking behind her parents: they mentioned that there had been "an incident" yesterday. I asked what had happened.

Sharon stepped out so that I could see her face. Her nose was a mass of scrapes. When she smiled, I could see dried blood around her two upper front teeth. Sharon told me that she had fallen onto the sidewalk while waiting for a bus with her sitter. I said I was sorry to hear it, but that she'd soon be better. Then I handed her off to Cathy, so I could talk to her parents.

"I have to ask you . . ." Karen began, "could this possibly be an accident?"

I reviewed the facts silently. Sharon had been quite upset by David's accident. She had talked about the blood a great deal. She had even asked to take him food from our Seder. I didn't think there was anything accidental in her behavior. Now— what should I tell the parents?

I looked at Karen's worried face. She could handle the truth. She was strong and smart, and she was asking a direct question. Besides, the answer wasn't so terrible.

I shook my head. "There's not much chance it was accidental," I said. "This is the girl who was called a 'wet baby' and peed in her pants an hour later."

"I didn't know that."

"Yes you did. It's just been a while."

"Well, I think you're right about the accident," Karen said. "Sharon's been trying to do it all week. She's been falling off sofas, chairs, our bed. I asked her what was going on, but she couldn't say."

I thought: Why didn't she tell me these facts before *she asked for my opinion? Is this a quiz?*

I said: "Look, it makes sense. David's accident was traumatic for these kids because they saw it. There was a lot of blood."

"I know. That's what scared Sharon. She couldn't really talk about it until she'd had her own accident. But she got it all out yesterday."

"Good. Then she's accomplished her goal. So it's done, and it's fine."

"Is it?" Karen asked me. "Is it normal to do this?"

The real issue had appeared at last. Abnormality is the hidden fear of every parent.

"Karen, for any young child, 'normal' has a very, very wide range. Sharon needed to accomplish this for her own health. It's fine."

Karen nodded. "Also, I was thinking that she may be overreacting because she underreacted to her own surgery in the fall."

"Sounds right to me," I replied.

Karen turned to her husband, who had not yet said a word. "Patti says it's okay."

He didn't need to be told; he had heard the entire conversation. He laughed and put a hand on her shoulder.

"Good. So relax." And I believe she did.

After the Sonfelds had gone, I related the story to Cathy.

"Well," she replied. "Looks like it's time for another meeting."

We held it right before dismissal, when everyone was seated on a chair. I asked Sharon to come up and tell about her "accident." Then I asked David to come and stand beside her.

"See how David's nose looks?" I asked the children. "It's perfect . . . it's all better. How does it feel, David?"

"Fine." He shrugged. By now it was no big deal.

"That's how Sharon's nose will look *and* feel in a few days."

As the two kids went back to their chairs, we began the usual litany of past injuries. There were some new ones. Jason had caught his finger in a door over vacation.

Suddenly, Mary Ann's hand shot up. She began to speak before I could call on her.

"When I was in Aspen," she began. She paused and could go no further.

It's finally coming up for this kid, I thought. I nodded encouragingly and she began again.

"When I was in Aspen I was in a ski lift and my mommy jumped out and I didn't get a chance to and then I fell. Way down."

The children looked and were silent.

"Did you hurt yourself, Mary Ann?" I asked gently.

"No." She shook her head.

"Were you scared?"

"I was very scared."

"Were you crying?"

"Uh-huh."

"I would have been scared, too." I turned to the other children. "Luckily, when Mary Ann fell, she landed in a pile of soft snow."

"It wasn't so soft," corrected Mary Ann. "It was pretty hard snow."

"I'm glad you told us, Mary Ann. Now you can feel better about it. And I know that Mom and Dad won't take you on that lift again."

"No." Her face brightened. "But I can ski on Fanny Hill and Assay Hill. I can really bomb that one."

"I'm a better skier because I *never* fall," said Benjamin, and we were back to business as usual.

At dismissal, Sharon's mother asked how I had handled the discussion of her daughter's bruise. I briefly described the meeting.

"Sounds like you're running a trauma workshop in there," she commented.

"Do I have a choice? This year that's my job," I answered with as much equanimity as I could muster.

I thought: Now who's going to run the one that Cathy and I need to join?

• • •

The next morning at 4:15 A.M., I awoke with a shudder. I had dreamt that Amanda's parents were killed in a plane crash. It was terribly real. One of the other parents had called me at home to tell me the news. Afterward, she stammered, "Wh— what do we tell the children? Maybe we should just lie. There are only seven more weeks left of school."

"There will be no lying," I said through my tears. "The children have been through too much pain. If one of them found out the truth and told the others, it would undo all the work we've done. How could they ever trust another grown-up?" While I was trying to figure out what to say to the children, I mercifully awakened.

• • •

I needed a break, but none was in sight. Without warning, Jason, Lee and Harris began to act as if it were September. Lee's tantrums resumed with vigor. He screamed when he didn't get what he wanted. He turned over a wooden baby carriage in which Amanda was sitting, dumping her on the floor, because he decided it was his turn to use the carriage. He banged pots and pans, and threw sand on the floor. He cried vociferously whenever he was disciplined, which was often.

I could not imagine what had produced this sudden, intense change. My curiosity was relieved, however, by an unexpected source. A family friend told me that Lee was not sleeping at night. He would awaken many times and cry to be let into his parents' bed. His parents kept taking him back to his own room, but they gave in after many trips. Not that it helped: the only way Lee could sleep was sideways, with his head on his father's head, and his feet on his mother's head.

I realized why I hadn't seen Carla for a week: she was catching up on her sleep while Lee was in school. There wasn't much I could offer in the way of advice, since I hadn't been "officially" told. (If asked, I would have said to keep putting him back in his bed, no matter how long it took. Kids can often sleep in their parents' bed with no harm, but this was a test of wills which had to be won by the parents.) I could only hope that the conflict would be resolved soon. Lee was driving us all crazy.

Then there was Jason, who had returned to his earlier, bolt-of-lightning stage. He ran around the room in his manic style— at the easel, at the Lego, at the sandbox all before I could exhale. He was practically throwing himself from one wall to the next. After roof time, he wanted to be the first one down the stairs, so he pushed to the front of the line so hard and so fast that he nearly fell. I grabbed the back of his collar just as he was tumbling down the first step. That morning, a teacher had found him sitting on top of some cubbies near our classroom at eight thirty-five, ten minutes before school started. His father had taken him to the early drop-off room. He had sneaked out, run down the back stairs and climbed onto the cubbies without anyone's knowledge.

Clearly, something was going on: the child was not himself. (Or he was more himself than ever.) It occurred to me that the behavior might have something to do with a recent back injury his mother had incurred over vacation. A phone call was definitely in order.

The most difficult child, however, was Harris. Jason and Lee were thorny situations—if you knew how to handle them, you wouldn't get cut. But Harris was out for blood. He bit Sharon on the ankle, but only succeeded in tearing her favorite pair of leggings. He poured sand on Lee's head. He hit indiscriminately; whoever was near him got hurt. We put him in time out, but it didn't help at all. When I called his home to discuss his behavior, I learned from his baby-sitter Opal that his parents were in London. She was staying with him for the week.

That's the kind of information a teacher needs to have in advance. (I knew the Whites had been planning a trip, but I thought they had gone during our vacation.) Naturally, Harris was nervous without his parents at home. But why was he so overly aggressive?

I resolved to speak to him the next morning before he got into trouble. Unfortunately, that was impossible. Harris walked into the room, right up to Lee, and tried to bite him on the hand. In my haste to stop the bite, I pulled Harris away a bit too roughly.

I removed our culprit to a nearby chair, and sat down next to him.

He looked at me angrily.

"I hate you. And I'm never coming back here again."

"Did I hurt you?" I asked.

He nodded.

"I'm sorry, Harris. It was an accident."

He nodded again.

"When did your parents leave?"

He told me that they had been gone all week, and that this afternoon his aunt Susan was coming to take him to her house.

"All the way to Kentucky?"

"Yes."

"Do you like staying with Opal?"

"No. She spanks me and she pinches me [he touched his inner thigh] and she says 'shut up' to me."

"When did she pinch you?"

"Today. She wanted to put on my shirt and I wanted to *do it myself* and I said all the bad words and she pinched me very hard." He showed me his thigh again.

Other stories followed. The former abusive baby-sitter, Lonnie, had apparently visited Harris again. "But she didn't hit anymore."

He had learned the word "asshole" from "a strange man who came right through the door when it wasn't locked and talked to Lonnie." He went on.

There was a lot. If even half of it was true, it was a lot.

I checked Harris's thigh: there was no mark. But there were just too many details for the whole story to be a lie. I looked at Cathy, who had been listening. "We've got to tell," said the look on her face, telegraphing my own sentiment back to me.

We had already informed the Whites of Opal's carelessness with Harris on the street. All of us knew that Harris complained about his baby-sitter. The Whites had promised to talk to her, and we had believed them. But this was no longer a case of neglect: this was abuse.

I shuddered. Today was Friday. Harris was going away with his aunt, so there would be no more nights with Opal. He would be in Kentucky all next week. But he would be back, and so would his parents.

We would have to do something to get the Whites' attention.

And it would have to be drastic.

MAY: SERIOUS STUFF
AND HAPPY HOURS

I awoke with a feeling of fatigue, and thought seriously about staying home. Cathy would be all right with a substitute in the room. The kids wouldn't be too bad with Harris out of town. At the last moment, I decided against it. I dragged myself into the shower with the promise of a taxi to school and a long nap afterward. It was a lucky decision: otherwise, Jason would probably be dead.

He courted accident as soon as he arrived in the classroom. Everything small enough to fit went into his mouth. He ate errant crumbs from the floor. I stopped him from choking on a bead. He nearly ran headlong into a steel dolly which was being unloaded in our hallway. He was truly out of control. When we got to the roof, I was determined to stay within five feet of him. Our playground seemed safe, but Jason was a disaster in the making.

A combination of nervous energy and athletic prowess, Jason was everywhere at once. When he ran, there was no use trying to keep up with him. I watched him as carefully as possible. I was more worried about the trouble he could get into when he alit somewhere.

After about ten minutes, Jason and Lee went over to our large, make-believe train. They began to play "Conductor," and headed for Disney World. They seemed safe enough for the moment. I stationed myself between the train and a nearby pillar.

Our sandbox had been removed and had not as yet been replaced by its long-promised successor. What remained was the old sand (were they planning on reusing it?) and one of the four pillars that had supported the sandbox roof. The pillar had a small step attached to it.

We had asked many times for the pillar to be removed, but after eight months it stood there still. The children enjoyed jumping off the step, but we were always chasing them away. The pillar was too close to the playground wall to allow for jumping.

The wall itself was a model of safety. It was over five feet of brick and topped with a chain-link fence. There were three rows of barbed wire on top of the fence. Certainly, no one could get out or in.

Out of the corner of my eye, I saw Lee leave the train and run to stand on the pillar's step. I warned him off and he moved away. Jason was still on the train.

At that moment, one of our girls asked me to look at her finger. She thought she had a splinter. I glanced down at it for several seconds but could find nothing. Then I looked back up at the pillar to make sure that Lee had not returned to it.

I beheld a heart-stopping sight. Not even thirty seconds had elapsed since I had last looked at the pillar. Yet, there was Jason, halfway up the nearby chain-link fence. I learned later that he had run to the pillar, stood on the step and chinned himself onto the top of the wall. Only one three-year-old in a thousand could have done it, but Jason was that one kid. I had just a few seconds to reach him before he either impaled himself on the wire or plunged six floors to his death.

"JASON!" I screamed in my loudest, most ferocious voice. He froze. At the same time, I began to run. Michael Jordan had nothing on me that day: I leapt as high as I could, and managed to grab the back of Jason's shirt. As I fell to the ground, he fell on top of me. Because we landed on the playground's rubber padding, we were both uninjured.

I stood up, overwhelmed with fear and anger. I was shaking all over. My face was hot: it was probably as red as a stop sign. I must have been a terrifying sight, because Jason was too frightened to cry.

"Just WHERE were you going?" I screamed at him. Everyone on the roof was listening now. "Can't you see that the fence is there to keep you from falling down to the STREET? You're going to sit out now for a long, long time."

I picked him up by the arm, and dumped him unceremoniously by the back wall. At least I knew he was safe there. Then I sat down on a nearby bench and tried to get control of my emotions.

Cathy comforted me. It was a terrifying incident, to be sure, but I had won the day. Jason was still alive. We talked about his extraordinary behavior. Surely, his nervous energy must be coming from his anxiety about his mother's injury. Cathy and I decided on an immediate conference with his parents. We also needed to inform our director of the incident, so that she could have the pillar removed immediately. (The pillar stayed, but the step was gone on the following day.)

After a few minutes, I glanced in Jason's direction. He was huddled on the floor. He didn't seem angry, or even chastened: he was simply sad. I felt my anger dissolve.

Our attempts at discussing his mother's injury with Jason had failed so far. He listened, but he wouldn't speak. I decided to try again. I sat down next to him and gathered him into my lap.

"Jason, I'm probably going to get chalk all over my pants sitting on the floor with you—even on my tush!"

He looked up at me and giggled.

"But it's so important to talk that I don't care," I continued. "Do you know why you're running around and getting into so much trouble lately?"

He just looked at me.

"I think it might be because you're worried about your mom. What do you think?"

"It's because I always rush," he whispered.

"Maybe so," I mused. It was a good answer, although it didn't get to the heart of the problem.

"You've got to try and stop, Jason. You've got to *look* and *think* before you go somewhere. Otherwise you could really get hurt."

Jason nodded. He'd probably heard it a thousand times before.

"Okay. You can get up now." I hugged him. "But remember: you have to be very careful, or you have to sit out again. I can't let you hurt yourself, Jason."

He hugged me and got up. I stood also. We both looked to see if there was chalk on the seat of my pants. There was none, and only one of us was disappointed.

I arranged a conference with the Aronsons for the following morning. We learned a great deal. Jason had been very difficult at home, as well. He had exhibited the same wild behavior at a party over the weekend. His father attributed it to his lack of discipline on their recent trip.

"He was in the water all the time, playing with older kids. There was really no need for the kind of discipline we have at home."

"Makes sense. You were on vacation," I told them. "But we were also thinking that he's upset about his mom's condition."

We learned that it was indeed the case. Jason and his sisters had seen their mother taken to the hospital by ambulance. Jason's behavior had been wild ever since.

We asked the Aronsons to talk to Jason about his mother's back, which was improving slowly. He needed to know that Anne would be "all better" soon. They promised to do so. Anne wanted to know if the roof had been fixed, so that such incidents could be avoided. We assured them that it had been taken care of. All four of us felt better as the conference ended.

The rest of our week was calmer. Jason improved, although not dramatically. Without Harris in the classroom, there was a lot less noise. We had not a single game of "Kill the Beast" on the roof. Instead, the children organized games of "One Hundred and One Dalmatians," which consisted entirely of crawling around pretending to be dogs. One highlight was watching Jenny go over to a piece of gym equipment and lift her hind leg, as if she were peeing on a lamppost. The game was gentle and fun (and completely devoid of Cruella De Vil, the movie's villainess). We knew it couldn't last. Harris was due back on Monday.

Cathy and I had discussed Harris's story with our director. She felt that the first step was to inform the child's parents and give them a chance to act on the information. Accordingly, I called the Whites' home on Sunday night. I was more than a little nervous, but it had to be done.

Harris Senior answered. After a bit of small talk, I related the story of Opal's pinch. I explained that this was a serious incident which needed prompt attention. An immediate parent-teacher conference was necessary.

Harris Senior was genuinely upset. His son and Joanna would return from Kentucky tomorrow night, so the conference could take place on Tuesday morning.

"But only one of us will come," he told me. "The other parent has to stay and put Harris on the bus."

I couldn't quite believe my ears.

"This is an extremely grave matter, Harris," I said carefully. "We must have both of you here. I'm supposed to notify the Board of Health in cases of abuse. I'm not doing so only because I feel assured of your complete cooperation."

(I didn't tell him that with no physical evidence, there wouldn't be much the Board of Health could do. I simply made the threat.)

I got his immediate attention.

"What can we do?" he asked anxiously.

BEHIND THE PLAYDOUGH CURTAIN

I suggested a breakfast date for Harris Junior at Louisa's house. Afterward, Louisa's parents could put both children on the bus. Harris Senior enthusiastically agreed.

Next, I mentioned that I had spoken to Harris's therapist, Dr. Adler. Harris Junior had told her the same story about Opal. Harris Senior said he would speak to her on Monday. I was happy to hear it; maybe the one-two punch of therapist and teachers would be more effective. Somehow, we had to make them see that Opal should not be around Harris anymore.

After school on the following day, I arrived home to find a long message on my answering machine. It was from Dr. Adler. She had spoken to Harris Senior but had *not* recommended firing Opal. "She has real strengths in setting limits, and I see such terrible housekeepers that I can appreciate Opal's good points."

I was mystified until I realized that the doctor, an excellent therapist, had not been told the entire story. I called and left a long message on *her* answering machine—ah, technology!—filling her in on Opal's frequent lateness, her yelling and her ignoring of Harris on the street. "This isn't one incident," I concluded. "It's the straw that broke the camel's back."

Dr. Adler returned my call at 9 P.M. No, she had certainly not been told any of those details. She would call Harris Senior back and make that clear.

I thanked her, then paused.

"Look—something *else* is going on in that home. I don't know what it is, but I can feel it. Something is wrong . . . there are issues we're not hearing about."

Dr. Adler took a long time to reply.

"You've mentioned that before. Of course, there are things I can't tell you because they're said in confidence . . ."

I hadn't remembered telling her my feeling, but it had been with me for quite a while.

"Okay," I replied, somewhat relieved. "I don't need to know. As long as *you* know, then it's all right."

Dr. Adler promised to call Harris Senior and tell him to "listen to what the school said very seriously."

I thanked her again and hung up. I knew I'd sleep a lot better after our conversation. Still, as I drifted off, I couldn't help wondering just what the missing piece was.

• • •

I got to school early Tuesday morning to find Joanna White in the teachers' room, getting coffee. We walked down the hall together, chatting. Yes, she had loved London. She and Harris Junior had caught the flu in Kentucky, but they'd had fun otherwise. As we entered the classroom, I was pleased to see Harris Senior. My suggestion of the breakfast date had been met enthusiastically by Harris Junior, who was currently with Louisa.

Cathy arrived, and we got right down to business. I again related the pinching story, and how we had learned of it. I dwelt on the fact that this kind of treatment was the wrong thing for their child.

"Well, what should we do?" asked Harris Senior, getting right to the heart of the matter.

"I think Opal is probably not the right person to take care of Harris anymore," I said. Cathy agreed.

"Wait a minute," Joanna interrupted. "There's something else. A lot of this is really my fault. I've never really given Opal a strong, clear message that she can't hit Harris at all." She paused, gulped and went on.

"I'm conflicted about it. Hitting was so much a part of my own childhood. It's how we were all raised out there in rural Kentucky."

Harris Senior interrupted. "And when she was just there, she saw it all again."

So there it was—the missing piece—ambivalence stemming from abuse in her own childhood. Joanna didn't want to hit her child. But she wasn't sure it was wrong. She had turned out okay. So she hired someone without giving her a clear message on how to discipline her son.

I was feeling so much pain that I could hardly speak. Wasn't her own childhood enough to convince Joanna that hitting *any* child was not okay? I forced myself to answer her in as normal a voice as I could muster.

"You're a brave woman to tell us this, Joanna. It's very hard to talk about it, I'm sure. But Harris is Harris. He isn't you. And you have to do the best thing for *this* child, regardless of what you think might work for children in general.

"Harris is struggling for his own impulse control. He was hurt as a very young child, so he's still struggling to feel safe in a world which grown-ups control. You have to make sure that he isn't hit by *anyone*."

"I know that now," she replied quietly. "I'm sure I can deliver that message to Opal very clearly."

I took a gamble. "I know this is an issue that your husband feels strongly about."

Harris Senior nodded. "I was hit in school. I always vowed that a child of mine would never be raised with violence."

I thought: So why aren't you stopping it, for God's sake!

I said: "Then perhaps you need to take a more active role in this situation."

He nodded.

"Maybe you need to be there during the talk with Opal."

"It's a good idea," he replied.

We spoke a little more about the possibility that Opal would not be able to deal with this new rule. Cathy and I felt that this would most likely be the case. I related a conversation between Opal and me: Opal said she had told Joanna that unless she had "a freer hand" with Harris, she would have to quit.

Joanna was appalled. There had never been any conversation of the sort. We urged them to think in terms of replacing

Opal even as they were delivering the strong message about hitting. They promised they would.

Harris Senior asked me to call at night to let them know how Harris's day had been. He'd been so difficult to discipline in Kentucky, so verbally difficult, that they were worried about his first day back in school.

Joanna said she'd get home at 6:30 P.M., so I could reach her afterward. That was a heartening sign. Harris Senior said he'd be picking up Harris today, because they hadn't yet talked to Opal. This was even more heartening. They thanked us profusely and hurried down the hall.

Although it was time for school, I asked Cathy to keep the door closed. I sat down on the dress-up bin and burst into tears.

"Are you all right?" Cathy asked me.

All I could manage to choke out were the words "the missing piece."

I lowered my head and allowed myself the luxury of a moment's tears. But I dried my eyes quickly; there wasn't time for anything else. Then Cathy opened the door and our day began again.

Harris was exactly as his parents had billed him: verbally difficult. He made Amanda cry by telling her that he wouldn't marry her. He teased Jason. He stamped the floor and yelled, "Damn it, I'm angry!" (I assumed this was modeled behavior: he had to be copying an adult. Unfortunately, it was pretty cute.) Because he was mostly using his words and not hitting, we were rather lenient. We spent the day issuing serious reminders to him rather than sitting him in time out. All in all, he'd been a lot worse in the past. I'd be happy to report that to his folks tonight.

I waited until 8:30 P.M. to call Joanna. Harris was in bed, but he was not yet asleep, so our conversation was punctuated by intermittent asides.

Joanna's evening had been a long one. Harris had tested her

over and over, but she had held firm. She had not allowed him to hit her, or to step out of his room once he had been sent there as a disciplinary measure.

"I'm determined to get it right this time. I know a lot of this is my fault. I've never set any limits when I come home from work. I've just been too tired to have any conflict at all. But I see it has to change."

"It sounds like you've made a good beginning," I assured her.

We discussed Joanna's childhood. Everyone she knew was beaten for discipline. They called it "getting a whoopin'." Sometimes, her friends would do a few bad things directly after an initial offense, since they knew they'd be beaten anyway. The more I heard about this form of child-rearing, the less sense it made. Joanna seemed to feel the same way.

We spoke of Harris Senior's difficulty in controlling his temper (another missing piece). When he saw Harris Junior acting up, he often became enraged and began to yell. (Aha! Here was the role model for "Damn it, I'm angry!")

"He has his own issues," Joanna said.

"Who doesn't?" I replied.

Joanna mentioned that she was having the talk with Opal tomorrow, and she would be very firm. The first thing her son had told her tonight was that Opal hit him when he'd "been a bad boy." She was unsure about Opal now, and was thinking about calling another woman who had been recommended to them. I urged her to proceed on both fronts.

We talked for forty-five minutes. She apologized for taking up so much of my time. I told her it was perfectly all right, gave her my home phone number and told her to call any time. We said good night, mutually hoping for the best. I hung up shaken. I kissed my family and went directly to bed.

When is the time for teachers to reflect? All of us have to find our own time and space. It can't be during working hours:

we're taking care, trying to improve lives. For me, it can't be in the late afternoon or evening: I'm busy with my own children, husband, friends or interests in general.

The only time left is the night. So, at 3:30 A.M. I was in the kitchen, thinking of Jeremy and his baby, of Cory and her brother, of Harris and his parents, who were doing the best they could. We'd set them all on the right road; somehow, we'd have to make sure they stayed on it.

• • •

The next day, Harris was better. He played well with the other children. He made a beautiful Mother's Day printing, following my complicated directions perfectly. His behavior continued to improve during the week: he wasn't perfect, just calmer. When I told him he'd have to sit out for five minutes in the gym for not sharing, he simply nodded. I was the last to arrive in the gym that day, and found him sitting patiently on the side, waiting for me to tell him when he could get up. One of the other teachers came over to me.

"Did you tell him he had a time out?" she inquired.

"Yes, but it was about twenty minutes ago."

"Well, he remembered. He went right over and sat down the minute he came into the gym. That's remarkable."

And it was. I let him up two minutes later, with lots of praise for remembering the rules.

A few weeks later, Harris had a lovely new baby-sitter. Dana was kind and affectionate, but she knew how to discipline when she had to. Cathy and I were thrilled, but Harris was ecstatic. His father told us he had jumped into her arms on her second visit to their household. Things were definitely improving.

The rest of the class was on automatic pilot. They could play and laugh and work all by themselves. They made their own good time. Cathy and I often watched and listened in admiration.

Here's a short exchange we caught in the classroom:

> HARRIS: When I'm thirty, I'm going to marry Mary Ann.
> MARY ANN: When I'm forty, I'm going to marry Harris and Jason.
> JASON: When I'm five, I'm going to marry my mommy.

One day, Sharon came to school without her usual good cheer. She wept when Mary Ann and Jenny shared a toy and left no room for her. She lolled around, unable to interest herself in anything.

Cathy approached her.

"What's the matter, Sharon?"

Sharon thought hard and shrugged.

"I don't know. I just feel bad. I don't know what it is."

Cathy decided to go for the laugh.

"Ah. I see. That happens to grown-ups a lot. It's nothing to worry about. It's called free-floating anxiety."

Sharon giggled, and so did Benjamin, who was standing nearby.

"Free *what*?" they both asked.

"Free-floating anxiety. You know, like this." Cathy stuck out both her arms and pretended to fly.

They couldn't pronounce it, but they thought the term was hysterical. They proceeded to "float" all over the room. Sharon's dark mood lifted and she was able to enjoy her day.

In the block area, the boys were building complex structures that had names and functions as well as beauty. Lee, Avi and Jason spent one entire morning constructing Robin Hood's castle. A pathway even extended up to our door (with special permission—otherwise blocks were not allowed out of their area). Lee—little Lee!—created an "entrance" out of crayon and paper. He placed it on the front of the building. We saw planning, cooperation and much pride of accomplishment. The boys were happy with themselves, and with the kudos they garnered from classmates and teachers alike. Of course, there was the usual sign of four-year-old development:

> PATTI: Boys, I really love your building.
> LEE (with exasperation): It's not a building, Patti, it's a *castle*.
> PATTI: Oh, I see. Well, it's a great castle. Tell me about it.

There was no use explaining that castles were buildings. This was the age where a sneaker was not a shoe, and neither was a sandal. These items had their own names, so they had their own identities. The understanding of broader categories would come in time. Meanwhile, the block building was the important thing.

Several months ago, we had instituted "Ladies' Day" in the block area. Every year, the boys always dominated block building, even when I selected equal numbers of boys and girls to play in the area. Invariably, the girls would leave, and the boys would simply take over. As I watched, I came to the conclusion that it was not just the greater aggression of the boys, but their different style of building that was responsible for this phenomenon. Boys used more blocks and more space in a shorter period of time. Girls also built complex structures, but they were more contemplative about the act of building. They took longer to choose and place their blocks. They frequently talked as much as they built. In a defined space, with a limited number of blocks, the boys would naturally have the edge.

Our goal was to develop confidence in the girls so that they would be able to hold their own in the block area. It's not politically correct to say there are gender differences, but after you've been teaching awhile, there they are, as undeniable as a rainy day.

Hence, the arrival of "Ladies' Day." The rules were simple.

You didn't have to build if you were a girl, but you couldn't build if you were a boy. At first, the girls would enter the area eagerly, but leave after a few minutes of desultory play. They had not yet developed block-building skills. When Cathy or I began to sit with them and model the process of building cooperatively, they began to make progress. (Kids enjoy doing almost anything if a teacher participates.)

The remaining teacher ran the class. At first, this was not an easy task: the boys simply couldn't think of anything to do. The playdough, sandbox, dress-up area and puzzle table were all available, as was the art area. But many of the boys walked around as if they were in an empty room. Initially, they needed direction as much as the girls did.

By May, however, our system had reaped its rewards. Boys and girls played confidently in all areas of the room. In the block area, the girls built complex structures filled with windows and ramps. They had an open, airy delicacy that reminded me of a spider's web. The boys enjoyed painting and playdough, and were proud of their artistic creations as well as their work with Lego and blocks. We kept "Ladies' Day," but we added "Gentlemen's Day" as well. The rest of the week was shared time in the block area, just as it was in the rest of the room.

When children reach this stage of easy cooperation, there are times in class when there is not much for a teacher to do. The best idea is to get out of the way and observe. If there's a problem, you're close enough to intervene. Otherwise, be quiet and take notes.

Despite the year's troubles—or maybe because of them—our students had become an extremely close-knit group. They strutted their stuff for us one morning: as Cathy and I watched in delight, they put on a puppet show.

Jason had brought a pile of blue paper squares from home. He handed them out so the children could color them. When he wanted them back, he walked around calling, "Tickets, tickets!" The children obligingly handed them in.

"Tickets for what?" Amanda asked him.

"Tickets for a show," he replied.

"Let's make a show—a puppet show," Amanda suggested.

"Yeah—a puppet show!" cried Harris excitedly. The two of them went up to the loft.

"Ladies and gentlemen—the show!" Harris called out.

"Who is watching?" shouted Amanda.

"We are, we are!" Jenny and Sharon sang out. They pulled over some chairs to make an audience in front of the loft. Many of the other children followed their example.

Jason handed out the precolored tickets. When he finished, he decided to become a puppeteer, and climbed the stairs to the loft.

"No. Go down. You're not in the show," Harris yelled at him.

"But I want to do the puppets," Jason protested.

"You are *not* the boss," Amanda told Jason imperiously. Chastened, he descended the stairs and resumed his former occupation: he collected the tickets he had just handed out.

The puppeteers and the audience had previously put on clothing from the dress-up bin. Since they continued to wear them for this next activity, they looked absolutely like theatergoers and performers from a Broadway show. The effect was hilarious, but Cathy and I controlled our laughter. One loud giggle could make the kids self-conscious and end the game.

It's not that they didn't want us to watch. They frequently glanced our way. It's just that we were supposed to participate or admire; we were supposed to take them seriously.

Harris spoke up. "Ladies and gentlemen, thank you for waiting."

"The show begins!" announced Amanda.

The show was not as wonderful as the preparations. (How could it have been?) Harris's puppet, a giraffe, sang "tra la la" and the words "master of the show" (to the tune of *Les Miz*'s "Master of the House") over and over. Amanda's puppet, a red something-or-other, popped up and down repeating the words "bubble in the forest." The audience was quickly bored.

Sharon got up from her seat. "The show is over," she announced.

"No!" shouted Amanda, in distress. "It's NOT over!"

I spoke up. "Well—it could be intermission, then. That's the time when the audience gets to walk around before the next act."

"Okay, it's intermission," agreed Jenny (pronouncing it correctly). "Let's go get some water, Sharon."

Clearly, she'd been through intermissions before. I was about to hand the girls some cups when they moved a few feet away and pretended to drink water from a make-believe fountain. The rest of the audience followed suit. After that, there was an intermission whenever they were feeling restless.

The next act was a lot more interesting, due to the presence of David. He had been sitting on the loft from the beginning, just watching. Now, he decided to participate. He draped a blanket on the sides of his head and began to dance, with a silly smile on his handsome face. He was genuinely funny.

The audience laughed. Encouraged, David put a blanket on the head of a puppet and danced with it. The audience was in stitches. He danced alternately with a doll and a stuffed bear, all with blankets on their heads. The children held their sides and nearly fell out of their seats. David was a smash hit.

Because the spotlight was no longer on Amanda and her cohort, she declared that the show was over. She ceremoniously descended with Harris right behind her. The children stood up and left their seats. At that moment, Mary Ann and Cory stepped up with brooms in their hands and began to "mop up," just as if they were in a real theater. It was a priceless imitation of life.

I checked my watch. The event had taken twenty-five minutes. The kids had prepared, performed and finished up with almost no help from us. It would have been extraordinary in nearly any preschool classroom. In ours, it was miraculous.

• • •

May raced along, filled with happy hours for the children and relative calm for their teachers. The parents also seemed to be doing well. Cory's mom quit one of her two jobs to spend more time with her children. Naturally, her children were thrilled to see more of her.

Jeremy's mother was flourishing in her new part-time job. She seemed a lot happier these days.

"Jeremy talks about the baby a lot now," she told me. "This weekend, when we were in the car, he said, 'The baby couldn't make it, but I made it. And I'm not the only one. Evan made it too.'

"Bernard, who was driving, turned around and said, 'And we're so glad you did.'"

I was thrilled. In one short conversation, Jeremy learned that it was okay to talk about the baby at home, too. Jeremy's parents were validating his feelings for him, and showing him how much they loved him.

Jason's mother's back injury was healing nicely, and he was calmer. "As I get better, he gets better," she told us. It certainly seemed to be the case.

Avi's mother got a job in a large Israeli company with New York offices. She also learned through amniocentesis that the child she was carrying was a boy. One morning, as she brought Avi over to the art table, he said to her: "*Ema,* I'll draw the penis and you draw the rest of the baby in your tummy."

He drew what looked like a long pole. She drew a creditable outline of a fetus, which she connected to the pole.

"Is that the baby? He looks like a donkey!" laughed Avi. He drew "donkeys" all morning.

Of course, there were blips in the radar—but they were minor. Amanda's mother informed us that she was having her daughter take the entrance exam for all private schools. Most children took it in the fall, as their families were looking at schools for the following year. There was no need to take this exam now. For Amanda, it might be detrimental. Given the extra months, her spatial abilities might improve.

A word about these tests. I'm sure they're accurate up to a point—depending on the competence of the tester. The problem lies in what they are actually testing. Childhood intelligence is so fluid: a child could make a great cognitive leap the day after he or she is tested. If a kid has a cold and doesn't feel like answering much, the test could reflect nothing at all.

Cathy and I discussed the situation. Should we tell Amanda's mother about the spatial problems when we hadn't mentioned them before? Janet Fisher might overreact to what was probably a minor difficulty. Should we say nothing and let Amanda take the test, with an outcome that could be detrimental to her? That option just didn't seem fair to the child. We decided to speak to her mother.

When I told Janet about our feelings, she became upset.

"Why didn't you tell me about this problem at the conference?" she wanted to know.

It was a fair question, which I met as honestly as I could.

"We thought that Amanda might improve in this area over the next few months. It didn't seem like a good idea to worry you over something that might change all by itself."

"Do you think the spatial problems would show up on the test?"

"They would show up now. But there's no telling how it will be in the fall."

I told Janet about my own experience with my younger child.

Laura and I had arrived early for the test, and were amusing ourselves with pencil and paper. I asked her what she wanted to draw;
she replied "shapes." We drew rectangles, squares and circles.

"Can you draw a triangle?" I asked my daughter.

She shook her head; she had never seen one.

I drew one, and she copied mine. She was so delighted with
the new shape that she drew it over and over. Then it was time
for the test.

The first thing she said when she came out of the tester's
room was, "Mommy, the lady asked me to draw a triangle and I
drew such a good one!"

If we'd been on time for the test, the tester would have
recorded that my kid couldn't draw a triangle.

The story made Janet feel better. She decided not to test
Amanda until fall. Subsequently, she asked for the names of
every spatial toy we had in our classroom. She went out and
bought as many as she could find, and worked with Amanda
every night for weeks.

Had I done the right thing in telling Janet, when it resulted
in so much extra pressure for Amanda? I still don't know. My
intentions were good, but we all know which road is paved with
those. I guess that's why I had to take the heat.

It was comforting to see that Amanda was apparently unaffected. In class, she was her usual cheerful, intelligent self. I
had an interesting conversation with her that very week. She
had overheard Jason insult Lee, and then say he was "just kidding." She came over to me with this observation:

"Patti—if someone does something bad and then says they
were kidding, they're lying."

"That's often true, Amanda."

"I *never* lie."

"Everyone lies sometimes, honey. We just try to do it as little
as possible."

"Not me."

"How about that time when you didn't tell the truth about your new baby-sitter?"

Amanda paused. "Well, I *learned*. I never do it anymore."

I couldn't argue with that line of reasoning, so I let it ride. *She'll be a great lawyer*, I thought.

We rolled along in this fashion until the Memorial Day break. When we returned there would be just three weeks of school left. It would be time to start talking about the end.

• • •

Lots of people left the city over the holiday, but my family stayed home. My husband, returning from three days of being sequestered on a jury, was diagnosed with Legionnaire's Disease. We spent an anxious weekend hoping to avoid the hospital. He pulled out of the worst stage (and later made a complete recovery), but I returned to school on Tuesday with absolutely no reserve strength for my students.

I came in because it was the right thing to do. The children, good as they had been, would need my attention. I was expecting a halcyon day; instead, I encountered chaos.

Right from the beginning, there was trouble. Cory wouldn't separate from her mother. Jason ran around the room touching everything. Sharon moped. Mary Ann wouldn't stop talking. As I tried to sort out the problems, our school secretary walked in.

"Harris isn't coming to school today," she announced in a voice that could be heard in Hoboken. "He has the measles."

All conversation ceased. The mothers and I looked at one another in fear. Measles? Every child who came here was supposed to be vaccinated against the disease. We could be dealing with quarantine, or a lawsuit. Every parent in the school would have to be notified. So would the Board of Health. It was a scary proposition at the very best.

"Don't worry," our secretary said, as if she had read our minds. "We already have a call in to Harris's pediatrician.

"Oh, and by the way," she continued. "We got a call from Louisa's mother. She's sending in money so you can buy Louisa an ice pop after school. Her daughter feels bad that she never gets one because she goes home on the bus."

An ice pop? Each afternoon, at dismissal, an enterprising ice cream man set up his cart right in front of the temple door. Many children wanted an ice pop, so there was always a long line. Sometimes the wait was six or seven minutes. The lobby was very crowded at one o'clock: five classes left at the same time. Was I supposed to desert my job of dismissing thirteen children and speaking to their parents or sitters, just to wait in line with one little girl whose mother was too busy to pick her up? It was nearly unbelievable that anyone would suggest it.

As if to confirm the impossible, Louisa arrived at that moment and handed me a note with two quarters taped to it. I sat down on the nearest furniture I could find. First the measles, and now the ice pop, on top of this whole, lunatic year. It was simply too much.

I pulled myself together, however, and turned to our secretary, who was still in the room.

"Linda, who called you with the diagnosis of measles?"

"Harris's father," she replied.

"Ahh. The daddy. Yes—it sounds like a daddy situation if ever I've heard one. Linda, if you'll stay and help Cathy with the children, I'll just go call Harris's mother and find out what's *really* going on."

Our room erupted in knowing laughter. As I left, I heard the mothers cheerfully exchanging "Incompetent Daddy" stories. So far, so good.

The result of my phone call was even better than I'd hoped. Harris had a few spots on his tummy. Joanna had left for work with the understanding that Harris Senior would take their son to the doctor as soon as possible. Meanwhile, Harris Senior had called his own mother, who had made the diagnosis over the phone.

I returned to our room with the good news. The mothers and Linda were vastly pleased. (Harris was in school the next day: he had suffered a mild allergic reaction to an antibiotic.) We moved on to the question of the ice pop. I asked Linda if she knew what our director thought I should do.

"She's against it," Linda told me. "She doesn't want you to leave the other children at dismissal."

"Very sensible. I'll handle it from here." I thanked Linda, and walked over to Louisa.

"Louie, I know how excited you are about having an ice pop." (She had flown about the room telling everyone the news.)

"I'll buy you one today, but just today. Otherwise, your mommy or Corinne will have to come and do it for you." I would explain to her mother tomorrow, when she came for Louisa's school birthday party. (All children with summer birthdays had a "school party" near the end of the year. Louisa was as excited as if it were the real thing.)

Louisa nodded and ran off to play with her friends. I couldn't help smiling as I watched her. Each day she arrived wearing a new outfit. Cathy and I were mystified by her immense wardrobe, until we learned what her father did for a living. As a theatrical costumer, he was able to acquire many fanciful children's outfits. Louisa was the primary beneficiary, but we all benefited just from being able to look at her. The kid was a visual feast.

Today she wore a blue-and-white-checked gingham dress à la Dorothy Gale of Kansas, topped off with a little pink cardigan. Naturally, she wore her ruby shoes, and she carried a small, white purse. I didn't check the contents of her purse: our "bag lady" had been carrying one all year. I assumed it held her usual assortment of hair barrettes, Chap Stick and stickers.

I turned my attention to other things. Ten minutes later, however, I heard Benjamin's voice from the loft.

"I smell gum!" he announced in a voice like an air-raid siren.

Cathy went over to investigate; it didn't take long to find the culprits. Under the loft, Louisa and Mary Ann had squeezed themselves between the play stove and the wall. There they sat, happily ensconced, chomping away on two surreptitious pieces of gum.

Cathy spoke to them seriously. "Girls, you know there is no gum chewing allowed in class. Now bring me your gum right away."

Mary Ann complied. But Louisa said, "I don't have it in my mouth anymore."

"Where is it?"

Louisa pointed behind the stove.

"Then pick up the gum and give it to me. Gum doesn't belong on furniture."

Louisa dove obediently behind the stove—but she was there for several minutes.

"I can't get it off," she reported in a muffled voice.

"Well, you just keep trying," Cathy responded. "And when you're done, bring it to me."

Louisa came out from behind the stove. But when she opened her hand to give Cathy the gum, it contained a veritable bouquet of old, dried pieces along with the wet, squishy new one.

"There's paper, too," she offered, as she saw our jaws drop.

"Go and get it, then," said Cathy. "Don't leave anything behind."

We glanced at each other. It was apparent that Louisa had been chewing gum for weeks now, and stashing it behind the stove. We looked inside her purse; it contained a giant pack of Juicy Fruit. Cathy confiscated the gum, and we held a short meeting on the evils of sticking gum on furniture. (It was sneaky. It spread germs. It brought roaches. It was definitely *not okay.*)

I bent down and spoke to Louisa.

"Will you remember not to bring any more gum to school?"

"Okay," she sighed, and she took my hand, looking up at me with her huge blue eyes to see if I was really angry. I wasn't; how could I be? Louisa was as adorable as ever—and clearly as unrepentant.

Next, Cathy took the kids to the bathroom while I hung back, tying Jeremy's shoes. After a minute I looked up to see the children walking back our way.

"What's up?" I asked.

"We have to go to the other bathroom," one of them explained.

"Yeah. Geoffrey is locked up in our bathroom," said another.

The kids all looked as if they had seen the latest installment of *Nightmare on Elm Street.* I asked them if they were worried about Geoffrey. They nodded in sync; I was peppered with questions.

"Why is he stuck?"

"Is he going to die?"

"Will he be there forever?"

I answered everything in the negative. But with these kinds of questions, the children clearly needed a second look.

"First, go with Cathy to the other bathroom," I told them. "Then we'll go back and see how he's doing."

While they were busy, I went and checked on Geoffrey to make sure the situation wasn't too frightening for my kids to see. There he was, behind the locked door. Luckily, he could see and hear his teacher through a metal grate near the bottom of the door.

After bathroom, I turned my students around and back we marched. We were met at the door by the very same secretary who had delivered this morning's bad news.

"You can't come in here," she announced. "Geoffrey is in there."

"On the contrary, we *must* come as near as we can. My kids are frightened; they need to see for themselves that Geoffrey is all right." She stepped aside and let us into the tiny vestibule adjoining the bathroom.

I spoke to Geoffrey's teacher. He had been in the bathroom with one other child, who had managed to take the tape off the door's lock before he left. The door had closed with a click, leaving Geoffrey alone. His screams had brought help.

I muttered under my breath. This bathroom didn't need a lock. For years, we had been begging to have it removed. Here were the nasty consequences of inattention. After speaking to Geoffrey for a while and seeing that he was all right, we went back to our classroom. Linda was bringing the culprit over to see that he had done no real harm. And behind them, the men were just arriving to open the door. The children begged to watch the rescue, but one of the men told me in a whisper that they had no key, and would have to break a pane of glass to get in.

"No—we're not watching—back to the class for Sharon's chocolate chip muffins! Sarah, will you bring Geoffrey into our classroom when he's out so he can have a muffin, too?" His teacher promised.

Ten minutes later, Geoffrey was in our room. He was as glad to see us as we were to see him. We all munched on muffins as he told us how far back he had to stand while the men broke the glass. Naturally, before we went to the roof, we had to go to the bathroom to see the missing pane of glass. The children were disappointed not to find the shards still lying around. But everyone was happy that Geoffrey was fine.

In the gym, we had a lot of dead people, and a couple of lock-ups as well. After all the difficulties of these months, our children did a terrific job of working out their anxieties in play. The following day was just as hard. The children were wonderful; the maelstrom around them continued to swirl.

We began with Louisa's school birthday party. The children sat around our tables, which were set up as a long rectangle. We had everything ready—candles, cups and napkins—but Louisa's mother was late. We talked about where she could be.

"Maybe she's stuck in traffic," Jenny said.

Benjamin and Sharon assented.

Amanda thought that she had gotten stuck on a bus.

"Maybe she got killed," worried Louisa. All faces turned to me.

"No. Pretty clearly not. Because someone would have called the school and told us. Besides, that's the kind of stuff that practically *never* happens."

"Then maybe her feet got killed," continued Louisa.

I thought: This kid is talking about death too much lately. She worried that Geoffrey would die, and now her mother. What's going on?

Before I had a chance to ask, however, in walked Elaine.

"Whew! What traffic!" she lamented.

I turned to Jenny. "You got it right, Jen, and a few of your friends did, too." All three of them beamed.

We started the party right away. Elaine greeted each child by name, and had something nice to say to each of them. After she gave out the cupcakes, she turned to her daughter.

"Do you know why I like this party so much, Louie? It's because all of your friends are here to share it with you."

Cathy and I sighed: wonderful parenting, as usual. But there was something in Elaine's manner that was different. She seemed tense when she wasn't speaking to the kids. When I explained about the ice pops, she snapped at me.

I soon discovered the reason. Her mother had found a lump in her breast and was being biopsied on Tuesday.

"It may be cancer. I'm a wreck. I don't know what to do." She began to cry.

I told her how sorry I was, and asked what Louisa knew.

"Nothing yet. But you know how close they are. If she's going into the hospital, I'll have to tell her something."

I mentioned Louisa's frequent talk of death. "She may sense what's going on, or have overheard something. When you get the results of the biopsy, we'll talk about what to tell her."

I squeezed her arm and walked away, thankful that there were only two weeks left of school. I could make it. By now, I could take whatever fate hurled at me. This was a happy thought, because after that fastball to the noggin came a curve around the knees.

It was the final day in May. Mary Ann brought in an audio tape of *Peter and the Wolf.* She was disappointed that none of the children would stand around the cassette player and listen to it with her.

"It's not surprising," I told Cathy. *"Peter and the Wolf* requires a lot of concentration. We'd have to sit them down and ask them to do nothing but listen. They really need to be older, probably."

When I returned from my lunch break, however, there they were in chairs lined up around the recorder. Cathy was explaining the story and the kids were listening and asking questions.

Most of them were really attentive. I glanced at our three youngest. Jason was sitting quietly, concentrating. (Yes!) Louisa was wiggly, playing with her bracelets. Every so often she'd look up and ask, "Is that the wolf?" Lee was paying no attention to the words. But he swayed and hit the sandbox like a bongo drum whenever the music was on.

Cathy looked at me with her eyebrows up, as if to say, "Is this appropriate?"

I responded enthusiastically. *"Great* job, Cath. I never would have believed it possible."

"Could you have even imagined this in October?" she asked me.

I shook my head. "Miracles can happen, I guess—especially when helped along by elbow grease."

We laughed together. *What a nice day*, I thought. *No bad news, no hysteria—just us and the kids, for a change.*

Not thirty seconds later, Amanda's baby-sitter, Aya, appeared at our door, with her husband at her side. She was crying copiously; he looked petrified.

"May I see you?" she mouthed.

I got right up and moved with them away from the door. "What's the matter?" I asked.

"My pains have started and I'm only five months pregnant," she sobbed. "I tried and tried to call Mrs. F. but she is not in at work. I have to go now to the doctor and I don't know who will take Amanda home."

I told Aya not to worry: we would make sure Amanda got home. I mentioned that I had gone into early labor with my daughter, who was now a beautiful, healthy teenager. She and her husband smiled. I walked them to the elevator and wished them the best of luck.

Amanda met me at the door to the classroom. She had seen Aya, and wanted to know what was wrong. I told her that Aya was going to the doctor, and that was all I knew. We would call her mommy or daddy to come pick her up.

Amanda took the news well: she simply nodded and went back to her seat. I was grateful: if there were repercussions, I'd deal with them on Monday. Meanwhile, I could think of only one thing: what if the year ended as horribly as it began, with the death of an unborn child?

June: A Difficult Good-bye

Amanda's mother brought us news of Aya's condition the next morning. She had not gone into labor; she had a urinary tract infection. The incorrect diagnosis had been made by Aya's mother, over the phone. So Aya would have her baby, and I would have one less crisis to contend with.

The following morning, we met with Jenny's parents. They were in California during the scheduled conferences, and wanted to hear about Jenny's progress. We were delighted to oblige.

Jenny had learned to be more assertive. She could now tell her friends and her teachers exactly what was on her mind. She had become a leader in many of the games on the roof. Jenny had grown in self-confidence, even as she retained her sweet nature.

Cathy related a poignant conversation that had taken place around Mother's Day. The holiday reminded Jenny of how much she missed her grandmother. It reminded Cathy of her grandfather, who had died in October. Now her grandmother was alone. It was hard to miss someone you loved, Cathy told Jenny. And it was okay to cry. So the teacher and the child in her lap held on to each other and cried for a little while.

Jenny's mother cried, too, when she heard the story. She hadn't realized how much Jenny missed her grandmother. We all discussed the fact that Jenny's progress had begun after the family returned from California. Was there a connection? Was there some new sense of life's preciousness in the face of death, even for a four-year-old? We would never know; we were simply happy for Jenny.

"She doesn't seem so happy now," commented her mother. "Do you think it's because school is ending?"

"It could be," I replied. "We haven't discussed it yet, because I know the children are going to be upset. But if Jenny's already sad, then it's time to start talking."

We would have had our meeting that day in any event, because there was a distinct change in the room. The kids were raucous and jumpy. They kept bumping into things. They fought more than usual. Cathy and I looked at each other.

"It's time," I said.

Cathy called the children to the rug.

"Kids," I began. "I don't know if all your moms and dads have told you, but we're coming to the end of school. There are four days this week and five days next week. How many days does that make?"

We counted on our fingers, and arrived at nine.

One of the children asked if we would be their teachers next year. I explained that they'd have new teachers, but that we would come and visit them.

There was silence in the room. I went on.

"I'm sad because we had such a good year together, and it is hard to see it end. Is anyone else sad?"

Sharon, Jenny and Cory nodded. Others raised their hands in agreement. I called on Jeremy.

"Well, I'll be here for summer camp, so it will be okay."

Louisa called out, "Patti and Cathy will be my teachers for camp."

"Cathy will be your counselor, Louie," I explained. "I help run the camp, but I'll come and see you every day."

(I helped administrate in our summer program: the job was more money but less fun. This summer, however, it would be a much-needed respite from the classroom.)

Jason raised his hand. When I called on him, he said, "Lee has paper in his pocket."

"Well, that's not about school ending, so we'll talk about it later. Anyone else have anything to say?"

"I do," added Cathy. "I'm sad about it. I'll miss you all."

Lee piped up. "I'm not sad. My mommy told me not to be sad so I'm not."

I thought: The same mommy who came up to me this morning and hugged and kissed me? Who insisted on knowing why there was a rule that I couldn't teach her son two years in a row? That's the mommy who told you not to be sad?

I said: "That's fine, Lee. You don't *have* to be sad, but it's okay if you are. Endings are sometimes hard. And, if you feel sad, it's okay to show it or say it."

Our meeting ended with this comment, because the children ran over to hug and kiss their teachers. *This is going to be a hard two weeks,* I thought.

The following day perfectly illustrated that assessment. Four kids came in crying. Sharon had been weeping since breakfast, her mother reported.

"She's been so low that I actually took her temperature to see if she's coming down with something," Karen added.

"I'm afraid it's gonna get worse before it gets better," I told all the parents. "Endings are very hard."

"I'm going to cry too on the last day," said Carolyn Jacobson. Her son had been nearly hysterical. "I don't want to come here! I'm bored with the toys! There's too many days left! I want to go to next year's class!"

We calmed the children as best we could. The hardest case was Lee. The boy who didn't have to be sad was simply terrible instead. (His father was on a long business trip, which magnified his difficulties.) He insisted on our undivided attention, and collapsed into swollen, red-faced tantrums when he didn't get his way. We try to avoid putting children in time out for the last few weeks, so Cathy took him out of the room to calm him down. The moment he returned, however, he attempted to bite Avi. I had no choice. I sat my little culprit in a chair. He whined, he yelled, he stomped his feet, he begged to get up. But I just pretended I didn't hear him (and inwardly counted the days left that I would have to listen).

When Lee returned to a mildly appropriate state of reasonableness, I let him off the chair. Then, before anyone had a chance to start crying again, we introduced some new activities. Children can throw themselves into their work even more effectively than grown-ups. They can bury their emotions and lose themselves in play. It's one of the great strengths of childhood, but it comes with a catch. The activities must be truly interesting to hold their attention.

For this reason, I always save some very special projects for the last few weeks of school. Today, we were planting lima beans. Each child put a paper towel into a small plastic cup, pushed three lima beans between the cup and the towel and poured a little water in. Then Cathy and I labeled the cup with each child's name. These plants grew fast: in just a week, we would see results.

As the children finished their planting, Mary Ann's mother entered our classroom with another surprise. She dragged in a cardboard box even bigger than the one she had donated in October.

"We just got a new television, and I thought you might enjoy the box it came in," she explained. We thanked her with joy.

After the children had painted it, however, the box presented a problem. The older children were quickly bored with the "Down in the Box" game which had captivated them in the fall. The younger kids were too small to get in and out of the box. What could we do with it?

Suddenly, I had an idea.

"This box is a little too big for 'Down in the Box,'" I declared. "I think we should make it into a house."

I turned it sideways, so the opening faced the children. I cut off the two short flaps, so the longer flaps could function as double doors. Next, I cut a window out of the back panel.

The kids giggled as they watched me work.

"Yeah, it's a house," said David. "Could Benjamin and I go in?"

"Sure," I replied. "But take a marker. This house needs to be decorated inside and outside."

There it was—something new that the class could do together. They went to work eagerly. The older kids drew flowers, trees and people. The younger ones scribbled and drew "designs." Even Lee participated. And while they worked, they negotiated beautifully.

"Don't color on my drawing."

"Okay."

"I'm making the mommy."

"I did the mommy already."

"Okay—the sister, then."

"There's not enough room here."

But there was. For all of them.

"What a wonderful idea," Cathy said as we watched the children. "Look how calm they are. Have you done this before?"

I shook my head. "No—it just came to me when I saw they needed something new to do with the box."

When the kids asked for doorknobs, I poked holes through each flap and passed pipe cleaners through them. I tied the pipe cleaners into circles, so that each door had a "handle." When the decorating was finished, dramatic play began. Some children went inside, and others knocked at the door. They were invited in for conversation and major giggling. Then everyone would come out, and the game would begin again. The house was a happy, nick-of-time addition to our classroom.

We also brightened up the week with a field trip to a nearby firehouse, and a stop at a bakery around the corner. Both visits went well, despite the fact that we had never taken the children out of school before. The kids were too young to stay in a line, but they held their partners' hands and managed to stay between Cathy in the front and me in the rear. We walked slowly, so we could talk about the trees and flowers and garbage cans and laundromat we saw on the way back to school.

"They're really growing up," Cathy commented with pride.

"They are," I agreed. "But it helps that four of our 'active' kids are absent today."

Cathy defended our group. "They would have done just fine," she said staunchly, "even if *everyone* was here."

Perhaps she was right. Certainly, she was feeling an emotion that all teachers experience at the end of the year. We had worked very hard to teach these kids the basis of civilized behavior. And, to a large extent, we had succeeded. No matter what happened later in their lives, a piece of us would remain within them. It was a just reason for pride.

We felt the same emotion on Friday, during a rollicking combination of a Shabbat snack and a birthday party. I never held these two events at the same time: there would be an overabundance of parents, and two children would have to share the spotlight. But Cory's mother had scheduled this visit several months ago, and Jason's mother had only this day available for his party. We had no choice, so we went ahead.

We pushed the tables into a long rectangle, as we usually did for birthdays. The children sat down, with Jason at one end and Cory at the other. That way, at least the two stars would be separated when it was their turn to shine.

Jason's mother was the first to arrive. Her son immediately jumped out of his seat to hug her. With Jason hanging on to her shirt, Anne took paper plates out of a bag and began to pass them out to each child. Normally, this isn't allowed in our school. We ask the parents to bring only the birthday treat; we provide the plain, everyday paper goods. (This eliminates any competition among parents for who can provide the nicest party. Otherwise, we'd have kids eating from Tiffany dinner plates.)

We made an exception because Jason was so excited. He left his mother to do the work, and went twirling and jumping around the loft, singing, "The plates! The plates! Barbie for girls and Turtles for boys!" But because of his lisp, it came out "Bawbee faw giwls and Tuwtles faw boys!" With his high-pitched voice and semimaniacal movements, he seemed like Rumpelstiltskin moving in for the kill.

Cathy and I winced. The worst possible choice for plates: sexism and superheroes. Neither Barbie dolls nor the Teenage Mutant Ninja Turtles were *ever* allowed in our room. None of the kids complained, however; both the boys and the girls looked perfectly happy. Many of them saved their plates to take home after the party. (Madison Avenue wins again.)

Meanwhile, Jason's singing and jumping were getting out of hand. His mother seemed not to notice, so I took him aside.

"Jason," I said seriously, "this is too much running around. Please sit in your chair until Mom is ready for you to help give out the cupcakes."

That wouldn't work, I knew: he was too far gone. As I said it, however, I took him firmly by the hand and walked him over to his seat. "Cathy," I whispered to my assistant, who was standing nearby, "keep him here." She obliged—just in time for me to turn around and greet Cory's mother, who walked in with her mother-in-law (invited) and twenty-month-old Edward (not invited, but welcome). We made room for them at Cory's end of the table.

Jason's mother handed him the cupcakes, and he scampered around the table, dropping as many as he delivered. Finally, he was finished. The candles on his cupcake were lit, and we sang "Happy Birthday." Jason tried to blow out the candles all during the song, but, fortunately, he was too far away. Meanwhile, little Edward was whining at the other end of the table: he wanted to eat his cupcake *now*. (The eating would have been preferable to the whining, but his mother wouldn't allow it. And I couldn't be in two places at once to tell her it was okay. Clearly, with this particular birthday boy, I had to be close to the fire.)

After the song, it was time to eat and drink. Sharon whimpered, "But I don't *like* milk," as soon as she saw the carton, although we hadn't given her milk for eight months. (It was hardly necessary to tell us again.) Edward was yelling, while squirming on and off his chair. Jason was bouncing and sticking his fingers into the cupcake. The other kids were eating or asking for help taking the paper off the cupcakes.

Into this chaotic scene dashed our school secretary. She announced breathlessly that in two minutes a man taking pictures for the temple would be coming into the room. Before I could object, she was gone.

After our birthday party, the teachers sponged off the table. So the children wouldn't have to get up, we passed the garbage can around the table to collect the birthday remnants. Some of the children got up anyway to wash their hands. Others ran to their cubbies to put their plates away. Some merely wanted to stretch.

The best-laid plans . . . I thought to myself with a sigh.

When we were all seated again, the action moved to the other end of the table. It was time to light the candles and say the prayers for Shabbat. But Jason could not stop talking and laughing, even though he was sitting in his mother's lap. She was apparently unwilling to stop him, so the job fell to me. I walked over and spoke quietly.

"Jason, if you can't be quiet for Shabbat, I'll have to ask Mom to take you out of the room."

Now Anne spoke up. "Hear that, Jason?"

"I don't want to stay," he replied. "I want to go."

Anne looked up at me.

I paused. There was nothing I would have liked better at that moment than to have Jason take a walk with his mother so the room could be calm. But it wasn't right: no matter how annoying he could be, he was entitled to participate. *Try harder,* I told myself.

"Oh no. I want you to stay. There's good challah and grape juice, and you know the Shabbat song where I touch each child's head? Think how funny it will be when I try to touch *your* head with your crown on!"

It worked. "Yeah!" sighed Jason. Smiling happily, he snuggled down into his mother's lap. She looked up at me gratefully.

I glanced down to the other end of the table. The children had been unaffected by Jason's clamor: they were quiet and attentive. Under Cathy's auspices, Cory's grandmother was just lighting the Shabbat candles. All was still as we began to recite the blessings.

Boom! The door burst open at that very moment. In came our secretary, another woman and a man holding a large video recorder with two huge lights that beamed directly onto our table. The effect was frightening: even the grown-ups were taken aback.

This is the guy taking pictures? I thought. *You might just as well have brought in Cecil B. De Mille.*

The children, however, behaved magnificently. No one got up and ran around. No one began to hit his or her neighbor. No one cried. Instead, they stayed calmly in their seats and asked about a thousand questions. My favorite was, "Why is he *doing* this?" which echoed my sentiments exactly.

"This is a man taking a movie of us having Shabbat," I told them. "So let's show him how nice it is."

We proceeded with our regular routine. The children were splendid. Nobody flinched. (The thought occurred to me that they may have been used to having video cameras stuck in their faces, but certainly not in school.) Shabbat went off without a hitch.

When the video entourage left, I was able to explain their presence more fully. "Remember on our walk we saw that the temple was getting ready for a big party? Well, this is a movie that will be shown then. You were all very good while the man was here, and it was a very big surprise that he came! I would have told you in advance, but it was a surprise for me, too!"

As the children settled on the rug to hear Jason's mother read a story, I asked myself: *Imagine if this had happened in October? Bodies, wounded, everywhere.*

We had done a good job.

• • •

On the Saturday before the final week of school, I figured Jason out. It was 4 A.M. when I realized that I had been so busy dealing with his impulse-control problems that I hadn't spent any time thinking about what made this child tick. Yes, he got wild when he got anxious—I had learned that from the incident with the wall. But he also jumped around when he was excited, or very happy. In fact, *all* of Jason's emotions were displayed through his body. When he felt affectionate, he *had* to hug and kiss his teachers. When sad or ashamed, he folded into a little ball, and remained that way until his spirits improved. He wasn't just a kid who couldn't control himself: he was a child who channeled all his emotions into his motor activity.

What difference did it make, especially at this late date? For one thing, it changed my perception of him. He was less of a disaster and more of a *type*. A teacher armed with this information might be able to find a way to channel this child's energies. I had no time left, but I could inform his teachers for next year. And I could tell Cathy, who had always adored him.

I made my surprising announcement as we were setting up

the classroom on Monday morning. Recognition spread slowly over Cathy's face.

"You're right—definitely. But why didn't we think of it before the last week of school?"

"I needed the missing piece, which was Jason's behavior at his school party on Friday. It jogged my thinking process."

"Does it make you feel better about him?"

"I think so. Now, it's not just that he acts out; it's his MO."

"MO?"

"Didn't you ever watch 'Kojak'? His *modus operandi,* or method of operation, in English."

Cathy laughed. "And it probably always will be."

We had no time to continue, however. The children were arriving to begin their last week of school.

It was quickly apparent that nobody was feeling too good. Children, teachers and parents alike knew something precious was coming to an end. Each of us reacted accordingly.

Many of the kids reverted to earlier behaviors. Lee took things from other children and cried like a baby when he had to give them back. Harris and Jason ran all over the room: they had to be watched constantly. Benjamin hurt his knee, and was positively shaking with fright. Mary Ann tried to monopolize our time by talking to us constantly. Jeremy hugged us or patted our backs with an intensity that was upsetting.

Sharon and Jenny moped around, but Amanda, Cory and Avi played cheerfully, asking no questions. After his parents told David that he and Benjamin would be in different classes next year, David began to pull away from his best friend. He played at least half the time with the girls. Benjamin filled the void with art projects, much to the delight of his mother.

One night, Harris's mother called to ask if she should keep her son out of school for a day. Her company was having an outing, complete with special passes to the circus.

"Of course, Harris should go with you," I told her. "A special day with Mommy is too important to pass up."

"Thanks," replied Joanna. "I thought so, too. But I want you to know that it was a tough decision for Harris. When he heard he would have to miss a day of school, he almost wouldn't come."

. . .

Each morning, the parents lingered in our classroom. They stood around, making conversation, unable to separate from us or from each other. One father remarked, "It looks like a coffee klatch."

"Separation is hard for everybody," I assured him. "Parents are not immune."

Neither were teachers. Cathy was miserable because she was leaving teaching. She'd be a great success in her new field, but that was not the point. It didn't ease the pain of saying good-bye.

And me? I cried at ridiculous things. I sobbed when I read that Picasso's *Guernica* was leaving the Prado, its place of residence since Spain had returned to democracy. (Of course, I cried when it left the Museum of Modern Art, too, but that was with joy for the people of Spain.) The painting was only going to a new museum a few miles away. What was so sad about that? And what did it have to do with me?

It was all connected, I realized, to a feeling of loss. Cathy and I were not only leaving the children, we were losing the ability to influence their lives. Who would these children talk to when they left us? Would their parents continue our work? Would their next teachers love them as much as we did? There were no answers to these questions. In the end, we told ourselves that it didn't really matter. We had done our best: we had given the kids a good beginning. No one could take that away from them—or from us, either.

The best thing to do was go on. In fact, we had the perfect culminating activity: we transplanted our lima beans. One by one, each child and I removed the lima beans from the cup and examined the roots that had grown. Next, we planted them in pots, with soil and water, so that they could sprout into bean plants.

In past years, I had begun this project in March. Now I resolved always to do it in June. It was such a fitting metaphor for the end of the year. We had given the kids their roots; now it was up to them to grow and flourish.

We also did science experiments. The general favorite was "sink and float." The children put different items in a big bowl of water to see what would sink to the bottom and what would stay on top. Then we allowed them to take all the items out and begin again. Fishing out the "sunk" items from the bottom was the most popular part of the experiment!

Although we all kept busy, the end of the year was never very far from our thoughts. We discussed it in our meetings, along with the related topics of death and separation. On Thursday, David was upset because he saw a baby bird fall out of its nest. The parent birds were unable to pull it back up, and they wouldn't allow anyone near enough to help. The baby bird fluttered and squawked each time David's mother tried to rescue it. In the end, they left the park with the situation unresolved.

"The baby bird died," David told his friends solemnly. This brought on an eerie discussion of dead animals that the children had seen in the park. I was amazed at the number of them: dead squirrels, bees, rabbits, skunks, "a white bird in front of the museum."

"Yes," I agreed. "Animals die and plants die, too." I avoided "all living things die." That was not today's topic—only the everlasting human subtext.

The children looked so upset that something inside me yelled, *ENOUGH!*" We didn't need to take these deaths to heart on the next to the last day of school. It was just too much to ask.

So, although I knew the facts of nature, I didn't reveal them. I pointed out that David hadn't seen the baby bird die. Then I read *Are You My Mother?*, a book where a baby bird leaves the nest and finds his mother at the end. The sighs of relief in my classroom sounded like escaping steam. It may not have been right, but it was very reassuring.

Later, at snack, Jason said, "I'm homesick."

Others repeated the phrase.

I asked, "Who knows what the word 'homesick' means?"

Jeremy replied: "You're sick and you're home."

I answered: "That's what it should mean, but it doesn't. Anybody else have an idea?"

Mary Ann gave it a try: "You're sick so you have to go home."

Jason interrupted: "*I* know. It's when you just have to go home *right now.*"

I nodded. "That's right. It's when you miss home and you want to be there."

We were treated to another chorus of "I'm homesick!" with almost everyone participating. School was just too tough these days.

"Me, too," I agreed. "I miss my kids and my Warren."

Cathy asked, "Does anyone know who Patti's Warren is?"

"Yeah," smirked Benjamin. "Her cat!"

"No!" countered Cathy. "Her husband!"

"But I miss my cat, too!" I chimed in. Everybody laughed, and the spell was broken. We went on to a relatively normal story time, roof and dismissal.

As we rode up in the elevator, Cathy said, "You know, we've just dismissed the kids for the last time."

"That's right. Their parents will take them home tomorrow right after our end-of-the-year party. Are you ready for it?"

"I'm a little nervous," she admitted.

"I don't blame you. I am, too. It's difficult to say good-bye, no matter how long you've been a teacher. So go home, get a good night's sleep and be prepared for the things you won't get to say."

"That I *won't* get to say?" she repeated.

"Yup. It all just goes by too fast."

That night, in bed, I thought about our late director, Maggie Kaplan. Tomorrow would be the last day of the first year without her. Our program had undergone a lot of changes. In a very real sense, Maggie had taken her school with her when she died. But she had left her values and her concern for children within many of the teachers who had worked for her. That was her legacy, and it would be with us forever.

Tomorrow's gonna be a killer, I thought as I turned off the light. *I'd better get some rest.* But I failed to take my own good advice. Although I conscientiously laid my head on a pillow for six hours, I couldn't sleep at all.

• • •

On the final morning, I had no time to consult my feelings. I was too busy helping everyone else deal with theirs. The children seemed painfully upset.

I looked around. Cory was playing with a table toy. She was withdrawn, not speaking to anyone. Once in a while, she would come over to Cathy and me and bend over our laps like a baby who needed a burp. Then, of course, came the long, hard hug.

Louisa sat in a corner of the loft, dispensing mints from her ever-present purse. She was a joyous combination of Queen of the May and a bag lady right to the very end. Sharon and Jenny stuck together as they walked around the room, although they didn't have much to say to each other. Amanda worked with playdough, seemingly unaffected. But she asked a lot more questions than usual. Mary Ann could not stop hugging, kissing, touching or talking to her teachers, as if she were the only one in the room who needed our attention. It was extremely annoying, but we did the best we could.

Jeremy was huddled in a corner, looking at book after book. He had come to school in the arms of his mother, screaming "I HATE school. I don't want to go there!"

Cathy took him out of the classroom to calm down while I spoke to his mother.

Ostensibly, Carolyn told me, he was crying because he had forgotten a picture he had drawn for Louisa.

"But that's not it. It's the end of the year that's bothering him. And he's constipated again. He's always going to be that way when he's upset, right?"

My heart flew. She had figured out the connection between Jeremy's condition and his emotions! It was the final piece she needed to understand her child. I assured her that she was right.

"But why is he *so* upset? He wasn't this bad at the end of last year, and Evan wasn't so sad when he left the three's."

"Jeremy's had a very hard year, Carolyn, and we've been his support system. But I think you're ready to take over now. Just keep talking to him."

She nodded. "I do, I do. I wish I could get my feelings out as well as he does."

We both laughed, and she hugged me.

"This was a terrible year for my entire family. When I insisted on having Jeremy placed in your class, little did I know how much I'd truly need you." With a quick hug, she was gone.

Jeremy returned to class with Cathy. ("It hurts my feelings that it's the last day of school," he had told her.) He was calm, but he was not happy. The other boys weren't faring much better. In the block area, David and Benjamin were building an airport for the planes, and they wouldn't speak to anyone else.

Lee, Harris and Jason were constructing a castle, while Avi watched and occasionally added a block. Because they were arguing over the placement of every block, I sat down nearby.

The four boys were so edgy that they only had the energy to disagree. They dared not hit each other while I was so close by, so they complained instead.

"I want that block."

"I had it first."

"You knocked down my part."

"That's my toy."

It was all I could do to keep them focused on the building. Suddenly, Harris got up and walked over to Cathy.

"You're not my friend," he told her.

"Why not?" she asked.

"You always put me in a chair."

"Well, you're *my* friend."

"I'm not listening!" He covered his ears and yelled, "AHHH-HHHHHHH!"

Cathy waited him out. When he stopped shouting, she spoke gently.

"Listen to me, Harris. I think we should try to get along better because we're going to be together all summer, when I'm your counselor."

He looked hard at her; still covering his ears, he ran away.

Avi, who had overheard the conversation, said consolingly, "Don't worry, Cathy. Harris is just having a bad day."

Weren't we all. The room was quickly degenerating into the helter-skelter activity that reminded me of the first day of school. (This was somehow fitting.) Even the girls were bickering.

Avi had found the microphone from our tape recorder and, having smuggled it onto the loft, was blithely pretending to fish with it by lowering it down. It was just a matter of time until someone got hit on the head.

Suddenly, I had my first inspiration of the day. I went over to Avi and took the microphone away.

"This is not safe, Avi," I explained. "But you can use this instead." I handed him a piece of yarn which I had grabbed from a nearby table.

The idea was an instant hit: everyone wanted a piece of yarn. They "fished" from the loft, they twirled around holding the yarn, they put it in their pockets or their cubbies to take home. Two feet of pink yarn for each kid kept the whole class busy for fifteen minutes. And the joy of a new activity broke the tension.

My second inspiration quickly followed. The children were constantly tattling on each other, so I changed our system of discipline for the rest of the day. My new rule was as follows: if someone—anyone—complained about another child, that child sat on a chair for two minutes. I was uninterested in guilt or innocence; any complaint at all resulted in a time out for the accused.

At first, the children were shocked at their power, especially the younger boys, who had been doing the bulk of the *kvetching*. They immediately complained about each other, so they all sat out. Once they saw how easy it was to be tattled on, however, they stopped their own tattling. Discipline was a breeze for the rest of the day. (I resolved to see if I could find a way to make this method work during the year.)

After free play, cleanup and bathroom, we celebrated our last Shabbat. It was a private affair, just for the teachers and the kids. Cathy and I had looked forward to it: we had ice pops for their treat, as we'd promised. But the atmosphere was fraught with tension. The kids wiggled and chatted when they were supposed to be singing. Jeremy spilled grape juice all over his shirt. As I bent to light the Shabbat candles for the last time, I felt tears welling up. I glanced at Cathy: she was in no better shape.

Suddenly, we were granted some comic relief. Jeremy, Benjamin and David, who were all sitting together, took their penises out of their shorts and began waving them around. Jeremy began to sing, "My penis is swimming in the ocean."

The other two boys joined in the song. After a minute of shocked observance, the rest of us laughed like crazy. Our sadness vanished. Surely that was the strangest blessing ever recited over the Shabbat candles in more than five thousand years of Jewish history!

Our next stop was the gym. The children played inside while the parents set up the good-bye party on the roof playground outside. After a while, I went out to see how many parents had gathered. It was my policy not to bring the children to the party until every one of them had a grown-up there. Why should a child get hurt because a parent is late?

We were still missing three parents. The ones who were present looked ill at ease: they asked how their children were doing.

I thought: Apparently, better than you are.

So I regaled them with the penis story, without mentioning any names. They all hooted—especially the parents of the girls.

"Who was it?" they wanted to know—especially the parents of the boys.

I demurred. "I'm not embarrassing anyone in a crowd." Jeremy's and Benjamin's mothers immediately guessed, but David's parents were mum.

As I walked back to the gym, Louisa's mother followed me. "You know that tumor my mother had removed last week?"

I nodded.

"Well, it was benign, but behind it was a malignancy. They found it when they operated, and they took it out."

Ahh, I remember thinking. *First the chaos, now the trauma. A perfect ending for this year.*

It was the final hour of school. There wasn't much I could do for Elaine except inquire what Louisa knew.

She had been told that Grandma had undergone a little operation but was fine. Elaine's mother had come right from the hospital to see Louie.

I told Elaine that I had seen no unusual reaction from Louisa. We briefly discussed the relative merits of the drug tamoxifen versus mastectomy. Then I ran back to the children, shaking my head to clear away the sadness. I had to be ready for the task at hand.

In a few minutes, a mother came in to tell us that all the parents were assembled. We brought the children out, and the party began. It had been arranged as a bring-your-own-food picnic, with dessert to be shared by all. Cathy and I split a tuna fish sandwich brought by my husband and my best friend, who were there for moral support. Even with their presence, I was moderately uncomfortable.

After the eating came the giving of the gifts. I would love to say that gifts don't matter, but they do. It's important to know that your work has been valued by the adults who benefit most from it. That doesn't mean they have to spend a lot of money. They simply have to remember to do something nice.

Cathy and I had privately joked that the only gift which would be even close to compensatory would be one hundred shares each of AT&T. It was that tough a year. But the parents did even better: they gave us drawings from their children (the usual), gift certificates (generous), and tee shirts with our class picture on the front! I jumped up and down while Cathy beamed: a perfect illustration of our complementary natures. (A parent kindly caught our reactions on film; a photo of that moment stands on my mantel today.)

Next came the speeches. Peggy Kaufman, Jenny's mother, spoke for the parents with sincerity and charm: they were so happy to have had their children in our classroom, and we were every bit as wonderful as they had heard. They wished us success in future endeavors, and they thanked us profoundly for the wonderful year.

It was my turn to talk. Cathy had asked me to speak for us both, and I had pondered long on what to say. I didn't want to be too serious, but I wanted the parents to understand how unusual the year had been. I settled on this:

"In my many years of teaching, this has been my most challenging and my most rewarding class. Cathy and I thank you for giving us the gift of your children and of yourselves for this year. Our gift to *you* has been that we have taught the children how to talk about their feelings—a necessity during the many painful moments of this year. We ask that you continue our work by talking to them in the same way. They'll share their feelings with you as they have with us. Thanks for a wonderful year."

Did they hear? Yes. Did they understand? I have no idea. They applauded loudly, and then demanded that Cathy speak for herself. She said that she had loved the year, and that she had learned more than she had ever learned in her life. She loved the kids, and she was pleased to be spending the summer with so many of them.

"That's enough, I think," she added, turning to me for support. I nodded, and we all applauded again.

After a bit, it was time for good-byes. Some kids hugged and ran; some lingered over kisses and promises of future visits. Jason, the huggy bear, wouldn't come near us. David, who had hugged us only once all year, graced us both with a tight squeeze. Harris merely looked at us until his father made him say good-bye. Amanda was matter-of-fact and Cory distracted.

We received the usual sweet hugs and kisses from Sharon and Jenny. Benjamin hugged and talked at the same time, as did Mary Ann. Avi hugged and kissed me but he wouldn't talk. He quickly hid behind his father. Lee gave us his usual delicious kiss.

Louisa loitered around the edges while her mother spoke to me.

"We really can't thank you enough," Elaine began. "We feel as if we gave you an Indian and you've given us back a chief. Louie learned about self-control, about sharing and mainly about respect. We couldn't have taught her that by ourselves. Thank you."

I had no words to reply. I simply swooped up Louisa for a giant good-bye hug, and let it go at that.

The hardest good-bye was to Jeremy Jacobson. He hugged Cathy for two or three minutes. She spoke quietly to him while she rubbed his shoulder. When she put him down, he walked over to me, climbed into my lap and put his arms around my neck.

"I love you, Jeremy," I whispered.

"I love you, Patti. And I'm going to see you. You're going to visit me in my new classroom."

I promised I would. He hugged me again, and went off to play with his brother. I was reminded of the Tin Man's line in *The Wizard of Oz:* "Now I know I have a heart, 'cause it's breaking." I looked up at my husband and my friend for a bit of extra strength. They were a welcome reminder that I had a personal world as well as a professional one.

The parents' good-byes were just as poignant in their own way. I was struck by how unwilling they were to let go. Several invited us up to their country homes. Many asked for lunch dates over the summer. All eight parents whose children were going to summer camp said, "We don't have to be sad. We'll see you in a week."

Several parents cried. One said she'd write me a letter—she just couldn't say all she wanted to. Another parent simply couldn't leave. She and her child helped us clean up after the party and even followed us down to the classroom. There, when she felt she was intruding on our privacy, she was finally able to say good-bye.

My husband and friend had arranged to meet me in the

lobby. Cathy and I checked the room once more, to make sure it was ready for summer camp. It was perfectly tidy, so there was nothing left to do but say good-bye to each other.

It was the hardest thing I'd had to do all day. We'd always be friends; we'd see each other all summer. But it would never be the same. A teaching partnership is like a marriage. You learn the rhythms of your colleague; you finish her sentences; you depend upon her every day.

Cathy and I hugged each other. We cried. The only words I spoke were the ones I'd told her yesterday: ". . . the things you don't get to say . . ."

She nodded, and brushed away the tears. "See you next week," she said—and then she was gone.

I glanced once more around the cool, quiet room. It seemed so dull without the children. All at once, I realized that there was more reason to be happy than to be sad. I felt victorious: Cathy and I had accomplished our goal. We had enriched the lives of thirteen families who would never be the same.

I turned away and walked down the hall. I didn't look back. I was thinking about the summer.